MODERN GERMANY
& HER HISTORIANS

C. Ruf, Zurich.

PROFESSOR ANTOINE GUILLAND

MODERN GERMANY & HER HISTORIANS

By

ANTOINE GUILLAND

**Professor of History at L'Ecole
Polytechnique Suisse**

GREENWOOD PRESS, PUBLISHERS
WESTPORT, CONNECTICUT

Originally published in 1915
by Jarrold & Sons, London

Reprinted from an original copy in the collections
of the University of Illinois Library

First Greenwood Reprinting 1970

Library of Congress Catalogue Card Number 70-110840

SBN 8371-4506-6

Printed in the United States of America

LIST OF CONTENTS

Modern Germany and Her Historians

INTRODUCTION

WHEN studying the history of the growth of German Unity, one is struck by the important part played in it by the historians : they were the promoters of that National-Liberal policy which reached its triumphant climax after the victories of 1866 and 1870.

They made this policy possible by preparing the nation for it by their doctrines : they became, later, the leaders of that German public opinion which betrayed itself, with such jealous nationalism, in the Luxemburg question. " Without their co-operation," the economist Schmoller said with justice, " the Empire could never have been set upon its feet." Again, Lord Acton said, " They brought history into touch with the nation's life, and gave it an influence it had never possessed out of France ; and won for themselves the making of opinions mightier than laws." [1]

The Germans were the first to recognize what they owed to their historians. " To attempt," said Hans Delbrück, " to define and explain the close relationship and, at the same time, the contrast between minds such as those of Ranke, Waitz, Giesebrecht, Häusser,

---

[1] " German Schools of History," *Engl. Hist. Rev.*, 1886.

Droysen, Gneist and Treitschke would be a vast and difficult undertaking; and one towards which so little has been done up to the present that the book to be written some day on this subject will be an original and imposing piece of work." [1]

The present work does not pretend to fill this gap completely. To do that it would have to assume larger proportions, for it would then be necessary to introduce all the manifestations of intellectual life—law, theology, political economy and literature ; for the historical method which was the principal means of expression of these national ideas was applied not only to political history but to all the allied branches of learning.

We have confined ourselves to political history, which after all is the most important. Moreover, it is in this that the Prussian national aspirations are best revealed.

All the great German political historians of the nineteenth century—Niebuhr, Dahlmann, Ranke, Waitz, Giesebrecht, Droysen, Häusser, Max Duncker, Sybel, Mommsen and Treitschke—were for a "Little Germany" under Prussian hegemony. For them it was an historical necessity arising clearly from the teaching of the past : and they set themselves the task of proving it, now by relating the history of Prussia or Germany, now by appealing to the history of other countries; for to them the process of forming a nation, subject as it is to certain definite laws, was the same for all countries.

As lecturers in all the great German Universities they propagated these doctrines from their professorial chairs and in their books, which carried their teaching

---

[1] *Prussian Annals*, October 1894.

much further—to the mass of people in the outside
world. They were men of great qualities : they were
either orators or writers : many of them were both.
They created by their works, which were fundament-
ally sound and clear and vivid in form, that powerful
German School of historians which has become the
exemplar and rival of the English and French Schools.

In temperament this school was purely Prussian.
As opposed to the great Catholic Germany it represented a limited German Union and was in its
nature Protestant and liberal. True, this liberalism
had nothing in common with that of Canning or
Gladstone : it was a Prussian liberalism—that is, a
liberalism which readily confused economic and intellectual liberty with political liberty, or rather
which, so long as it enjoyed the former, was not
sparing of the latter. And we know what power of
resistance this liberalism had after Sadowa and
Sedan ! Bismarck knew how to make these liberals
accommodating in their principles by throwing them
the bone of the *Kulturkampf* to gnaw and by
opportunely parading before their eyes the bogies of
Revenge and Revolution. By that time there was
little of their liberalism left—on the other hand their
imperialism had grown wonderfully.

As the defenders of Prussian traditions and the
future supporters of Bismarck's policy, these men,
who first appeared in public life between 1840 and
1848, were then real *historians of the New German
Empire*, although their works, with the exception of
Treitschke's, were written before the formation of the
Empire.

The study of these, then, means the examination
of an important factor in the accomplishment of
German Unity, and to understand this thoroughly it

is necessary, before looking at the men, to consider on what sort of soil they grew up and what circumstances fashioned them.

The first element in the composition of the national historians is German patriotic sentiment. We know how slow this sentiment was in appearing among the German nations. At the close of the eighteenth century all the great writers of the classical period—Klopstock, Wieland, Schiller, and Goethe—were cosmopolitan in feeling. Herder regarded the patriotic sentiment, which the ancients had known, as " monstrous." [1] Lessing, in his turn, wrote: " I cannot understand this love of one's country. To me it seems, to say the best of it, an heroic weakness which I am happy not to share."

But one must be careful not to take too literally the utterances of these philosophers and poets. In the heart of every German, however emancipated he may seem to be, there is always a corner left for sentimental love like that of Jean-Jacques Rousseau for the church-tower which saw his birth.

However much these men might call themselves " citizens of the world" in theory, it is none the less true that in reality they were powerfully attached to the land of their birth, to their race, and, above all, to the principle which it represented in the world. If a stranger appeared who threatened to destroy their home and that " heritage of common recollections" which makes up their native land, they immediately became ardent patriots. This is what happened after Jena, and it was Napoleon who revived this patriotic sentiment which had been dormant so long.

---

[1] " It is a horrible thing," said he, " an unnatural feeling, a species of barbarism unworthy of a civilized people."

Yet never was a man received, at first, with such enthusiasm by this idealistic nation, so quick in discovering genius. Hegel called Napoleon "the soul of the world." Johannes von Müller, the historian, in loud-sounding phrases celebrated "this hero of modern times," and compared him with Frederick the Great. Goethe, full of admiration for him, cried to the patriots who were beginning to bestir themselves: " Shake your chains as much as you will: this man is too strong for you: you will never break them. You will only drive them deeper into your flesh!" Heine, the sceptic who ridiculed everything, still held from his childhood one idea of adoration: " The Emperor." [1]

And if you think that this is but the enthusiasm of speculative philosophers or the dreams of poets, listen while a calm and deliberate man, Dr. Döllinger, tells us what feelings animated German youth at that time: "With me and my schoolfellows the need of an ideal was a part of ourselves, and I remember how Napoleon fired our imagination, although he was in truth not exactly a fitting object of such unbounded enthusiasm. . . . At Würzburg I formed one of the crowd of curious youngsters who followed at Napoleon's heels about the town when he came there to inspect the fortifications. I can see him now in his green uniform and three-cornered hat, his dark complexion and sharply cut features making him appear to my eyes like a figure carved in bronze." [2]

And there were in Germany hundreds like him!

---

[1] " Ideas : " " The Emperor rode calmly straight through the avenue : no policeman stopped him . . . the trumpets pealed . . . and the multitude cried with a thousand voices, ' Es lebe der Kaiser ! ' (Long live the Emperor !)."

[2] " Conversations of Dr. Döllinger," recorded by Louise von Kobell, translated by Katharine Gould, London, 1892.

Ranke, the historian, found a schoolmaster, far away in the country, who worshipped Napoleon as a hero of the human race, and who attributed to him a mission from God (eine göttliche Mission).[1]

But these feelings changed abruptly. He who the night before was called a liberator suddenly became an "intractable despot." One day's work was enough to bring about this change : Jena.

Never was a foreign yoke felt more heavily by a nation than that of Napoleon by the Prussian nation after Jena. The Emperor meant to annihilate this kingdom, and he thought he had succeeded in doing it. For a moment, indeed, Europe might have shared his illusion. With its treasury exhausted, its army scattered, so to speak, its towns captured, its territory diminished by half,[2] Prussia might well believe its last hour had come. "Prussia is done for," wrote Napoleon to the Sultan; "she has disappeared from the map of Europe." And Gentz, in whom the wish was father to the thought, wrote on his part: "It would be more than absurd to try to revive that Power."

But all these men were mistaken. They did not know that at the root of this State there was a latent force which a mere stroke of bad luck could not thus annihilate. In default of anything else, its history might have taught them that.

It is a strange history, indeed, that of the fortunes of Brandenburg, the cradle of Prussian power, "that

---

[1] L. von Ranke, " Zur eigenen Lebensgeschichte," Leipzig, 1890, pp. 19, 46.

[2] Napoleon himself said to Count Rœderer: " I have taken a billion from Prussia." He said also : "After all my wars have only cost me a million of men, and the majority were Germans."

country of sand-pits," as it has been called,[1] "watered
by sluggish rivers flowing at the foot of alder woods,"
with its wide plains, broken here and there by hills,
and towards the north by little lakes, ponds, and bogs.

How did these flat unfertile regions, the poorest
in Europe, manage to form a powerful State ?

This is explained by the work carried out by its
princes, an admirable line of rulers to which no nation
can show a parallel, from the first Margraves, who
have no peers in Germany for endurance, tenacity,
and practical knowledge, down to those exalted personages the Great Elector, Frederick William I and
Frederick II.

At the time of the Great Elector Prussia had no
standing in Europe : it consisted of three disconnected
fragments, the duchy of Prussia, Brandenburg, and the
duchy of Cleves ; beside this there was some territory
ruined by the Thirty Years War. This Great Elector
had the great good fortune to be able to receive in his
country French Protestants driven out of France by
Louis XIV. They came there in large numbers :
they civilized the country, they made a town of Berlin,
they drained the swamps and in a short time transformed
"the Sandpit" almost into a fertile garden. Who can
ever say what Prussia owes to France ?

With the two kings, Frederick William I and
Frederick II, Prussia entered the concert of the Great
European Powers. And yet the first, Frederick
William I—a contemporary of Louis XV—in spite
of this was a king without any display, who loved
only what was real and positive, was hard to his
people as he was to himself, using his cane and
believing in the existence of the God of Israel who

---

[1] M. Ernest Lavisse, " Origines de la monarchie prussienne."

punished "to the third and fourth generation those who did not obey His commandments": quite persuaded that he must make the people "happy in spite of themselves":[1] displaying with all this a vigorous activity, practically without a court, reducing his ministers to the level of copying clerks: entering himself into the details of various matters, avaricious and rough, and like a Grandet in his old coat, seated at his plain wooden desk, receiving his tradesmen's accounts: they knew they could not cheat him out of a penny; he saw everything. He filled his treasury, created a wonderful army which he filled with giants, and trained at the same time exemplary public servants, whom he paid ridiculously, and who did a preposterous amount of work.

Yet more astonishing still is his son, Frederick II, a typical Hohenzollern, with a keen and active mind without a suspicion of fanaticism, never mistaking the shadow for the reality, as skilful in conquering a province as in strengthening it and making the vanquished forget the barbarity of the process: a man of indefatigable activity, always the first at his work, from earliest morning spurred and in uniform ready to mount his horse: scrutinizing in his tent, between parades, the accounts presented to him, playing the flute or writing French verse. With all this a genial simplicity, the simplicity of a truly superior man who knows what life is worth, who despises appearances and lives only for reality: a cynic in conversation, unmasking with delight human hypocrisy,

---

[1] "Thank God," said Count von Moltke, "the old regime of supervision and parental authority, that old theory which has been so much reviled, that the people must be made happy in spite of themselves, still exists in Prussia in spite of progress."

but a man of duty—that "confounded duty" (*verfluchte Pflicht*), as he called it, "from which one cannot get away."

It has been attempted to explain the whole history of Prussia by this feeling of duty. "This feeling," said Colonel Stoffel, "is developed to such an extent among all classes of the country that astonishment never ceases when studying the Prussian people. Having no reason for seeking the causes of this fact, I confine myself to stating it. The most remarkable proof of this attachment to duty is furnished by the personal character of the employés of all grades in the various administrations of the kingdom. Paid with a truly surprising parsimony, most often burdened with families, these men work the whole day with a tireless zeal without complaint or even seeming to desire an easier berth. 'We take care not to interfere with it,' said Bismarck to me the other day. 'This hardworking and badly paid bureaucracy does the best part of our work and is one of our most valuable assets.'"[1]

One thing is certain, and that is that nothing contributed so much as this to win the sympathies of Protestant Germany for Prussia. In the seventeenth and eighteenth centuries all the innovators, Puffendorf, Thomasius, Leibniz, and Spener had already turned their eyes towards this country which seemed to them one of the most advanced of States and one most anxious to make progress. Prussia was the first State in Germany to make education free and obligatory. Into its universities, breaking away from the old scholastic spirit, it had introduced modern ideas. At a time when professors in Germany still lectured in Latin, it was also the first to extol the use of the

---

[1] Colonel Stoffel, "Rapports militaires," p. 104.

B

national tongue.[1] This spirit of innovation could be found everywhere in its administration, in which, by the reform of small matters, the Government had made progress which among other nations did not begin until after the French Revolution. From that time one can understand why the more enlightened Germans, jealous guardians of the intellectual superiority of their country and its moral worth, inclined towards Prussia.

After the battle of Jena the movement became general. At first sight this is a matter for surprise. Was not Jena a defeat for Prussia? Yes, but in the flashing lightning of the battlefield these Germans, who hitherto had relied upon this nation, saw their hopes about to founder, and in a splendid outburst of patriotism they hastened to prevent it. There were already at this time a number of Germans in Prussian service at Berlin: Baron Stein from Nassau, Prince Hardenburg and Major Scharnhorst from Hanover, Gneisenau and Fichte from Saxony, Niebuhr from Schleswig-Holstein. Others were still coming in. And they all recognized at the same instant the same truth: " We must regenerate Prussia for the salvation of the whole of Germany."

What is still more surprising is that these men, seeing the Prussian Government failing in what they had called its mission in Germany, took this heritage

---

[1] It was the Prussian University at Halle that substituted the study of Germanic Law for that of Roman Law exclusively.

On the subject of the usage of the national tongue in University courses, Thomasius said : " The Greek philosophers did not write in Hebrew nor the Romans in Greek. Each people uses its natural tongue, and the French do this with success at the present day. Why should we Germans deprive ourselves of this advantage, as if our language were not suited for the purpose ? "

to themselves and tried to associate the whole nation with it.

This was not to be realized until later, when that ruler should appear who would understand that Prussia, in order to triumph, should rest upon the support of the people. But it was truly from the year 1807 that this idea had its origin, during the reign of Frederick William III. And yet if it had been dependent upon this king alone, it would never have been taken up. Timid, irresolute, and narrow-minded, he betrayed at this time the greatest weakness. Instead of bearing up against misfortune like Queen Louisa, so as to draw strength anew from it, he cringed in the first place to Napoleon. "Your Majesty," he wrote, "has heightened again the dignity of the throne by the brilliance of your virtues." It was not until he found the Emperor inexorable, and that he could ask no more without losing his dignity altogether, that he resigned himself to the struggle. And what sort of a struggle? A veritable death-struggle. The very existence of Prussia was at stake. Happily, in this great crisis from which Prussia would come out either annihilated or renewed in strength, he had the sense to go not to the quacks, as was his habit, but to a great doctor, Baron Stein, who had diagnosed the disease already with a relentless penetration and was ready to apply the remedy.

Among the figures of the founders of German Unity in the nineteenth century that of Baron Stein, the first chronologically, is one of the most outstanding. Not that Stein had foreseen all the problems which had to be solved, but that he saw, at least, the whole breadth of the problem which was to unite closely the future of Prussia with that of Germany.

In this sense it is that the historian Treitschke could say of this man's work, "Each step forward in our policy constantly brings us back to Baron Stein's ideal."

And Baron Stein is truly the forerunner of the National Liberals who placed economic before political liberties. He was by no means one of the vanguard. Many of his contemporaries showed a more penetrating mind than his, as, for example, Prince von Hardenburg, who wrote in 1805:

"The French Revolution, of which the present wars are but the continuation, has given France, amid the storms and bloody scenes, an unexpected impetus. Forces which were dormant are now awakened. The old organism, which had outlasted itself, with its defectiveness and weakness, its crimes and prejudices, with the good that was in it as well, has been carried away and destroyed. . . . It was supposed that, by adhering more closely to the old organism and by pitilessly persecuting the new principles, the Revolution would be most effectively resisted, but in this way it was most particularly favoured and its development facilitated. The force of its principles is such, indeed, that the State which refuses to accept them will be obliged either to acknowledge them or to perish itself. . . . A Revolution, in the best sense of the word, brought about by the wisdom of the Government and not by a violent impulse from without, this should be our aim, our guiding principle. Democratic principles in a monarchical government, this seems to me to be the formula appropriate to the spirit of this age." [1]

Baron Stein would have nothing to do with such a

---

[1] Cavaignac, "La Formation de la Prusse contemporaine," p. 340.

Revolution. To him political reforms were subordinate to social and administrative reforms. To this side of the question he directed his entire attention.

These reforms, however, were not easy to carry out. To do this it was necessary to destroy all the privileges of Prussian nobility. But this consideration did not deter this old nobleman of the Empire. " In North Germany nothing may be expected except from the peasantry and the middle class: the rich noble wants to enjoy his property and the poor noble wants a place and a livelihood: the official is possessed by a hireling spirit. If these classes are not roused by some stimulus they will remain inactive and do mischief by their example." [1]

Of all these reforms which he had in mind, Baron Stein carried out but two: the municipal, which gave the towns self-government, and the administrative reform, which was not, however, completed. But what survived the work was the spirit. Prussian in tendency, this Southern German could see no future for Germany save in a close union with the Hohenzollerns. This was the reason he gave: "The Hohenzollerns are true Germans: Prussia is a Protestant State, in which for two hundred years a great and many-sided life and a spirit of free investigation has been developed which can neither be suppressed nor misled by jugglery." On the other hand, he said of the Hapsburgs: "The Hapsburgs cannot hope to lead the Germans, because the true German spirit among them has been adulterated by the Jesuitic spirit, fatal to all truth. . . . Austria is no guarantee for the future."

Once this idea is clearly caught, the whole plan of

---

[1] Seeley, " Life and Times of Stein," i. 406.

the future Prussian policy is indicated at the same time. "But at the same time Prussia must not be alienated from Germany, and she must receive sufficient power to be able to help in its defence without over-straining her resources and putting her political existence to hazard: she must be powerful and inde-pendent."[1] In the eyes of Stein the strengthening of Prussia meant not only enlarging its institutions so that they became the institutions of the whole of Germany, it meant also the extension of its territory by incorporating German territory annexed by any foreign country or held by sovereigns who, like the King of Saxony, "had forgotten their duties as German Princes." From 1810 he recommended certain annexa-tions. "To give strength and a continuous frontier to Prussia we must incorporate with her Mecklenberg, Holstein and Electoral Saxony."[2] But in order to become truly great, Stein thought that Prussia should above all initiate moral reforms. He said Prussia should become through its virtues a pattern for the Germans. And so from the beginning he devoted all his care to inculcating in the Prussian people those virtues which he thought necessary for national life: the sense of duty, the spirit of sacrifice, and the feeling of patriotism. To do this Stein was led to reform the two institutions which are the reservoirs of national life: the school and the barracks.

It would be difficult to say which of these institutions, in the history of Prussian development, played the most important part. They were in truth comple-mentary one to the other. When it was said in 1866, " It was the schoolmaster who won the battle of

---

[1] Seeley, "Life and Times of Stein," iii. 131.
[2] Ibid. iii. 182.

Sadowa," it was not intended to convey the meaning merely that Prussia was better educated than Austria, but that Prussian schools were better than Austrian schools in the matter of instruction in morality and citizenship. King William I said this on the morrow of that famous battle when he praised that "humane, moral, and enlightened spirit of the Prussian school" (die Gesittung der Schule) [1] which developed in the children "diligence in their work, the feeling of duty, perseverance, order, economy, and obedience."

This doctrine had passed from the school to the barracks. "The Army, which represents the nation itself," said Colonel Stoffel, "has all these qualities." [2] Indeed, from the year 1807 it had become a school of citizenship and patriotism. In this, it is true, Stein had found a matchless collaborator in Major Scharnhorst, who was the principal organizer of the nation in arms. He it was who was the soul of all these reforms.

He said: "We have come to value the art of war more highly than military virtues. This at all times has caused the ruin of nations. Courage, the spirit of sacrifice, and perseverance are the foundations of a nation's independence. As soon as these virtues no longer move our hearts, it is practically all over with us, even at a moment of great victories." [3]

---

[1] Speech on August 5, 1866.

[2] "Rapports militaires," p. 26.

[3] Clausewitz explains, at a later date, the causes of the defeat at Jena in the same way : "The enormous effects of the French Revolution are, it is evident, to be sought much less in the new means and ideas of the French mode of waging war than in the altered science of State policy and administration, in the character of the Government, and in the condition of the people, etc. That the other Governments saw all these things incorrectly, that they

Stein was not mistaken when he said that it was "by its virtues and the excellence of its institutions" that Prussia could make a moral conquest of Germany. He did not live long enough to see this realized. His brief entrance into public affairs did not give him time to gather the fruit of his work. When Napoleon hurriedly turned him out of public affairs, he only had time to scatter the seeds of future harvests.

In his retirement and inability to serve his country, of whose general policy, moreover, he disapproved, hopeless of seeing his plans realized, Baron Stein wished to prepare the public for those ideas.

He set himself to try to find the best way of doing this. On thinking it over, he thought history would be the best means.

Stein had a natural inclination for historical questions. In the time left to him by his public occupations he had given himself up to history. "History," he wrote to his nephews, the sons of Count Arnim, "raises us above the vulgarity of the present and makes us acquainted with what the noblest and greatest men have accomplished, and what indolence, sensuality, vulgarity, or the perverse application of great powers have marred." [1]

With a positive and exact temperament, a dislike for anything but fact, detesting metaphysics, which he called "the dangerous occupation of a dreamer," Stein was already marked with the characteristics which distinguished, later, the political historians with a tendency towards Prussia.

with ordinary means wished to hold their own with forces that were new and crushing—that was all mistaken policy."

Quoted by Colmar von der Goltz, "The Nation in Arms" (English translation, 1887), p. 113.

[1] Seeley, "Life and Times of Stein," i. 66.

At the time when Stein was thinking of using history for political ends, Germany had no historians. To find his doctrines he had to go to English history, which he had studied considerably. "English literature," he said, "among the modern European literatures deserves best to be accurately known, as it has the most good historians to show, who have faithfully represented incidents and characters, rationally and with special knowledge developed causes, and in whom chiefly morality, public spirit, and thorough knowledge of the foundations of civil order reign. For these reasons is the study of the English language and literature, and particularly the historical part of it, solidly and in every way beneficial." [1]

Now that he had time to spare he wished to foster an interest in historical studies among the German people.

"Since my retirement from public affairs," he wrote to the Bishop of Hildesheim, "I have been animated by the wish to awaken the taste for German history, to facilitate the fundamental study of it, and so to contribute to keep alive a love for our common country and for the memory of our great ancestors. It was also my purpose to endeavour that the multitude of documents dispersed by the revolution of the year 1803 might be carefully collected and preserved from destruction ; this, however, depends principally upon measures taken by the Government, and cannot be accomplished by the determination of individuals." [2]

---

[1] Seeley, "Life and Times of Stein," i. 66.

[2] Ibid. iii. 441. Stein urged the Prussian Government with great insistence to favour this national enterprise. "It seems to me," he writes, "that our nation has a greater and more general interest in its history than in the knowledge of any

To do this it was necessary to gather together the scattered forces in the country and to found a great historical association. This association, which first saw the light on January 20, 1819, and which was, so to speak, the cradle of national historical writing in Germany, had Baron Stein as the author of its being, [1] and it is very strange that the founder of Prussian political policy in the nineteenth century was also the creator of that historical school in which Hohenzollern policy was to find its strongest support.

Baron Stein in the first place upheld all the ideas which became the creed of Prussian historians.

In studying historical writing of a Prussian tendency one finds it distinguished both by its exclusive nationalism and its hostility towards the French Revolution.

The point of view of these historians is that laid down at the beginning of the century by the jurists of the historical school. We know that this school, begun in Germany by Eichhorn and Savigny, was developed by the reaction against the Revolutionary ideas. In his work " On the Mission of our Time in Legislation and Jurisprudence," [2] Savigny, taking up the doctrines of Montesquieu, tried to show that

---

erica from the Cape or some new species of Brazilian ape."— Ibid. iii. 491.

[1] The principal historians who made up this society at the time of its foundation were Dahlmann at Kiel, Niebuhr at Rome, the brothers Grimm at Cassel, Heeren at Göttingen, Pertz at Hanover, Savigny at Berlin, Eichhorn at Göttingen, A. W. Schlegel at Bonn, Fr. Schlegel at Vienna, Schlosser at Heidelberg, Büsching at Breslau, Docen at Munich, Görres at Coblenz, v. Hormayer at Vienna, Hüllmann at Bonn, Pfister at Turckheim, v. Raumer at Breslau, Rudherdt at Würzburg, Rühs at Berlin, and Voigt at Königsberg.

[2] " Ueber den Beruf unserer Zeit zur Gesetzgebung und Rechtswissenschaft " (1814).

laws are the exact reflection of the life of a people, that they have never been imposed by legislators, but that they have arisen from the nation itself. This book became the textbook of all the Prussian historians. Condemning in politics all *a priori* notions, all abstract principles in the name of which reforms might be introduced, they held that no innovation could be introduced save first in the mind of the nation, and that the people themselves show us their true needs in their history. The study, then, of the historical development of a people was, in their eyes, the key of the political problems of the day.

Baron Stein was, with Savigny, Eichhorn and Niebuhr, the first representative of this tendency in Germany. While these were seeking the justification of these theories, one by the study of law in the Middle Ages (Savigny), the other by that of German law (Eichhorn), and the third that of the Roman institutions (Niebuhr), Stein was looking for an application of them in German politics. He wanted to show that the German State of Brandenburg, the centre of Prussian power, would become the centre of the whole of Germany, that is, by the force of circumstances the Hohenzollern institutions would so spread as to become those of the other German States. As to the political form, he said that as each State, in order to endure, needed to be faithful to its origin, Germany should become, like Prussia, an absolute and military monarchy. Prussia, he said, had become great through the old absolutism and could do so again in the present and future.

In writing this Baron Stein had in his thoughts Republican France, whose influence on the German mind he feared.

Baron Stein was a declared opponent of the principles of the French Revolution, Varnhagen von Ense says. His hatred of the Revolution was so unbounded that he included in one and the same contempt all the men who had taken part in it.

Burke, of course, was his gospel. He writes to Gneisenau: " Burke is indeed very voluminous. Your Excellency should stick to the Letter on the French Revolution: it contains a rich store of maxims and principles on constitutional and administrative politics." [1]

Admiration for Prussian institutions, hatred of the French Revolution, these two cardinal political notions of Stein were to become those of all the national historians. In the name of the philosophy of history derived from the theories of the historical School of Law they tried to prove two things: the fiasco of the French Revolution and the historical development of Germany with Prussia as its basis by showing that Brandenburg is to Germany what Wessex was to England and the Ile-de-France to France, the centre of the future German crystallization. [2]

But if all the national historians were agreed upon proving, by history, the Prussian development of Germany, a point upon which they were at first by no means agreed was as to what were those "primary institutions" which were to determine the policy of the

[1] Seeley, iii. 387.

[2] Treitschke, " Hist. und pol. Aufsätze," iii. 435. It should be noted, however, that all German historians do not share this point of view. " Prussia," said one of them, Hans Delbrück, " is not a national State." " *It was mere chance* which united under one head territories such as those of Prussia, Brandenburg and Cleves " (" Hist. und pol. Aufsätze," ii. 131). Elsewhere, he called Prussia " an artificial state "—a point which English and French historians have always upheld, to the great indignation of Prussian historians.

whole State. There were among them Liberals and Prussian Absolutists. About 1848 the Liberals were in the majority. Their leader was Professor Dahlmann, who endeavoured to prove that the constitutional forms were involved in old German law and that consequently, if Prussia wished to take over the government of German affairs, she should introduce into her own government Parliamentary institutions. On the other hand, the Absolutists, who were then but a small minority, said with more logic that if Prussia became the centre of the future German crystallization, it was for the Prussian institutions to shape the new State. " The true destiny of Prussia," said one of them, Ranke, the famous historian, "is to be and to remain a military monarchy. It is impossible not to submit to what is historically due."

It was the great victory at Sadowa which was destined to put an end to this difference of opinion. From that day forward, the Liberals were reconciled to the Absolutists and became partisans of " the great military Empire." Thenceforward Ranke's theory, which was that of Baron Stein, prevailed. Some fanatics, in their zeal as neophytes, invoked Darwin to support their absolutism, and, describing German history as a vast struggle for life, pointed out brutally that "the historical rôle of Prussia had begun on the day when that Power incorporated, one after the other, those German States whose death-knell had sounded." [1]

It must be recognized that this theory is one which certainly suits the State of those Hohenzollern whose

---

[1] Treitschke, " Zehn Jahre deutscher Kämpfe," p. 30. The same historian tells us : " Radicals hold that the State results from the free consent of its citizens. History, on the contrary, teaches us that States are more often formed against the citizens' will by conquest and tyranny " (" Deutsche Geschichte," iv. 350).

philosophy the Swedish Ambassador, Schlippmann, at the Congress of Münster, summarized in these words : " God no longer speaks to princes by means of prophets or dreams : but there is a divine call at all times when an opportunity arises of attacking a neighbour and extending one's frontiers."

While they were expounding these Darwinian theories, these self-styled Liberal historians were tending, in practice, to the most reactionary policy. It could not be otherwise. By adopting the theories of the historical school of law, that is, by setting up *the rights of States*, drawn from the histories of Empires, against *the rights of man*, drawn from human reason, "they extorted," as M. Albert Sorel admirably says, "from inveterate abuses, the principle of the perpetuity of abuses " : they " transformed very ancient usurpation into lawfulness " : they " subtly distilled accumulated injustice in order to extract from it a so-called historical right, and erected in front of the old regime the façade of a Palais de Justice with beautiful romantic designs to attract the attention of the passers by." [1]

It can be understood that these men would become more and more embittered opponents of the principles of the French Revolution. While vying one with the other in proclaiming that " the result of events is a judgment of God " [2] and that the conquered are always in the wrong, they could scarcely understand what was noble and great in that attempt : they could only see its partial failure. That proves how limited was their outlook. For, after all, to those who can see, history offers other spectacles. As Elisée Reclus says :

" The historian, the judge who calls up centuries

---

[1] A. Sorel, " L'individu et l'Etat," *Le Temps*, April 4, 1896.
[2] Treitschke, " Hist. und pol. Aufsätze," ii. 559.

and parades them before us in an unending procession, shows us how the law of the blind and brutal struggle for existence, so much extolled by the worshippers of success, is subordinated to a second law—that of the collecting of weak individual bodies into organizations more and more developed, learning how to defend themselves against the inimical forces, how to recognize reforms in their midst and even to create new ones. We know that if our descendants should attain their high destiny of knowledge and liberty they will owe it to their closer and closer *rapprochement*, to continual collaboration, to that mutual assistance from which gradually brotherhood arises." [1]

By extolling realistic policy as the only legitimate one, they have overlooked that great historical truth that all progress in the condition of men has been brought about by the great idealists, by those who, having known the world in its contradictions and unhappiness, have turned away from that and imagined it and shown it to be better, juster, and happier. It is owing to the idealists, as M. Albert Sorel again says, that "the notion of right has arisen out of the contemplation of injustice, and that the controlling idea of all human dignity, conscience, has arisen pure and supreme from the chaos of fanaticism and superstition."

At bottom the German historians have had a vague notion of this truth, for, in spite of their philosophy of history, which had urged them to justify force and guile,[2] they have always tried to show that force was not detachable from moral worth

---

[1] Elisée Reclus, Preface to "La Civilisation et les grands fleuves historiques," by Léon Mentchnikoff, Paris, 1889.

[2] Mommsen.

and that, after all, the pageant of the world made virtue stand out with greater lustre. Again, some of them, when discussing the justification of Prussian spoliation, far from setting it down to the law of interest, prudently draw back from this and exhaust to the utmost the resources of a skilful sophistry to cleanse their compatriots from any reproach of duplicity.

One must also guard against believing that the hatred of the French Revolution among the German historians was caused exclusively by the idealism which characterized that event. With some of them we must allow for fear, and, with many of them, for jealousy.

" I should have been quite ready to recognize as just the claims of the French," said Ancillon one day, " if I did not see therein danger for other nations." This is Burke's cry, and it is the cry which all the Prussian historians utter after him.

Yes, they are afraid of this Revolution, afraid for their country, for its institutions, and it is the hatred inspired by this fear that often manifests itself among them.

It is a saddening task to reckon, in the enlightened Germany of the nineteenth century, the men—scholars, authors, and painters—who have been truly sympathetic or even just to France. One would find a certain number of them—Ranke, for example, who appreciated the literature of the great century and thought Descartes " a profound and original mind." Julian Schmidt, again, who, in spite of his Prussian exclusiveness, recognized that Goethe would not have been possible without Boileau and Voltaire. But the others ! Painters, scholars, and authors compete in their verses, scientific works, and paintings as to who shall attack France the most. Was it not a German painter, Overbeck, who, commissioned to paint the schools of philosophy in fresco, on the walls of Bonn University, purposely left out the French School? To a German philosopher of that time, would men like Abélard, Descartes, Malebranche or Pascal count?

Another one, a critic, wrote a very long treatise on " Comedy " from which Molière's name was calmly omitted. The author no doubt had sworn it should be so, and had kept his word.

But it is above all in history, and among the historians of a Prussian tendency, that this hatred is manifested.

For a long while in France we have regarded the Germans as the most impartial of historians. We were mistaken. Their learning deceived us. Indeed, this learning was always immense, and the directing spirit of their work was admirable. Few scholars have equalled them in scientific abnegation, in earnestness and patience in their researches. But they were not able always to derive from this learning accurate and reasonable ideas.

This is due, I think, to two defects which are frequently found among their scholars, and which, perhaps, are only after all the manifestation of one and the same thing: the lack of insight and passion.

M. Albert Sorel remarks that in spite of "their knowledge of the precise detail of facts, the Germans often lack critical ability in the discovering of causes and are mistaken in their estimations of things as a whole. " [1] And, indeed, the reason is that these scholars, who are so diligent, so apt in all the requirements of learning, do not know how to draw general ideas from their subjects, or, if they do so, it is often with a most disconcerting eccentricity. It might be said that all

[1] *Revue des Deux Mondes*, April 1, 1873.

opinions, no matter how absurd, have been supported by German scholars. I do not speak merely of the paradoxes of those scholars who have taken upon themselves the defence of Catalina, or those who have taken the part of the Athenian Government against Socrates,[1] but of those eccentric writers or simpletons who, with regard to Hamlet, seriously set themselves the task of discovering why Shakespeare " had made him fat and asthmatic."[2]

What is the cause of these astonishing eccentricities ? Is it, as M. Victor Cherbuliez believes, "because in Germany, personal relationship between man and man being weaker, the power to impress and to impose one's opinion is consequently stronger "?[3] Perhaps. But one thing is certain, and that is that passion is stronger among them. The Germans acknowledge this themselves. "Simple, impartial history," said Treitschke, "could not agree with a passionate and quarrelsome nation." And this is also true in their scientific world. Whoever is familiar with the old German reviews knows that it is not uncommon to find in them the most virulent attacks of one scientific rival on another. For a comma omitted or misplaced, the terms blockhead and fool would be readily used, and the abuse would be all the more coarse the more insignificant was the matter in question.[4]

---

[1] Dr. Forchammer, for example, who considered Socrates a " rascal " who deserved his fate.

[2] Here is the ingenious explanation of this commentator : " It must be that, being uncertain in his resolutions, he must have been of a lymphatic temperament, *ergo* he was inclined to stoutness."

[3] " L'Allemagne politique," Paris, 1870.

[4] Treitschke also said : " Among us scientific discussions degenerate too often into personal questions and end in disgusting

In political history, it is above all against France
that this Germanic passion is exercised. It is difficult
to imagine nowadays the things that were printed
about 1840 on the French nation. One of the best
known historians of that time, Heinrich Leo, who was
by turn Hegelian and romantic and compiled a
" Universal History " which enjoyed for a long time
a great reputation, wrote in all seriousness sentences
like the following :—

" The French are only a nation of apes (*Affenvolk*).
The Celtic race as it is found in Ireland and France
has always been moved by an animal instinct, while we
Germans only act under the influence of a holy and
sacred thought. Through the Gallic mask petulance
together with vanity and arrogance always penetrates."

In the same work this historian called Paris "the
ancient home of Satan," and regarded Necker as an
idiot.

One of the peculiarities of the historians of that time
was to search in the past history of France for all the
causes of ill-will that the Germans might have against
the French.

Heinrich Heine was scarcely joking when he tells
us, "Once in a beershop in Göttingen a young Old
German declared that Germany should take revenge
on the French for Conradin von Hohenstaufen, whom
they had beheaded at Naples. You have forgotten
about that long long ago. But we forget nothing." [1]
Edgar Quinet met this young Old Germany, no longer
at Göttingen but at Heidelberg, in the form of a

---

quarrels." The author of an interesting pamphlet, M. Flach, Der
Deutsche Professor der Gegenwart, said, in his turn, " There is
only a small minority of German scholars who are polite and
amiable."

[1] Heine, " Germany," i. 210 (English translation, 1892).

historian who wished " to go back to the Treaty of Verdun between the sons of Louis le Débonnaire." [1]

These scholarly imaginings are not always without their ridiculous side, as witness the wrath of that German publicist who accused George Sand of having stolen her name from that patriot-student Karl Sand who murdered Kotzebue.

Heine was right in saying, " A French lunacy is far behind a German one, for in this latter madness, as Polonius said, there is method." [2]

It is but right to acknowledge that the serious historians never descended to such absurdities, but with them hatred of France was not on that account less lively or vigilant. One might say that public affairs on the other side of the Rhine were their principal preoccupation. They could never think of their national state without taking up arms against France and recalling " all the insults undergone " in the past.

The Prussian statesmen and generals retained the conviction " that there was still an account to settle with France." [3] And in their philosophers—above all

---

[1] Heine said : " The Germans are altogether more vindictive than the Latin races. This comes because we are idealists even in hating. . . . We hate in our enemies the deepest, the most essential part in them—that is, thought itself."—" Germany," i. 108 (English translation, 1892).   [2] Ibid. i. 269.

[3] Expression of Treitschke's, " Deutsche Geschichte in XIXe Jahrhundert," i. 555. See General von Roon's correspondence on the outbreak of the war of 1870, letter of July 28th : " How fortunate ! what we have hoped for from childhood has happened . . . our revenge for the misdeeds of the Gallo-Francs for two hundred years " (Ibid. 429). " Yes, I admit it. I would sacrifice willingly one or more sons for that great purpose— vengeance for all the insults undergone during the last two hundred years " (Ibid. 454).

in their historians—they found faithful supporters of their hatred. The latter " lived with this presentiment of revenge," like the historian Menzel,[1] who wished " to wash in streams of French blood the shame and misfortune inflicted on the Germans by Louis XIV and Napoleon." They still stirred up the fire of hatred. " Nothing is expiated yet," they cried, "and the French flag still flies over Strassburg Cathedral."

One can quickly recognize the power of these feelings in 1840. It was the historians who brought on the Gallophobe movement. From that time on they lost no opportunity of reviving patriotic recollections. In 1843 they celebrated the thousandth anniversary of the Treaty of Verdun, a particularly national date, for it was from that time that Germany had an existence separate from that of France. The Prussian Government took advantage of that occasion to establish a national history prize, which was called definitely the Verdun Prize. The national historians on their part founded a " National Historical Review," which they placed under the ægis of this glorious anniversary.[2] They were three: Leopold Ranke, Giesebrecht, and Adolph Schmidt.

" Could we choose a more suitable moment ? " said they in their Preface. " Is this not the year in which we celebrate the thousandth anniversary of our country's independence, and at this time, when the unity of our country, which as yet is more in our wishes than in actuality, is spoken of so much, it naturally

---

[1] The historian Menzel (1798–1873), surnamed "the eater-up of the French," said that the gladiator dying at Rome should fill the German tourist with a patriotic indignation against a people who used " Germans " for their amusement.

[2] *Zeitschrift für Geschichtswissenschaft*, edited by Dr. W. Adolph Schmidt, Berlin, 1844.

occurred to us to set the cornerstone of a branch of knowledge which more than anything else, although in a limited domain, contributes to bring together the whole German people. This branch of knowledge, history, we wish to cultivate with one accord, for it is closely allied to politics : in fact, it is its mother and teacher. May it at least be able to prove to us that within its domain there is no profound difference between the German people, and that all the efforts put forward, whether east, west, south, or north, do not form irreconcilable oppositions." [1]

That was the second step on the path of national history. From that time on all historians would help by their works to make their fatherland understood and beloved and would help to solve the political problems of the time. Even the most learned of them, those who seemed the most objective, were not the last to extol it. The scholar Giesebrecht, a model of scientific exactitude, cried in an outburst of enthusiasm : " It is wrong to think that knowledge has no fatherland and that it soars above frontiers : our science should not be cosmopolitan but German." [2]

What Giesebrecht meant by German science was a quite realistic manner of treating historical and political problems. From about 1850, under the influence of that great experimental movement which influenced the mind of all, it was attempted in Germany to

---

[1] Preface, pp. iii, iv.

[2] " The principle which gives unity and life to the German scholar is the love of Germany," said Fustel de Coulanges. "The scholar is a patriot. . . . Most of the historians belong to the Liberal party : nearly all of them dislike the institutions of the old regime, but this hatred, instead of being directed against Germany, is vented on foreign countries" (*Revue des Deux Mondes*, September, 1872).

apply to the moral and political sciences the processes
and methods of the natural sciences.

The theory of the historical school of law, which
regarded each State as a living organism developing
itself according to its own laws, was carried out with
the most scientific exactness. In politics they expected
to find the very laws of the historical development
of a people. From this to the drawing of practical
conclusions for the needs of the politics of the
day was but a step, and this step was taken by the
historians.

In the short space of three years, 1853–55, there
appeared one after the other five works,[1] which at
first sight seemed to bear no relation one to another,
for one dealt with the French Revolution, the next
with Roman history, the third with German history
at the beginning of the century, the fourth with the
beginnings of the House of Brandenburg, and the
last with Imperial Germany: and yet all these
works emanated from the same spirit, applied the
same method and looked towards the same goal:
to write history from a Prussian national point
of view.

This school it is we are going to study in its best
known representatives: in its two forerunners first:
Niebuhr and Leopold von Ranke, who set the
method and prepared the way for the others: next in
the two great Liberal historians of the generation of

---

[1] (1) Sybel, " Geschichte der Revolutionzeit," Düsseldorf, 1853 ;
(2) Mommsen, " Römische Geschichte," Berlin, 1854 ; (3)
Häusser, " Deutsche Geschichte, vom Tode Friedr. des Grossen
bis zur Gündung des deutschen Bundes," Berlin, 1854 ; (4)
Droysen, " Geschichte der preussischen Politik," Berlin, 1855 ;
(5) Giesebrecht, " Geschichte der deutschen Kaiserzeit," Brunswick, 1855.

1848, Theodore Mommsen and Heinrich von Sybel: and finally in Heinrich von Treitschke, the corypheus of Imperialism.[1]

---

[1] All these historians were more or less concerned with politics, and their works have profited thereby in becoming more striking and practical. Karl Hillebrand recognized this when he said in 1874, " Our historical writing has never been done by statesmen or politicians. In Germany we have had no Guichardini, no Clarendon, Grotius, or Mignet. What practical experience in public affairs, however small it be, adds to the historian's understanding, is proved in the works of recent historians—Häusser, Sybel, and Treitschke. What a difference between them and their predecessors, Wachmuth, Schäfer, Leo, and Schlosser ! "

CHAPTER I

THE FORERUNNERS

NIEBUHR

I

NIEBUHR is famous above all as the founder of
historical criticism. It is agreed, also, that
no one, by his works, has given so powerful an impetus
to historical research and that every modern school has
its origin in him. But it is the patriot Niebuhr that
we know least of, who, when writing his "Roman
History," was convinced that he was thereby serving
Prussia, his country of adoption. And it is this
Niebuhr that we wish to consider now.

Niebuhr was one of those numerous Germans who
were drawn to the banks of the Spree by the mis-
fortunes of Prussia and who devoted themselves
entirely to the regeneration of that State.[1] He had
been called to Berlin a little before the Battle of Jena
by Baron Stein, who entrusted to him the control of
the Bank of Prussia. Niebuhr was a financier of the

---

[1] He belonged to a Hanoverian family settled in Denmark.
His father, Carsten Niebuhr, a great scholar, famous for his works
on Arabian language and literature, lived at Copenhagen. There
it was that the historian Georges Berthold Niebuhr was born on
August 27, 1776.

first rank.   Before revealing himself to the world as
a scholar, he had begun his career in the Danish public
service.   Before coming to Prussia he had been in
turn Secretary to the Minister of Finance at Copenhagen, Assessor in the Department of Commerce of
the East Indies, Director of the Royal Bank of Copenhagen and of the Commercial Company of the East
Indies.   In Prussia he was also deputed on several
occasions to negotiate loans in England and Holland.
Nominated Privy Councillor to the King, Frederick
William ,III, whom he accompanied in this capacity
in the campaign in Saxony in 1813, he became later
Prussian Ambassador at Rome from 1816 to 1822.

But although he had spent the greater part of his
life in public affairs, Niebuhr did not like them.   Of
delicate health, with a nervous system strangely
developed at the expense of his muscular system,[1] he
had been from infancy of a studious nature, little
inclined to active life.

He said of his childhood, during which he seldom
passed beyond the house and garden, " The actual
world was impenetrable to my gaze : so that I became
incapable of apprehending anything which had not
already been apprehended by another—of forming a
mental picture of anything which had not before been
shaped into a distinct conception by another.   It is
true that in this second-hand world I was very learned,
and could even, at a very early age, pronounce opinions
like a grown-up person : but the truth in me and
around me was veiled from my eyes—the genuine truth

---

[1] Description of Niebuhr by Dr. Arnold : " In person Niebuhr
is short . . . his face is thin, his eyes remarkably lively and benevolent . . . yet with nothing of what Jeffrey called, on the other hand,
the beer-drinking heaviness of a mere Saxon " (" Life of Thomas
Arnold," by A. P. Stanley, 2 vols., 1844, ii. 373,

of objective reason. Even when I grew older and studied antiquity with intense interest, the chief use I made of my knowledge for a long time was to give fresh variety and brilliance to my world of dreams." [1]

Of a pensive and imaginative [2] nature, Niebuhr had no liking for anything but letters and the sciences. At twenty years of age he had acquired a very great amount of learning: ancient and modern languages, including Arabic, mathematics, geography, history, financial science, political economy, he knew everything. [3] But like most intellectual natures, alive and accustomed to problems of learning, he was but ill suited to unravel the problems of practical life: he was too much inclined to look at questions from their many aspects, and that weakened his will. He argued instead of acting, which Baron Stein picturesquely described when he said, " Niebuhr is no use save as a dictionary whose leaves one turns over."

Stein thought he had made in him a great acquisition for Prussian politics: he was soon to recognize that he had been mistaken.

Nothing, moreover, could be more in contrast than

---

[1] " Lebensnachrichten über Niebuhr," English translation, 1852, p. 354.

[2] All his life he complained of his imagination, which he called a dangerous enemy of justice, thought, and even morality.

[3] Niebuhr's learning was enormous in the most varied branches of knowledge : linguistic knowledge, Greek and Latin archæology, classical philology and history. He knew twenty languages. It was an amusement for him to learn them. It was he who discovered the key to the *Osca lingua* and who deciphered the first inscriptions in that tongue. He had learned several Slav tongues. At Memel, where he took refuge with the King of Prussia after Jena, he learned the Sclavonic language. " It is necessary to understand all nations, were it possible, in their own tongues " (Ibid. i. 223).

the natures of these two men. Stein was of the statesman type, with practical views, with a decided and
firm will, going straight on to his goal, disregarding
obstacles. Niebuhr, on the contrary—a supple and
immense mind—took in everything but hesitated in
action. Then Stein would treat him brusquely and
the sensitive nature of the scholar would recoil,
wounded by the least offence. As compared with his
master he was like the earthenware jug to the iron pot.
In his correspondence Niebuhr often seemed possessed
of the hallucination of persecution. One day he wrote :
" Stein has done me more harm than any one else :
for he has trampled underfoot the most sacred of
friendships and he has sacrificed the confidence of that
friendship to the most unworthy of men." And why
all this ? Because one day, without meaning any harm,
Baron Stein had shown Prince von Hardenberg a con-
fidential letter of Niebuhr's. The Prince it was whom
he called the most unworthy of men. Can we not
imagine in this Jean-Jacques Rousseau crying out
of his benefactor, with an outburst of madness, "David
Hume is the most unworthy of men !" ?

With a character such as this, we can understand
that Niebuhr was little suited for public life. During
the whole of his life it oppressed him. "I am fed up with
this life," he constantly said in his letters. He sighed
continually for the time when he could return
altogether to his beloved studies.[1] He felt he was
made for that alone. "My true vocation," said he,

---

[1] "Lebens.," i. 538 (not in English translation, see original) :
" I am often seized with regret when I think of my beautiful
researches into history. . . . Shall I ever renew it ? Shall I ever
be able to restore it to fresh life ? " (Ibid. i. 216, English translation).

"is history, and I would like to devote my whole life to it." [1]

The time was not long in coming when he could realize this dream. In 1810 Wilhelm von Humboldt, who was laying the foundations of Berlin University, asked Niebuhr to be Professor of Ancient History there. That was a great day for the scholar; at last he was going to serve his country in the way that he understood it. " It was a happy time," he said, "when the Berlin University was opened. To have enjoyed the enthusiasm and happiness of that time, and to have lived in 1813, are enough to make a man's life happy, notwithstanding much sad experience."

The foundation of Berlin University is, after Stein's reforms and before the Zollverein, the third great work of the otherwise unfruitful reign of Frederick William III. We know how much Prussia, by the interest she took in intellectual affairs, had deserved at all times the gratitude of enlightened Germans. True to the spirit which had always guided the Hohenzollerns in the formation of great schools, the King wished to make of this University a centre of free research, and Wilhelm von Humboldt, entrusted to staff it, called into it the first scholars of Germany. With Niebuhr he sent for Fichte the philosopher, Schleiermacher the theologian, Savigny the jurist, the doctors of medicine Kohlrausch, Hufeland and Reil, and Böckh the philologist.

What could also be seen from the first was that

---

[1] " Lebens.," i. 42 (English translation). He said too : " Hence also I am no mathematician but a historian ; for from the single features preserved I can form a complete picture and know where the groups are wanting and how to supply them " (Ibid. i. 187, English translation).

this University would have a new spirit. Intellectual
Prussia was not old Germany, poetic and gloomy like
one of her forests, the Germany which preferred in her
studies the periods of faith and the dawn of history,
the Germany of the Nibelungs, loving Dante's Italy,
Calderon's Spain and the countries of a rich and
powerful civilization : the Germany which still could
be seen in the south with the Frankforter Böhmer, a
forerunner of Janssen, who was already striving to
prove that German decline dated from the Reformation:[1] the Germany of Görres, that visionary
pamphleteer, as eloquent as Lamennais, an artist like
Michelet, a demagogue and romanticist, who published
" Lohengrin " : no—the military Prussia of the Gneise-
naus and Clausewitz, the rationalist State, of rigid and
hard Protestant principles: that country, of which the
Southern Germans said in scorn " where there only
grew æsthetic tea, criticism and country squires," had
nothing in common with the old cosmopolitan Germany, which included in its complex character all
the wealth of German genius. The Southern
Germans were not mistaken therein. The Christian-
mystic scholars of Münich University, the Baaders
and Puchtas, at once saw in Berlin the enemy. That
University in which Fichte and Schleiermacher taught
Protestant rationalism, where Savigny expounded
the theory of the national development of peoples,
where Niebuhr inaugurated his pitiless art of criticism,

---

[1] At bottom the contrast between these two attitudes of mind
is a religious one. Great Germany was a Catholic Germany : Little
Germany a Protestant Germany. At the beginning of the
century the Protestant converts to Catholicism were numerous :
Schlegel turned Catholic as well as Count Stolberg. The first
of these said that he did not like the "Protestant heroes," and
called Frederick the Great " a national enemy."

which like a "surgeon's knife cut away the flesh of
tradition and left naked the skeleton of truth,"[1]
where Hegel developed his theories on the State
which suited Hohenzollern policy so well, and which
his disciples were to apply later, Gans in law and
Droysen in history: in short, this University, the
bulwark of Hegelism and scientific rationalism, foretold to the people of the South the rising of a New
Germany, powerful and full of fight, which would
consume the other.

II

When accepting his Chair, Niebuhr considered how
he might best serve his country. He saw that it
would be by inspiring a passion for truth. Nothing
seemed to him more suitable for this than knowledge.
He had a religious respect for this. He spoke in a
mystic tone of the scholar's place in society. He raised
him far above earthly competitions and rivalry. He
wished him to hover in an ideal world. "Let us forget
and despise the things of this earth, let us not be concerned with foreign matters, but follow our path as is
our duty, and so we shall not bury the talent which
our Heavenly Father gave us ; but let us cultivate
it and leave our children and our children's children in
possession of an increased store of wisdom, and enable
them to mount higher and higher the stairs of knowledge and science, and extend their successive investigations over the whole field of the human mind, over
the whole of this globe and the universe."[2]

Niebuhr thought that knowledge well applied should

---

[1] The remark is that of Field-Marshal von Moltke, who saw
in Niebuhr a true representative of the Prussian mind.

[2] "Lebens.," i. 67 (original, not in translation).

ennoble the character.   He said to his students, " If we
do not reveal the mistakes we discover, even though
others would not easily discover them : if, when laying
down the pen, we cannot, before God and our conscience, declare to ourselves that we have never tried
to deceive ourselves or to deceive others: if we have
never shown our enemies, even those whom we hate
the most, in such a light as we could wish ourselves
to be shown at our last moment, we have made a
wrong and irreligious use of study and literature."

These were the lessons which he wished to impress
upon the minds of his audience, and no branch of
learning seemed better suited to serve this object than
history.   To study history, said he, one must be fair
and honest.   One must beware of the desire of making
impressions, of vanity : our life should be a life of
duty under the eye of God.

The subject he had chosen was the history of the
first centuries of Rome.   No subject seemed fitter than
this on which to exercise this spirit of truth with which
he was possessed.   His first task was to look clearly
into the obscure problem of the origin of so great a
people: and then to show what this people, thanks
to its institutions, had really been in history.[1]

Until the time of Niebuhr the critical historian who
touched upon the origin of Rome was satisfied, like
Voltaire and Bayle, to discard the facts that seemed,

---

[1] Roman history had always been the favourite study of
Niebuhr : his first important writing, which appeared in 1804,
was entitled " A Treatise on the Roman Laws of Ownership and
the Agrarian Laws " ("Das römische Eigenthumsrecht und die
Ackergesetze "), which, in his opinion, gave the key to the understanding of the complete development of the Republic.   In this
work he already outlined the whole plan of his future " Roman
History."

to them, to be opposed to common sense. Beaufort, the best known representative of this tendency, thus explained the matter : " In history the probable alone is likely to be true."

For this quite arbitrary method—one which could at best give but approximate results, Niebuhr substituted another method—that of scientific criticism. He was not truly the discoverer of this method : before him it had been applied by Wolf in 1795 for the elucidation of the Homeric question, but this was the first time it had been extended to the history of a whole people.

We know what this method comprises : the point is to gather together all the evidence one can about the history of a people, to subject this evidence to the most exacting criticism, and to retain only what has the character of strict authenticity.

In the case of a period like the history of primitive Rome, about which we have nothing in the shape of documentary evidence except the dialects and the old literary remains (songs and epic fragments), there can be no question of establishing facts which shall be strictly exact, but at least we can, by the study of these songs and epics, make some advance in understanding the people who created them. By means of the name we can seek out the thing, and by means of the thing, the idea which caused the thing to be so named. We thus obtain valuable information about the intimate life of peoples, the historical data for which are extremely vague.

It was by applying the philological method that the German scholars of our century were to derive so much information for the reconstruction of primitive civilizations. Niebuhr had a passion for philology. He called it " mediator between the remotest ages."

" It has recognized its calling," he says, ". . . to

D

afford us the enjoyment of preserving an unbroken identity through thousands of years with the noblest and greatest nations of the ancient world : by familiarizing us, through the medium of grammar and history, with the works of their minds and the course of their destinies, as if there were no gulf dividing us from them." [1]

To a young man who wished to devote himself to the study of philology, Niebuhr gave great encouragement. "Philology," said he, "is the introduction to all other studies. . . . I am so fond of philology myself, that I could not select for a youth so near and dear to me as you are any other vocation in preference." [2]

It seems that by the application of the philological method for collecting information about times that are quite involved in obscurity, one can scarcely produce anything more than a psychological history, or a history of institutions. [3] At least this is what has been recognized by contemporary historians, who have given up hope of learning anything exact about the early history of Rome.

But Niebuhr, as a man of imagination, was not satisfied with this. Having acknowledged that the early legends of Rome were poetical, he tried to

[1] Preface to the "History of Rome" (English translation, 1847), i., p. ix.

[2] "Lebens.," ii. 223 (English translation).

[3] That is what Niebuhr wished to do. "I am not inquiring who built Rome or who gave laws to her : but with regard to the questions, what Rome was, before her history begins, and how she grew out of her cradle, some information may be gleaned from traditions and from her institutions. What by long meditation on the subject has to me become clear and certain, I am now about to communicate" ("Hist. of Rome," English translation, i. 286).

distinguish what might be true in these legends which had been embellished by poets and by the people, who are the greatest of poets. Niebuhr said, and with great truth, "To have formed these legends which so strongly influenced popular imagination, there must have been some truth at bottom." Perhaps, but how is one to distinguish this truth? How can one fix the point at which legend took leave of truth? Niebuhr attempted this, and thanks to the special insight which he had for Roman history and the psychology of the Roman people, he succeeds in giving us several hypotheses which have the appearance of truth: but they are only hypotheses after all, and their doubtfulness is none the less.

In the history of early Rome, if he belittles the legends about Romulus and Remus, and even Numa Pompilius, he believes, on the other hand, that there is a basis of truth in the story about Tullus Hostilius.[1]

He regards the fall of Alba as historically certain. He recognizes that in the reign of the Tarquins legend predominates in the marvellous episodes of Scævola, Cocles and Clœlia, but he believes in the existence of Tarquinius Priscus, and he attributes to this king the construction of the stone wall around the city and the great system of sewers which drained the Velabrum and the valley of the Forum.[2]

And so on to the Punic Wars, where he ends.[3]

---

[1] "History of Rome" (English translation), i. 220 and 346.

[2] Ibid. 357–541.

[3] It was the intention of Niebuhr to write a complete history of the Roman people up to the point where Gibbon took it up. Above all he was going to deal with public law. The first part of his "History of Rome," which appeared in 1811, comprised the whole period of the kings; the second volume, which dealt with the history of the old Republic as far as the Leges Liciniæ, was published in the next year.

But in spite of his imagination Niebuhr is none the less a strictly scientific historian. His "Roman History" inaugurated the modern historical method, which has completely transformed the science of history.

Niebuhr has thus both the characteristics of contemporary historians: the method of investigation and the scientific conception of history.

His manner of investigation was that of the exact sciences: it consisted in the first place in determining the truth of the historical facts, then in grouping them, and then in drawing no conclusion which could not be deduced strictly from these facts alone.

In the matter of the early period with which he dealt, Niebuhr compared his work with anatomy. "I dissect words," said he, "as the anatomist dissects bodies," and he added, "I am trying to separate from foreign matters a skeleton of fossil bones collected too carelessly."

If he had written the history of the posterior centuries of the Republic and the Empire, he would have dealt with epigraphy and numismatics, he would have examined epitaphs and inscriptions, and would have deduced therefrom the manner of administration of the Roman provinces. But in that he was satisfied to point out the way.

Niebuhr's conception of history was closely dependent upon his method of research. By the comparison of dialects and mythology, of laws and religions, he led up in history to that theory of evolution which in the course of the century, in Germany, was to transform the historical sciences or form others from them: linguistics, phonetics, æsthetics, folk-lore, comparative mythology, the history of religions, etc. The "Roman History" was one of the first applications of this method. It formed part of that great scientific movement which was Germany's glory in this century.

It was the time when Benecke began his suggestive lexicographical works : when Augustus Böckh wrote his admirable work "The Political Economy of the Athenians" : when Franz Bopp originated the comparative study of languages : when Frederick Diez began to collect matter for his "Grammar of the Romance Languages" : when Wilhelm Grimm revived the old legends and German popular stories, while his brother Jacob laid the foundations of historical grammar. All these labours were due to the same inspiration, inaugurated the same methods of research, and served their country in the same way.

The whole of this magnificent intellectual impetus, which followed so closely on the disaster of Jena, showed that the people who were capable of it were not yet nearing their ruin : and the secret of Prussia's success was the turning to her own advantage a great part of these intellectual forces. If there was no such a thing as Prussian science, there were at least German scholars who placed all their talent and science at the service of the country of their adoption. Niebuhr was in the front rank of these scholars. In writing his "Roman History" he wished, by the examples which he set before the Prussians' eyes, by the political lessons he deduced from this history, to serve Prussian policy.

Let us try to show how he succeeded in this.

III

Niebuhr, like all the patriots of the generation of 1807, Stein, Scharnhorst, Fichte, Gneisenau and

Schleiermacher, attributed the Prussian disaster to her bad government, as its carelessness and lack of strength had gradually impaired the intelligence of the governing classes. But the people themselves had not been contaminated, and it was of them that he expected the regeneration of the State.

"If you knew this people," he wrote to one of his friends, "you would find it worthy of your love. Nowhere would you find such strength, seriousness, spirit of obedience and magnanimity. If this people had been well governed, it would have been invincible, and in spite of the violence of the hurricane which burst over the country, the same spirit fills it still." [1]

This nation needed leaders, but Niebuhr remarked with horror that those who might fill this part had lost confidence and faith. "Our young men," he said, "are backward and lack enthusiasm." [2] To remedy this evil, that is, "to regenerate youth and render it capable of great things," he determined to write his "Roman History," which would "place under their eyes," as he said, "the noble examples of antiquity." "The evil time of Prussia's humiliation," he wrote later to Francis Lieber, "has some share in the production of my History. We could do little more than ardently hope for better days and prepare for them. What was to be done in the meanwhile? One must do something. I went back to a nation, great but long passed by, to strengthen my mind and that of my hearers. We felt like Tacitus." [3]

Niebuhr was not one of those writers who reveal themselves altogether in their writings. He was a

[1] Letter of October 22, 1807.
[2] "Lebens.," i. 385 (not in English translation).
[3] "Reminiscences," 90.

scholar and he wrote as a scholar. Yet there is in his style a certain rhetorical grandeur, an emotional feeling which in places breaks out into personal expression. Whenever he finds in Roman history positions analogous to those of his own country or time, he shows that [he takes an active interest in those events, and it is not difficult to find in his opinions the influence of contemporary things. His emphatic dislike for those great conquerors, Alexander and Cæsar, certainly has its origin in his hatred for Napoleon, "the great enemy of his country," as he calls him.[1]

From the political point of view, too, Niebuhr frequently shows in his work his personal preferences : what may be seen throughout is a lively sympathy for the oppressed.

Niebuhr had a liberal mind without being on that account a "liberal" in politics. Indeed, if one were to regard his political ideas alone, one would take him for a reactionary.

---

[1] Niebuhr had passed through various stages before arriving at hatred. Like many Germans at the beginning of the century, he had begun by admiring Napoleon. Désaugiers, the First Secretary to the French Legation at Copenhagen, who was an intimate friend of Niebuhr, said to M. de Golbéry, the French translator of the "Roman History," "We both admired the young General, whose fine speeches recalled to us the eloquence of antiquity." As for the army, Niebuhr's expression invariably was, "The peerless Army of Italy." The 18th Fructidor (September 5th) pained him deeply. The exile of the patriots, particularly Carnot, roused his indignation. That was the first blow to his idol. The 18th Brumaire succeeded in breaking the charm. The greater his admiration for Napoleon had been, the stronger became his dislike. On the return of Napoleon from Elba he was pleased for Prussia's sake, who would play "the principal part in the coalition."

He did not like, for instance, "middle-class liberalism." In Italy he took the side of detestable Governments against the national demands. In France he expressed a profound contempt for the "current constitutional doctrines." What was the reason for this? It was that he regarded them as an inheritance of the French Revolution, which he abhorred.

It has been said of Niebuhr that the strongest passion of his life was his hatred of the French Revolution.[1] This much is certain, at any rate, that he was one of those in his own country who most actively opposed it. He had been brought up by a father who, from the time of the taking of the Bastille, had instilled in his mind the idea that the French were not capable of creating and preserving liberty, and that all that fine outburst of enthusiasm ended in wars.

He was not, however, disturbed by it on any other account, for he saw in it the opportunity for Germany to take back the " German and Burgundian territories which the Welches [Celts] still held."

It was always from that point of view that Niebuhr regarded the French Revolution. Whenever he thought he saw its influence he set about opposing it. At times peculiar situations arose from this. As he was liberal in thought he was often torn between his aspirations and his hatred. Thus it was in 1830, when no one could say on which side he was. He execrated the folly of Charles X, which made the revolution possible. " Yes," said he to Dr. Arnold, " after what took place, I would myself have joined the people of Paris, that is to say, I would have given them my advice and direction, for I do not know

---

[1] Sir J. R. Seeley.

I should have done much good with a musket." [1]
But at the same time he was opposed to all the men
of this revolution, Manuel and Benjamin Constant,
Lafayette and the Tricolor Flag.

It was because in these men, who were influenced by
the most noble ideas, he saw a kind of tyrant of liberty
whose notions might be dangerous to the neighbouring
States whose emancipation he fervently desired. Now
Niebuhr detested essentially all constraint and all
tyranny. Deeply imbued with the rights of the individual, he abhorred all oppression, no matter whence
it came. "And if I lived in a State where one constitutional element of the whole was injuriously
repressed," he said, "whether it were the democratic
or a truly aristocratic element, I would strain every
nerve to give it fair play and put it in possession of its
rights." [2]

This feeling breaks out on every page of his "Roman
History": everywhere Niebuhr takes up the defence of
the oppressed because, as he remarks in the preface to
the second part of his work, which deals with the
struggle between the patricians and the plebeians as far
as the Leges Liciniæ, "the domination of one class
or clique is always suspect, unjust, and paltry."

This is a point of view which contrasts very strangely
with that of the future Prussian historians, who were
admirers of "coups de force." Niebuhr at Rome was
for the defenders of liberty, for Cato and Cicero against
Cæsar. Yet he regards the Empire as necessary,[3] but

---

[1] "Life of T. Arnold," by A. P. Stanley (1844), ii. 374.

[2] "Lebens." (English translation), ii. 395.

[3] It should be noted that these opinions of Niebuhr are not
to be found in his "Roman History," but in his Lectures delivered
to the Bonn University later, in 1824.

he takes no pride in it. On the contrary, he is disappointed, as, but for the profound corruption of Roman
society, Cæsar would not have been possible at Rome.
The Imperial epoch which then begins strikes him as
being "one of the most distressing spectacles of
history."[1]

From this, of course, Niebuhr draws a moral lesson.
He shows his listeners that a nation, without the
spirit of sacrifice, is very near to its ruin : that selfishness kills peoples as it kills individuals. He exhorts
them therefore not to follow the example of those men
who, like Phocion, through desire for repose and through
indifference, abandoned their country in a time of
danger.

It will be said at once when he speaks of these
events that Niebuhr was thinking of the evil days
of Napoleonic domination in Prussia. " Phocion," he
cried, "was particularly hostile to Demosthenes, a
hostility which all will understand who noticed the
conduct of certain men at the time of the Rhine Confederation. I knew people, whom I was far from
considering dishonourable, but who were incapable of
enthusiasm, of sacrifice and hope, who thought it a
lesser evil to be reduced to slavery by a foreign master
than to suffer the evils which follow a war of independence : who thought that nothing was more senseless
than sacrifices of any kind : that there was small chance
of success, and that the mass of people are indifferent
as to who governs them. How many times did I not
wish to die with those whom I loved ! And I should
have thanked God for that, and also because I had no

---

[1] See, on this subject, an interesting work by Charles Seitz,
Professor of History at Geneva University, entitled " Julius Cæsar's
Historians in the Nineteenth Century," Geneva, 1889.

children then who could say to me 'You are an enthusiast,' and then add indignantly, 'You are the cause of all our ills!' Those who were not of their opinion ran the risk of denunciation by them as fanatics and the authors of all the evil."

But it was not only the heart of youth that Niebuhr wished to influence, it was also the intelligence. In the Germany of 1810 no task seemed to him more urgent than this. The point was to form in future generations a sound political judgment.

Politics had long been a matter of indifference to German youth. What the young men sought in the Universities was science. History to them was nothing but a learned research. Moreover, there were no political historians at that time. They were still at the period of the literary history of Schiller and Johannes von Müller. There was one political essay in existence, that of Spittler, but how dull and heavy and poor in practical teaching! Niebuhr gave the Germans what they lacked: a real political history.

One feels in reading each page of the "Roman History" that, from the manner of settling political problems and elucidating the most involved historical questions, the author has taken part in public affairs and has conducted negotiations himself.[1]

---

[1] Niebuhr attached great importance to his travels in England : " My early residence in England," he said to Franz Lieber, " gave me one important key to Roman history. It is necessary to know civil life by personal observation in order to understand such States as those of antiquity. I never could have understood a number of things in the history of Rome without having observed England. Not that the idea of writing the history of Rome was then clear within me, but when, at a later period, the idea became more and more distinct in my mind, all the observation and experience I had gained in England came to my aid and the resolution was taken " (" Reminiscences," p. 65).

" All human events," said Goethe in astonished admiration, after reading the "Roman History," "should be dealt with in this fashion. . . . The agrarian laws have no interest for me in themselves, but what delights me is the art with which Niebuhr explains them, makes clear their complicated relation one to another, and obliges me henceforward to deal thus with all the public affairs that I undertake."

The first political lesson which Niebuhr wishes to draw from Roman history was how the process worked by which " the nation of shepherds of Latium came to control the fortunes of Italy and the world." In short, it seemed necessary to him to bring before the eyes of the German people, "who had no country or State," the history of this people who had been "the model of national development."

When speaking of Latium, Niebuhr evidently had Prussia in his mind. He saw a striking analogy between these two States in which individual energy had done everything. He wished to impress his listeners thoroughly with this truth, that the State is " strength," that no unity can come from small States, however cultured they may be. " Times change," he said, "kingdoms rise and become powerful and the little republics and principalities cease to be States. For a State can only take upon itself that name if it is independent in itself, that is, if it is capable of feeling the desire to live, of continued existence, and of making its rights respected. . . . Protected States may be very pleasant for people themselves alive in times of peace : they may even be favourable to art and letters, but the man who belongs to them has no fatherland : he lacks what destiny has found to be the best means of arming and strengthening man. For in slavery not only does half the man disappear, but without a State or a fatherland the best man can do nothing, while with a State and fatherland a mere citizen can do much." [1]

By relating the history of Rome, Niebuhr was to show the Germans how that State, which they lacked, could be created. Latium, to preserve its existence, had to annex all the country within its orbit. Prussia in its turn had to do the same, that is to say, had to conquer one after the other all the German States which had become isolated and consequently reduced to weakness. And Niebuhr mentioned these States; they were Saxony, Schleswig-Holstein, Hanover, and the free cities. To console the inhabitants of these countries for the loss of their independence, he had what he considered peremptory reasons : they would gain a great deal thereby from the material point of view.

"Bristol and Liverpool as free cities," said he, "would be far less important than they are as municipal cities. In the same way Hamburg and Schleswig-Holstein will not reach their highest point unless they are placed under Prussian authority."

Niebuhr, who was from Schleswig-Holstein, did not trouble himself with vain regrets. He pointed out to the student that it was a law in the historical life of peoples against which it was useless to struggle. "In ancient times," he said, "little republics were able, thanks to peculiar conditions, to become powerful centres of civilization, but they can no longer be so nowadays, when the tendency of States is to coalesce in national life." The distinct political lesson which his listeners drew from this was that the little German

---

Quoted by Treitschke, "Zehn Jahre deutscher Kämpfe," 1879, p. 35.

Courts must disappear in an enlarged and powerful Prussia.

Another lesson no less important which Niebuhr emphasized in his " Roman History " is that in politics all imitation is dangerous.

At the time when he wrote his work, men were not rare in Germany who, impressed by the lessons of the French Revolution, thought that the new German State might be organized on those lines. Niebuhr put forth his efforts to put his countrymen on their guard against this illusion, by telling them that every imitation from abroad is dangerous to the life of a people ; and that the people had no chance of doing any good unless it remained faithful to its genius and origin. " If, above all, the form kills," he said about Roman literature, " it will kill all the more if the form is foreign : that is why, in a sense, Latin literature was still-born." And it could be clearly seen that in saying this Niebuhr wished to show the Germans that, in order to possess a truly national State, they should look at home, not abroad : for there they would find a State in which the German qualities were best embodied : " Seriousness, sincerity (Innigkeit), originality, and love." That nation was Prussia.

But Niebuhr was not satisfied with that : he wished to show his audience as well that Prussia, from a political point of view, had realized its essential liberties without recourse to any revolution. " It is a mistake," he said, " to believe that liberty should come from below : history teaches us, on the contrary, that it is never more lasting than when it comes from above— from the powers that be : it must be granted by, not snatched from them." He concluded from this that Prussian absolutism, enlightened, supervisory and vigilant as it was, which had always recognized the rights of the intelligence, was the best form of government for the Germans.[1]

We must clearly seek out all this in the "Roman History." Niebuhr did not display these sentiments on every page: on the contrary, he discreetly concealed them, knowing quite well that this was the best way to give them effect. The Germans have made no mistake about it. While certain people have affected to see in this History nothing but a work of pure learning, the Prussian nationalists have recognized in Niebuhr for a long time their chief and forerunner. "The 'Roman History,'" said Treitschke rightly, "is much more a 'lived-out' work (ein erlebte Werk) than the result of scientific researches: that is why Niebuhr's contemporaries regarded it as one of those classical works which cannot be superseded even if it were refuted in every detail." [2]

IV

We find Niebuhr at the entrance to every avenue of modern historiography. He was the first to state historical problems in the way they should be stated. His philosophy of history, which is that of the "becoming," of the gradual evolution of peoples, is nowadays that of all contemporary historians. Before all the others, by the application of comparative

---

[1] Outside his "Roman History" and his Lectures, in which these doctrines are more or less concealed, Niebuhr developed these ideas in pamphlets and in a journal he had founded to serve as an antidote, as he said, to Kotzebue's "worthless and mischievous publication, on which our dull public browses" (Seeley, "Life of Stein," iii. 141).

[2] Treitschke, "Deutsche Gesch.," ii. 64.

science, he opened our minds to the intuition of the past. From the year 1811, moreover, before Augustin Thierry, before Michelet, he perceived the importance of the problem of races, which Mommsen, Taine and Renan were to draw upon so much for the better understanding of laws, art, religions, and literatures. There is another point in which Niebuhr was an innovator, and that is form.

Before his time, the history that was studied was the vivid and dramatic narration of Schiller or the altogether intellectual exposition of facts of Voltaire, which gave one the meaning of things rather than showed them to one. In both cases, however, it was general history which seemed to suit the intellectual race of the eighteenth century, which was attracted by ideas rather than facts and did not like the analysis of sentiments and sensations.

But with Niebuhr another period began, that of historians who sought a direct and rapid communion with the life of the past. Of a critical mind, above all, he had that kind of penetration which in the apparent uniformity of the past could seize upon the points of customs and character which are farthest removed from us. He was the first among modern writers to attempt to understand and determine the individual life of each nation.

At the time when he was writing his "Roman History" no one yet talked of historical resurrection. It was not until later, with Augustin Thierry and Michelet, that this expression obtained currency. Yet Niebuhr was the forerunner of these men.

In the solitude and silence of his study he arrived at the same results as they did. It is true he did it in a less brilliant manner. He gave less importance to local colour, to setting, and to customs. As a good philologist who follows up words which reveal states of mind, he always wished to investigate above all the intimate life of peoples and individuals. It is none the less true of him that he brought about a far-reaching revolution in history. This he characterized in the following manner:—

" Previous ages had been content to look at the ancient historians in the way many look at maps or landscapes, as if they were all in all, without ever attempting to employ them as the only means for producing an image of the objects they represent. But now a work on such subjects could not be esteemed satisfactory unless its clearness and distinctness enabled it to take its stand beside the history of the present age." [1]

Thus it is that he proceeds. Rome for the first time arises from its ashes. No such instinct of historical divination had yet been seen. Niebuhr identified himself entirely with Roman life. He grasped the soul of the times. He had, moreover, a little of the spirit of the old Germans by which to understand these obliterated Italic people. This is what enabled him to enter into the customs of these men with such ease and absence of effort. He compares them with those he sees round about him, with what is still primitive among the people of Jutland and Dithmarschen. The legends of Frisian peasants help him to explain the legends of Rome. The settling of the Greeks in Italy is made life-like by comparison with the migrations of modern peoples. He sees in it the complete reverse of the action of the " modern Anglo-Saxon who seeks in America virgin forests in which to live an independent life." He throws

---

[1] Preface to the " Roman History " (English translation), i. p. ix.

E

brilliant light on the condition of the primitive peoples of Italy by explaining to us certain customs of the Redskins of the Mississippi.

The mixture of the Italic races recalls to him the descendants of the Crusaders in Palestine and Cyprus or those of the Spanish Conquerors. He explains the cyclopean works of these primitive races by showing us the Peruvians at work upon their gigantic constructions. Again, he calls in the corporations of the Middle Ages to explain certain peculiarities of Italic towns. In short, his enormous learning is placed at the service of his historical intuition and brings to life again for us the things of the past.

The description of the physical features of places comes to the assistance of this resurrection and helps to make it completer: Niebuhr describes all the landscapes of Italy—the mountains, the valleys, the towns and the plains. Rome has no physical secrets from him. He has excavated and re-excavated it, and the giant rises before our eyes.

Of course Niebuhr did not possess this talent to the same extent as our contemporary historians, Renan, Taine, or Mommsen. In that again he was only the forerunner, but it is certainly from his time that the taste for the actual in history dates.

Niebuhr was truly haunted by this taste for the actual. We can feel in every page as we read it that he was not merely a theoretical writer. He recognized that he owed this taste to the fact that he had lived "at a time when we were witnessing many unheard-of, incredible events. . . ."[1] When a historian is reviving former times, he added, "his interest in them and sympathy with them will be the deeper the greater

---

[1] "Roman History" (English translation), i. p. ix.

the events he has witnessed. . . ." [1] And his correspondence, indeed, is full of picturesque passages such as we like to find nowadays in works on history.

Here, for example, in a few words, is a picture of the battlefield of Eylau after the war: " Even in the neighbourhood of Königsberg we saw single ruined houses: in the villages the majority are uninhabited: no cattle are to be seen in the fields: here and there —but very rarely—you may meet with a small flock of sheep or a few pigs: in the villages scarcely a creature appears: the few whom you do see look anxious and miserable. At Eylau the devastation has been carried up to the very gates of the town . . . we found, however, guides to the field of battle who explained it to us. I could not bring away any relics for you —we found nothing on the field but rags of uniforms." [2]

Elsewhere he describes the retreat from Russia :—

" For the last two days the fugitives from the Vistula have been coming in: a spectacle that I cannot describe. This is by far the most memorable epoch of my life : no danger, no difficulties it may involve could make me wish it erased. This thing ought to be witnessed close at hand." [3]

But there is one good quality lacking in Niebuhr: the gift of form. His " Roman History " is not pleasant to read : it is badly composed, diffuse, confused, involved, and unsystematic: it bristles with technical discussions, and is interrupted by parentheses which

---

[1] " Roman History," p. xiii. He also said (December 12, 1808) : " I can now [after the fall of Prussia] understand through and through the histories of many times and the fall of nations. . . ." (" Lebens.," i. 402 ; not in English translation).

[2] " Lebens." (English translation), i. 212.

[3] Ibid. i. 365.

bar the way and interfere with the progress of the narrative.

But it must be noted that these parentheses are in themselves very interesting. When, for example, he speaks of Perizonius and his talent of divination and of the earthquakes at Rome : when he describes to us certain diseases, when he compares Roman and Macedonian tactics, Niebuhr is full of curious information, but the narrative is encumbered by this wealth of erudition.

What makes this fault in composition worse is the language. Niebuhr could never write. In his dissertations he is, as a rule, rhetorical and bombastic : he lacks simplicity and moderation. "His style," said Taine with a great deal of justice, "is obscured by abstract words, crowded with long phrases, lacking arrangement and divisions and noticeable movement : one might fancy oneself at the bottom of the mines in the Hartz Mountains, in the light of a smoking lamp, near a miner scraping with difficulty the hard rock." [1]

Macaulay was right in saying of Niebuhr : " A man who would have been the first writer of his time if his talent for communicating truths had borne any proportion to his talent for investigating them." [2]

V

LEOPOLD VON RANKE

At the first glance nothing seems of less national character than the work of Ranke, the historian. If one glances down the list of his books one finds that Italians, Spanish, Turks, Servians, Greeks of Peloponnesus,

---

[1] "Essai sur Tite-Live," p. 104.
[2] Preface to "Horatius."

Venetians, Roman Popes of the great period, French and English are dealt with, but in the midst of all this German and Prussian affairs seem to be lost.

In his capacity of professor, too, this illustrious scholar, who cast so much splendour over the Berlin University, scarcely resembles the historians of the new school, those apostles of Prussianism who turned their University chairs into political rostrums. With a penetrating and discreet mind and aristocratic tastes, that man, who was one of the companions of a most pious and conservative King, Frederick William IV, and of his suite of diplomatists and statesmen, lived quite outside the political questions of the day. He never sought the position of a deputy. He lived only for his science, sharing his life between his peaceful study, peopled with books, his lecture-room at the University of Berlin, and the meetings of the Academy of Sciences.

His political inclinations even were by no means those of the noisy, blustering national historians who for a long time gave trouble to the Prussian Government. Towards the end of his life he seemed quite a stranger among that democratic society which invaded Berlin after the convocation of the Imperial Reichstag. With his fine old head covered with white hair, his courteous and pleasant manners, his politeness that seemed of another age, he would have been taken, said one of his contemporaries, for an old marquis of the time of Minna von Barnhelm.

And yet this man of the old school was in a number of respects quite a modern man. No one had such a penetrating insight into the politics of the day. At the time when the Liberal national historians were waging an implacable war against the policy of William I, Ranke, in the silence of his study, approved of it entirely.   Later, he had nothing to deny, nothing to ask pardon for.   He had always been a good and faithful servant of the Prussian monarchy, above all, disinterested and discreet.   He did not parade his ideas and sentiments in his works.   Like a good disciple of Niebuhr, he believed that the lessons would not be the less striking because he had taken the trouble to conceal them.   With him one must first break the shell before one gets at the kernel, but it is not less pleasant on that account.

Let us try to unravel all this. . . . We shall see that his labours are not less real because they were not very noisy : that he, too, by his historical conception and the lessons to be learned from his works, is connected with the powerful movement in Prussian historiography.   In going over his life and his activity as a historian carefully, we shall be astonished at what we find in it, and we shall end by recognizing that his part in the common work was not lacking in splendour.

VI

Ranke is one of the most characteristic examples of the way in which Prussia, from the beginning of the century, was able to win over adherents to its policy. By his ancestry he belonged to old Germany.   Born at the beginning of the last century (1795) in Wiehe, a little agricultural town of Thuringia, where life flowed peacefully and without trouble, he was brought up in a middle-class family, of good solid education and strong virtues.

Who would suspect that at the time when he was born great upheavals were taking place elsewhere? With its old castles in ruins dating from the time of the Empire, Thuringia, that country of legends where

still the mountain in which old Barbarossa sleeps
is pointed out, seemed completely dead to modern
life. Its schools,[1] the first in Germany, were nurseries
for grammarians and philologists. What was taught
there had not changed since the time of the Reformation. At a time when, in France and England, the
reign of the applied sciences had begun, when the
intellectual horizon receded until it almost reached
the end of the earth, these people still had their eyes
turned towards the past.

There was no political life. In those rich valleys,
on the fruitful plains dotted with fields and forests,
the inhabitants lived in peace under the fatherly
authority of the King of Saxony, and none of these
good Protestants found it strange at that time that
their King should be a Catholic.

But these things were not slow in changing. Life
from without appeared among them: it came, as it
did to many other corners of Germany, in the train
of Napoleon's armies. Jena and Auerstadt are at
the gateway of this country. When Davout's cannon
roared, Ranke, a boy twelve years old, climbed up
the mountains near Wiehe to hear the noise of the
guns. Later he saw the French marshals with em-
broidered uniforms bedizened with crosses enter the
town. At that time, like all Saxons, it was with
distinct sympathy that he greeted the arrival of the
French: he read with admiration the bulletins of the
Grande Armée. But gradually these sentiments
dwindled. At school the teachers made their pupils
read the Agricola and awakened their patriotic feelings.
Until that time Ranke had only been a Saxon: but
his teachers showed him that above that little Saxony

---

[1] Donndorf and Schulpforta.

fatherland there was the great Germany fatherland, the ideal fatherland. From that time forward he no longer regarded the French as liberators. On the contrary, he read with joy in his house the manifestoes of the Allies. A powerful feeling of patriotism did not yet stir within him, but hatred was increasing in the bottom of his heart: he sighed for the tyrant's fall.

Ranke has admirably related all this in his " Autobiography " : [1] he also tells us how he came to see that the Germans should be united to prevent the return of such disasters, and how he came to be convinced that Prussia alone was capable of creating this unity. But even at that time he did not think that dreams of liberty would suffice to do this. He had a prudent and reflective mind. At a time when all the young people were filled with enthusiasm for liberal ideas, when those patriotic associations, the Tugendbund and Burschenschaft were founded, he prudently kept aside. He even reproved the more hot-headed ones ; but this did not prevent him, however, from thinking that " the repression of governments is as unjust as it is revolting." [2]

Already at that time Ranke was, as he was to remain for the rest of his life, a good Prussian. But this, however, was not brought about by Ranke alone. In 1815, when Thuringian Saxony was annexed by Prussia, Ranke, who was then a student at Leipzig University, recognized that it was not without grief that he experienced this " snatching away from the Saxon fatherland." But his father, who was a practical man, at once saw the advantages resulting

---

[1] " Zur eigenen Lebensgeschichte," Leipzig, 1890.
[2] Ibid. pp. 31, 47, 79, 81.

from this, and made his son understand them. He was a Saxon magistrate of positive temperament, who for a long time had praised "the superiority of the Prussian administration and the usefulness of Frederick the Great's institutions": he predicted that "the future of Germany was reserved for Prussia." "He wished me," said Ranke, "to follow up my career in Prussia, and at length I fell in with his point of view." [1]

From that moment Ranke became a good and faithful servant of the Prussian monarchy: in 1818 he began his career in Prussia as Professor at the college of Frankfort-on-the-Oder. "There," he said, "in the company of Prussian officials, I learned to appreciate the vigilant and enlightened administration of my new fatherland." [2] Seven years later, in 1825, he was called to Berlin to fill the chair of Professor of Modern History at the University. From that time on the union was complete. The Thuringian died completely within him, and if his accent had not still been a little raucous and guttural, and thus betrayed his High-Saxon origin, he would have been taken towards the end of his life for a Berliner of Berlin, a Berliner of the old school.

In the question of political outlook the identification was complete. The man who had not shared, at twenty years of age, the illusions of the young Liberals was ready to accept the Hohenzollern policy, made up of sound administration and wise government. And some years later he could write with truth : "It is a real pleasure to be part of a State with whose ideals one so heartily agrees." [3]

---

[1] "Zur eigen. Leben.," p. 47.

[2] Ibid. p. 31. He said that his entrance into Prussian service was the principal event of his life.   [3] Ibid. p. 315.

VII

When he arrived at Berlin in 1825, Ranke was a young scholar who had never yet taken any interest in politics. By instinct and temperament he was conservative, and as a Prussian little inclined to innovations. The first time he had to give an opinion ón the questions of the day was at the house of Varnhagen von Ense, where he often went, and where he met a new kind of man which he had not seen before —" Liberals," he said, " who were enamoured of the political struggles of the French Chambers, and who thought more or less that the future of liberty in Europe depended on the result of these struggles."

Asked to take part in this, Ranke, who could not become enthusiastic about something with which he was not acquainted, began to study history.[1] The principal problem of the age seemed to him to be that of the French Revolution, and after examining it from all sides he tried to solve it. To him the problem was thus stated : " Has the Revolution a general interest which gains the support of the mind and heart and claims a complete sympathy, or is it only an ordinary event which has its origin in certain particular facts, and which was the result of a concurrence of circumstances which might have been different ? "

But who cannot see that to state the problem thus

---

[1] " It was under this influence," said he in his " Autobiography," " that I began to read in 1827 the most remarkable authentic memoirs of that time. I plunged myself so deeply into the reading of the *Moniteur*, that I began to feel a personal acquaintance with the instigators of the movement. I learned to know the motives they invoked, the tendencies which moved before them, and thus it was that I solved the problem."

is, in a manner, to solve it, or to show at least that it is solved already in spirit? Ranke had the same illusion as many historians who believe that historical facts always help to prove the value of the political principles whose result they are, and in this case he saw that, as the French Revolution had failed in its essential task, the principles under whose authority it passed were bad ones. "While fully recognizing," said he, "its universal importance and what it was for each one of us in particular, yet I deliberately took my stand among those who opposed it."

Ranke did not like idealists in politics. Having met one day, at Vienna, a Saxon fellow-countryman, the philosopher Schneider, who expressed to him his admiration for the French Revolution, he wrote contemptuously of this man: "He is one ·of the race of idealists, liberals, rationalists, who foster the grossest prejudices with regard to history. Their convictions may well have the appearance of strict continuity and relationship: but for all that their falsity is none the less obvious." [1]

This was precisely the reproach he levelled at the French Revolution. The idealism of its legislators was repugnant to his realism. He argued like Burke, whose thoughts had a great influence over him. The "Reflections on the French Revolution" of the great English publicist formed the creed of Ranke's political faith. [2]

But there was another thing in the case of Ranke. If he did not like the ideas of the French Revolution it was because he saw in them a danger for Germany.

---

[1] "Zur eigen. Leben.," p. 205.
[2] On the relationship between Burke and von Ranke, see Ottocar Lorenz, "L. v. Ranke," pp. 83–85.

In his opinion one of the most marked traits in the French character was the liking for spreading their ideas. " To spread their ideas," he said, "the French would willingly make war." He could see proofs of this in the whole of modern history, " from that day when young noblemen, in their love for glory, embarked for America under the command of Lafayette, down to the wars of conquest (Eroberungsgelüste) of the Revolution and Napoleon." Hence his notion of the particular psychology of the French people which he laid down at the beginning of his " History of France." " Endowed with a national spirit, powerful, ambitious, conquest-loving and warlike, the French people are always ready to take the offensive; they defend themselves unceasingly against real or imaginary enemies and oppress free nations." [1]

The consequence of this with Ranke is that in his opinion revolution and desire of conquest are synonymous terms among the French. He cannot see a movement towards liberty on the banks of the Seine without thinking that soon conquering armies will be marching on the Rhine. He shows this occasionally in an amusing fashion in his correspondence.

In August 1830, for example, when travelling in Italy, he learned, in a village hidden in the Apennines, the news of " the three vainglorious." At once he becomes excited. " What ' la grande nation ' requires," he cries, " is some one who will put her in order without upsetting her neighbours on that account."

In 1848, again, " he thought he could see a new danger to Germany at the hand of that nation always ready to make war (Schlagfertige französische Nation)."

---

[1] Preface to his " French History."

Yet Ranke was not one of those fanatical Teuto-maniacs who, whenever any one spoke to them of France, saw red at once. He had often spent holidays in that country and he had illustrious friends there. He even liked the Frenchman as an individual, enjoyed "his sociability and his delicate taste in the arts." He also recognized what civilization owed to "la grande nation," and this time I think there was no sarcasm in his use of this expression.

But what Ranke did not like in the French was their politics. He thought that if Germany wished to do any good she should take an opposite course to that of France and consequently take care not to borrow anything from her.

Ranke expounded these ideas throughout the articles published in the *Politische-Historische Zeitschrift* (Berlin, 1831-36), which he founded for the express purpose of combating French influence in Germany. " The sympathies for what was happening in France were so lively and wide-spread," said he, "that I allowed myself to speak my opinion on the situa-tion." [1]

Ranke's programme was clear and simple. " Let us make our own organizations without troubling to imitate our neighbours." This conformed with the philosophy of history which past experience had taught him.

"We have to undertake," said he, "a task which only concerns ourselves, a task that is entirely German. We have to form a real German State which will correspond to the genius of our nation. Above all, we must take care not to imitate the forms which the French nation have found satisfactory for themselves.

---

[1] " Zur eigen. Leben.," p. 60. Letter of March 1831.

French interests are quite different from our own . . . .
I do not blame them for having done what they
have : that they should be what they wish, or what
they can be, is their own business. . . . As for ourselves, all the efforts of our great literary period, all
the scientific discoveries of our great men, all that has
become great in Germany, has never succeeded save
by opposition to France." [1]

But this had no echo among the crowd. The
German middle-class was not ready yet for these ideas.
" Irremediably indifferent to politics," said one of the
historians who later was to have an influence in trans-
forming it, " the middle-class was satisfied with venerat-
ing Canning, with agitating against reaction, shaking its
fist at Polignac, before going back to its business or
going to bed." [2] It was evident that, to awaken it
from its sluggishness, something more than academic
phrases was required. Now Ranke, a man of aristocratic talent and refined diplomacy, excelled in discussing
questions, but lacked the passion necessary to make
another share his convictions. There was nothing
popular in him. His qualities were those of a historian,
not of a political writer, and still less a controversialist.
He spoke more to the intelligence than to the heart or
will. At the beginning of his undertaking he wrote :
" I need more than ever, moderation, restraint, intelligence, and wisdom." But that is diametrically opposed
to what he needed in order to succeed. The crowd
knows nothing of the subtle distinctions of thought, of
delicate distinctions and shades. It must be spoken to
in a direct and powerful language. As soon as Ranke

---

[1] " Zur Geschichte Deutschlands und Frankreich in 19. Jahrdh.,"
Leipzig, 1889, pp. 72, 73.
[2] Sybel, " Die Begrundung des Deutschen Reiches," i. 72.

began to give his reasons it would no longer listen to him.[1]

By wishing, moreover, to satisfy all, he did not succeed in pleasing anybody. "How I was mistaken," said he, "in thinking that every one would approve. Just the opposite happened : my old friends Varnhagen von Ense and Alexander von Humboldt, who saw the salvation of the world in the progress of the French Revolution, showed coldness towards me and became estranged from me. My friends of that time, Radowitz and Gerlach, who had just established a Conservative paper, could not tolerate me because I did not entirely approve of the Revolution."[2]

Ranke ended by renouncing his undertaking. Three years later the paper had ceased to exist. This check had this advantage for the historian, that it made him sceptical of all theories. Twelve years later he was completely won over to the policy of practice. In the midst of the Revolution of 1848, in the midst of the general confidence and joy, he understood that the votes of a parliament would never be able to complete the unity of Germany. He now expected nothing but from the good sword of Prussia.

This he said with considerable directness to the King, Frederick William IV, who, astounded by what was happening in those days in March at Berlin, had

---

[1] At the beginning of his undertaking Ranke seemed to take stock of the difficulties which met him. " I do not know," he wrote on November 21, 1831, " why I came to a decision so speedily. I have a sort of excuse for that. My studies up to the present have taken me to the threshold of contemporary history. I shall not easily find so good an opportunity of becoming acquainted with the affairs, position, and interests of contemporary society " (" Zur eigen. Leben., " p. 258.

[2] " Zur eigen. Leben.," p. 50.

asked his advice on the situation. Ranke summarily replied to his sovereign: "Grant a constitution. . . . The constitutional system should be considered, without affection or hatred, as the political form which modern societies affect. In the actual state of our affairs two things militate in favour of a constitution : in the first place the old Prussian administration, which was so great in its day, which rendered such great services, has ceased to exist. . . . The second reason is that men are accustomed nowadays only to consider political life under the constitutional form. The countries on the banks of the Rhine have judicial institutions, the ideas of which do not agree with those of the hereditary States of Prussia: and these institutions have in their own countries the force of laws. . . . If we do not take any notice of that, there is another thing which we should consider—our relations with the rest of Germany." [1]

In these circumstances Ranke showed a remarkable political insight. But, like a good Prussian, he did not wish that the constitutional institutions should take over everything. The King's authority should remain intangible. It was the cornerstone of the new political arch. The King should not receive the "word of order" from the street, and to assure Frederick William IV, who was shaken by the Berlin rising, he said to him: "At bottom the people have no interest in politics . . . what they want is just to live. . . . Their heart is good, but they are suffering. . . . They listen to the leaders. They only wanted, in the Revolution, an opportunity of showing their discontent. Put right their just demands and they will sever their connection with the professional rioters

---

[1] " Zur Geschichte Deutschlands," p. 592.

We must before anything find work for those who need it."

Thereupon Ranke develops the whole of a daring programme which is a sort of State Socialism, which the future imperialists might well have envied him. " We shall organize companies of workmen," he said, "who will be employed in public works, in the improvement of rivers, the cultivation of waste lands, and other works of this kind. On the other hand, to those who have little property we shall grant but few political rights."[1] In the question of Prussian politics Ranke is no less positive : " Prussia has a mission to perform in Germany : she should not flinch before her task : she should restrain the rebellious by force. You are master of the situation," he said to the King, " since you have the army."

Then follows a passage about the Prussian army : " It is a tree with ancient roots. Storms have smitten and stripped it of some of its branches, but since then it has grown . . . strong and proud. . . . The other troops have no such history : they are too weak to be called armies. . . . The Prussian army alone it was which put an end to the dangerous consequences which a union of constitutional ideas with destructive tendencies might have. Was it not this army that was able to protect the Frankfort Assembly ? "

Conclusion : " With so fine an army " we can dictate our conditions to the Germans ; we can subdue " the rebellious princes " ; we also can, " if Austria will not understand that to relieve her of her interests in Germany is to do her a service,[2] convince her of it by force of arms (Krieg wagen)." [3] And this word in

---

[1] " Zur Geschichte Deutschlands, " pp. 598, 605.
[2] Ibid. p. 611.   [3] Ibid. p. 615.

conclusion, worthy of Bismarck himself: "I have no doubt that Prussia, by approaching the revolutionary elements in this qualified fashion, will gain thereby a greater position in the world : but the action must be rapid, resolute, and energetic." [1]

Frederick William IV, intelligent enough to understand the situation but not energetic enough to deal with it (he himself said to the delegates at Frankfort who offered him the imperial crown: "Frederick the Great would have been your man; as for me, I am not a great king")—Frederick William IV, I say, was satisfied to lock up this advice in his drawer and leave to better times and another king the task of putting it into practice.

As for Ranke, who for a moment had left his historical works to give his opinion on the situation, he returned to them with more calmness than ever. He knew that the policy he recommended was the right one— that it was, as he said, "in the logic of the history of Prussia"; and while waiting until that man should appear who could, who ought to, realize it, he, for his part, went on preparing the coming generation for it by the political teachings which he intended to give with his historical lectures.

VIII

It is said that, at a congress of historians, a zealous Protestant, author of a history of the Reformation, equally noted for the orthodoxy of his opinions and for his partiality, accosted Ranke and said to him, with vainglorious pride: "We have this in common, you and I, dear colleague: we are both historians and

---

[1] "Zur Geschichte Deutschlands," pp. 611–15.

Christians." "But," replied Ranke, "there is one difference between us : I am a historian first and then a Christian."[1] This most authentic anecdote gives an admirable description of Ranke. The moment he approached history, he left his individual feelings at the door. His ideas were dear to him, but dearer still was his love of truth. This man, apparently so calm, became excited when truth was at stake.

"What I seek," he wrote in one of his letters, "is truth, not glory : I aspire with all my power to this truth . . . error ought gradually to disappear."

Ranke's career as a historian had no other origin than this same search after truth. When he taught history to his young students at Frankfort-on-the-Oder, he set about rewriting the history by going back to the actual sources, in order to be certain of its truth. This work decided what his calling should be. When studying the fifteenth century, and at the time when Louis XI was occupying his attention, Scott's historical novel, "Quentin Durward," which

---

[1] Ranke was by conviction a Protestant of an orthodoxy that had no narrow-mindedness in it, but which was no less positive on that account. He attended services, even to an advanced age, as long as his health permitted. In the evening he read the Bible to his family. "In the face of the problems of life," he said, "I humbly confess my faith as a Christian." He also said, "I am a Christian before I am a Protestant." But when he approached history he forgot his particular faith and only remembered that he was a historian. When speaking of Jesus Christ in his "Universal History," iv. 160 and 165, he said : "In writing this name, although I am a good evangelical Christian, I must still guard against the presumption of undertaking to speak in this place of the religious mystery, which, incomprehensible as it is, cannot be understood by historical intelligence. . . . The domain of religious belief and that of historical science are not opposed one to the other, but distinct in their nature."

deals with this period, came into his hands. " I read it," he says in his " Autobiography," " and found a great deal of charm in it, but one thing shocked me, and that was the liberties the author had taken with Charles the Bold and Louis XI, quite contrary to all historical tradition, even in matters of detail. I studied Commines and the contemporary accounts, and became still more convinced that a Charles the Bold, a Louis XI, such as Walter Scott represented them, never existed. The worthy novelist knew this himself: and I could not excuse him for having given his story characteristics destitute of historical value. By comparing his account with the truth, I was convinced that historical truth was far more beautiful and far more interesting than romantic fiction. From that time forward I devoted myself to the former, and resolved to avoid in my works all imagination and invention, and to restrict myself severely to facts." [1]

Ranke summarized his purpose as a historian in the Preface to his first work, " Histories of the Roman and German Peoples " : " I desire simply to relate the facts as they actually occurred." [2]

At first sight nothing seems simpler and even more ordinary than this purpose. To speak the truth —all sincere historians desire to do this. There is no doubt about this, but in practice it is a difficult thing to realize. It is not enough merely to wish to do so ; a peculiar grace is necessary, and this is granted to but a few.

This grace, which consists of certain natural gifts, which are perhaps negative qualities, such as balance of faculties, weight of judgment, wisdom, but also of positive qualities, such as goodness and faith,

---

[1] " Zur eigen. Leben.," p. 61.   [2] Preface, p. vii.

Ranke possessed in the highest degree. He never took offence, and sought always to be fair to every one, and said : "Before anything else we must be just and good."[1] He thought this could be accomplished by hard work, and a certain hygiene which he summarized in these words: "Man's duty is to be at peace with himself and to keep himself in a condition of self-satisfaction."[2]

Therein, it may be said, was the secret of his power. This wise man exuded from his lips the honey of Nestor. His experience is full of peacefulness. He

---

[1] He exercised this spirit of fairness towards himself as well. He was entirely without jealousy. One day he was candidate for the chair of history at Munich University. The King of Bavaria preferred Görres to him. "It is only right," said he, "that the King should have made this choice. Such a man, I think, should not live abroad and suffer miseries there" ("Zur eigen. Leben.," p. 189). See also in his Correspondence the moderate tone in which he speaks of one of his colleagues who quoted him freely without acknowledgment (1845).

[2] Like Spinoza, he thought that lowness of spirits and discouragement were a diminution of one's being, and that they were our worst enemies. "Among all the states of mind which we ought to combat,"¡ he wrote to one of his brothers who was prone to be discouraged, "there is that one which paralyses our powers at the moment we have need of them. It takes its place in the depth of our being, near love, enthusiasm, and will, and annihilates all those qualities which might make our activity good, great, and happy. This evil disposition, my dear boy, has long since planted its roots in you, and finds expression in your letter. It seems to me—but I don't know whether it is right—that such a disposition should be avoided, since it comes, as a rule, from something that is without us and outside our calculations : and that it introduces a foreign element which infects us. Nature has given us two means of striving against this disposition : carelessness or anger. You will find a third one which nature does not give to us, but which the good man (der gute Mann) gives himself" ("Zur eigen. Leben.," p. 174).

saw from above, he saw from afar: he saw rightly too. His vision was never troubled by passion or prejudices. At an early stage he reached that state of wisdom, the fruit of experience, which is granted only to old men. And this wisdom—there is no doubt about it—gave his intellectual faculties all their force and the whole of their range.

Ranke was not a genius: he was even lacking in originality, but he was very intelligent. Endowed with great gifts, he had shown, from childhood, a great universality of aptitudes. As a historian he was not a man of one idea or of one science. On the benches of the University, at a time when that enormous work of specialization beyond measure began, he devoted himself to the most varied studies—history, philosophy, law, literature, and theology. He showed, indeed, a kind of horror for that kind of scholar, so frequent in Germany, who is nothing more than a learned man. " This colossal race," he said, " works all the harder at a subject the more insignificant it is." [1]

Niebuhr even did not find grace in his sight. He thought him too erudite, and not sufficiently literary.[2] " There are other things than mere texts to examine," he said. The great ideas of history ought also to be

---

[1] In his Correspondence, for example, he reprimands his brother for studying " that unfortunate Cornelius Nepos about whom no one knows anything and about whom it is not worth while learning anything, for he is one of the most insignificant of Latin authors " (" Zur eigen. Leben.," p. 66).

[2] He said of Niebuhr : " I had difficulty in following him through the thorny discursions on the Roman Constitutions, just as with Ottfried Müller in the affairs relating to the Constitution of Greece " (Ibid. p. 41). Elsewhere he also says : " Niebuhr often loses sight of the universal connection of history. With him the individual question ends by devouring the general one " (" Ueber die Epochen," Preface).

investigated by the historian. [1] The interest which Ranke took in history was a human one. " To look at the world, past and present," said he : " to absorb it into my being as far as my powers will enable me : to draw out and appropriate all that is beautiful and great, to see with unbiased eyes the progress of universal history, and in this spirit to produce beautiful and noble works : imagine what happiness it would be for me if I could realize this ideal, even in a small degree. " [2]

Ranke had something of Goethe's spirit in his conception of history. He has expressed this admirably in the following lines : " The real interest we take in the world consists in our trying to make something within us of what is without us." [3]

Elsewhere he expounds the same thought in the following way : " History has no other task than to record the actions and sufferings of that multiple being which we are, at once savage, violent, powerful, good, noble, calm, soiled and pure : to follow it from its birth and in its shaping. I am re-reading the ' Universal History.' My heart beats rapidly when considering human affairs." [4]

---

[1] The Professor who had most influence over him at Leipzig University, where he studied, was F. Beck, whose " knowledge in the domains of history and literature was very wide." On the other hand he had little liking for Gottfried Hermann, too much of a grammarian for his taste, giving too much importance to the question of metre alone.

[2] " Zur eigen. Leben.," p. 261.

[3] Ibid. p. 219.

[4] In another part of his Correspondence, Ranke said that the first condition in the making of a real historian was to have an actual interest in men. " If one has a true sympathy for this race of varied beings of which we are units . . . for that being who has suffered . . . one is always pleased to learn how, at all times, it has lived ; to know its virtues . . . its vices . . .

In order to obtain this knowledge of man, Ranke assigns two tasks to the historian : the first is to place in its own type of truth the individuality of the great historical actors and the nations they represent : the second is to mark their rôle in the concatenation of universal history, which is to him definitely the supreme object of history. The individuality of nations and the concatenation of Universal History are the two characteristics of Ranke's history.

Ranke in the first place attaches a great deal of importance to the study of individuals. As opposed to Buckle, who believed that the great historical movements were determined by physical laws in which men had, so to speak, no part, and of which they are only the instruments, Ranke holds that history is nothing more than "the work of certain minds fulfilling more or less certain conditions, and each having a certain peculiar sphere of influence." [1]

Without going as far as Carlyle in his belief in the missions of historical men, Ranke was convinced that the development of a nation or a period depends upon the great men who have best personified its spirit. "It has not been doctrines that have overthrown the world," said he, "but the powerful personalities who are the incarnation of these doctrines." [2] Now it is a point to notice—and history proves it—that these great historical figures do not appear save as

---

its joys and sorrows, the development of its nature in the most varied circumstances, without any other object in view, just as one enjoys flowers without thinking of their classification."

[1] "The historian's task," said he, "is to explain history by human motives."

[2] "Zur eigen. Leben.," p. 570. "Geschichte der romischen Päpste," 1878, ii. 23.

the manifestation of a general tendency which exists without them, and that they belong at the same time to an order of the moral world of which they are the incarnation.[1] Great men are also, then, a product of nations, and they do not appear save " at a comparatively advanced stage of civilization."

We must study, then, with great care the nation and race, and, since they are made up not of unconscious and blind forces, but of compounds or aggregates of free individuals, we must try to determine the characteristics of " this collective individuality " which are to be found in each of its components.

If Ranke gives great importance to this " individuality of peoples," it is because in his eyes it determines their historical action—that is, their politics, their art, their poetry and their religion. It is by means of this that he explains the differences between peoples, races, and periods, and that is why he wished to be acquainted with it to the utmost detail, and why he prosecutes a full inquiry with respect to each people and all its historical representatives. Ranke discovered that this inquiry had never hitherto been sufficiently prosecuted, and he insisted that universal history, which is only known to us by tradition, should be subjected to new investigations.

This was an enormous enterprise which one man alone could not carry out with success. Ranke was satisfied to set an example. His first works, " History of the Roman and Germanic Peoples " (1824), " The Moors and the Spanish Monarchy " (1827), and " History of the Popes " (1834–36), covered the history of Europe from the end of the fifteenth to the beginning of the seventeenth century. Beyond anything else he

---

[1] Preface, " Wallenstein."

sought original documents, at first hand. He read all the chronicles, all the letters of the period. At Berlin he discovered in the Royal Library some narratives by the Venetian Ambassadors, rich in details explanatory of the political life at that period. This was a discovery that had a great influence on his career as a historian. It determined what manner of research he was to make, inclining him more and more towards diplomatic history. In fact, it added to his historical talent some of diplomacy's most marked characteristics : diplomatic delicacy, reserve, and a mind capable of understanding all shades of opinion, all of which he acquired by associating with those subtle Italian diplomatists who saw everything and said nothing, and for whom the diplomacy of intrigue and secret service had no more secrets.

For the writing of the works which followed immediately after—" German History at the Time of the Reformation " (1839–43), " History of France" (1852–56), " History of England " (1859–68)—he levied contributions on the archives of the principal cities of Europe.[1]

But to collect material was for Ranke only a part of the historian's task : to make a critical study of it was more important in his eyes. Ranke's criticism resembles in no way that of Niebuhr, although it was

[1] When writing his " History of France," for example, he paid frequent visits to Paris between 1839 and 1850. " I am surprised," he wrote, " that the French let me investigate part of their history here" (" Zur eigen. Leben.," p. 339). Of London, where he stayed often and for long periods in order to complete his " History of England," he wrote : " No nation has so much unpublished material for its history as the English nation. In the valuable State archives and British Museum I have found many unknown details which shed a new light upon the politics of the time " (" History of England," i., Preface).

derived from his. It is exercised not on the word but on the idea—that is, it is concerned more with the witness than with his evidence.

This can be understood : in view of the multitude of facts in modern history it would be impossible to establish the strict authenticity of each of them. We should be satisfied to examine their source—that is, the amount of good faith in their narrator. That is why Ranke concerns himself above all with the critical study of sources. He finds out in the first place whence the authors derive the facts which they relate, and whether they were actual witnesses or only repro-duce a story from hearsay : under what circumstances they wrote their works, what was their character, their mode of life, their manner of work, etc. And it is not until he is in possession of this information that Ranke accepts the evidence of a writer on any event.

This mode of criticism was not new. Many writers had employed it before Ranke. It was Sainte-Beuve's method, for example, in literary criticism.[1] To succeed in this more psychological instinct is needed than actual science. And Ranke was well provided with this spirit of subtlety.

Beyond this versatile critical genius Ranke had a synthetic spirit of the widest radius. Indeed, it is the combination of these two characteristics, one of

---

[1] See, for example, the portraits which Ranke has given us of the historians of the Renaissance—Machiavelli, Guicciardini, Giovio—in his " Critical Studies on the History of the Renaissance," which was included with his first publication, " The Germanic and Roman Peoples." Among the finest specimens of critical history we should mention his essay on the Spanish Conspiracy against Venice, his dissertation on the Memoirs of the Margrave of Baireuth, and on the Memoirs of Frederick II ; his fine passages on Clarendon, and his lucid exposition of the origin of the Revolutionary Wars.

which as a rule precludes the other in the same man, which makes up the originality of Ranke's talent as a historian. While devoted to the study of detail, his mind likes to soar to embrace the whole. Even as a young man, when [he began to write history, he said he wished " to write history from the highest point of view, to establish the inter-relationship of events," " to study the march of progress of mankind," " to reach the very core of history," and " to put an end to the regrettable fault of universal histories, all of which are fragmentary."

Ranke is still regarded as a universal historian. From his earliest works, he tried to write portions of universal history. But he never saw the magnitude of his task until he began his " History of the Popes." Enthusiastic over his discoveries, he then exclaimed : " Gradually the history of the most important periods of the world sinks into me almost without my knowledge : to make this history plain and to write it will be the purpose of my life. I am satisfied to know what I live for : my heart beats violently when I foresee the happiness which the elaboration of this important work will give me : every day I promise myself to bring it to a successful end : every day I take an oath not to budge by a hairbreadth from truth once I have recognized it as such. I am often reproached with extending my horizon too far : I am told that an aim nearer at hand would be more easily reached, that I do myself wrong by staying so long in foreign countries. But these words no more than strike my ear, and I continue my forward march without listening to them." [1]

[1] " Zur eigen. Leben.," pp. 89 and 164. " I have the conviction ever stronger in me," he wrote, " that in history, after all, nothing

Indeed, it was an immense political history of Europe, of each nation at the most brilliant period of its life, which he thus saw rise from the dust of the papers found in the libraries of Italy, France, Germany, and England.

In his "History of the Roman and Germanic Peoples," he attempts to prove that in spite of the abyss that seems to be sunk between the two great races of Western Europe, the Germanic and the Latin races, both these peoples have worked with the same object: the elaboration of European civilization: in his "History of the Moors and the Spanish Monarchy," he depicts for us the most brilliant period in the life of these nations at a time when "their history had a European significance"; the "History of the Popes" is conceived as an enormous fragment of European history at the time when pontifical power reached its fullest expansion, in one of those "decisive phases on which the fate of the world depends"; [1] his "History of Germany at the Time of the Reformation" shows the part in universal history played by Luther.[2] His histories of France and England are taken at times "when the history of these countries was involved in European history"—in France the reign of Louis XIV, in England the time of the religious and

---

but universal history can be written. All our efforts tend to illuminate this. Detail never seems better than when it is seen in its relation with the whole."

[1] Before writing this work Ranke had conceived a more universal one still, that of the birth of Protestantism in the face of the Roman Church and of its development as opposed to the renovation of Catholicism. He gave it up because it seemed to take him too far.

[2] "Our German history became at that period at once a universal history" ("History of Germany," v. 102).

political struggles of the sixteenth and seventeenth centuries."[1]

In all "these moments of universal history" what Ranke pre-eminently brings to light is civilization. This does not mean that Ranke wrote histories of civilization. On the contrary, his conception of history is purely political. One can even see that diplomatic negotiations take up a very large place in his books, but what Ranke regards, after all, as the aim of human activity is civilization. In this respect this national historian is still a German of the eighteenth century. His inspiration seemed human rather than strictly national. Above the rivalry of races, peoples, and religions, what he continually brings to light is the triumph of civilization. This word "civilization" (Kultur) comes continuously from his pen, as if it gave us the key to the general tendencies of his mind. In his "History of France," deploring the death of Henry IV, he cries : "If Henry IV had lived he might perhaps have spared Germany the horrors of the Thirty Years War and saved that late sixteenth-century *civilization*, which might have been surpassed in what concerns development of science and inventions, but which was far more comparatively widespread among all classes of society." Elsewhere in his "Universal History" he showed that if Julius Cæsar is so great it is because his victorious armies gave new openings to *civilization* and attacked

---

[1] "History of England of the Seventeenth Century." "England took a great part in the political emancipation of Western Europe : she had a Constitution which has become that of most modern States : her part in reform has been enormous : she personifies the union of modern feeling with tradition."

With the French people, it is the people's history that has most importance and most general significance. "European life has been tossed about between the two poles of the political life of these nations " (Preface, vi–ix).

in order to conquer barbarianism in an important part of the earth.

With this Ranke was not far from sharing Hegel's notion, which became that of all the Prussian historians —namely, that civilization is spread only by war: that " the bloody human battles are only at bottom the struggles of moral energy." [1] But Ranke did not parade these ideas in his works and he did not seek therein a pretext triumphantly to show the superiority of the Germanic race over other races. He was satisfied to believe that " God uses wars for purpuses which we do not know, and that it is moral influences which regulate the greatness and decline of men and nations." [2]

IX

With the characteristics which we have just recognized in Ranke's work—the universal tendency and

---

[1] " Epochen der neuen Geschichte," p. 7.

[2] Ranke expounded this point of view over and over again in his works. " Of ancient civilization," he said with reference to the Italians of the Renaissance, " they had nothing but the shadow . . . that is why the judgment of God weighed against them. . . . The evil had increased and passed from one palace to another " (" History of the Roman and Germanic Peoples," p. 77). The same of the Spanish of the sixteenth century : " Life among them withered on the plant, and they were present impotently at their ruin, from which they have not yet delivered themselves." He explained in the same way the decadence of the Turks : " Many of them, it is true, had certain virtues which adorn any man : their sincerity, kindness, and hospitality are praised : yet they have not carried it as far as to include the free development of the mind : they have always remained barbarians. Of the beauty of things they have only felt the sensuality. They have no desire to take the world into themselves, to truly identify themselves with it. They marched over the ruins of a civilization that had been nobler at one time " (" The Moors and the Spanish Monarchy," p. 76).

æsthetic inspiration—it scarcely seems possible to range his work among the creations of national history.

Yet Ranke thought so. He thought that he also by his works had contributed his help to his country's policy. In truth, he attached a different meaning to his task as historian from that of his confrères. The historian, in his opinion, had no other mission than to fortify political judgment. For that the historical method, well applied, was sufficient. By relating in good faith affairs as they really happened, he thought that was the best way of preparing future generations for the tasks which awaited them.

Ranke was a pupil of Niebuhr. " My conception of history," he said in his " Autobiography," " arose from the notion of the individuality of peoples as opposed to the French theories of Republics or Universal Empires." [1] Like Niebuhr, he believed that the State is only " a modification of national life, that is, Nation and State are one and the same thing."

This idea he made the foundation of all his works, and thus it was he thought to work as a national historian. And, indeed, we might say of his work that it is the expression of the historical development of the peoples of modern Europe: Italians, Turks, Spaniards, Serbians, French, and English. In telling this to the Germans, he showed them what they had to do.

But that was not good enough for the national historians. From 1830 on it was seen that the historian was expected to take a side. At the time of the rising of the Greeks, they found it strange that a national historian, instead of attacking Metter-

---

[1] " Zur eigen. Leben.," p. 47. He boasted that he followed up Niebuhr, who was the first, he said, to study the inmost conditions of the historical development of a people.

nich or celebrating in a lyrical tone Navarino and Missolonghi, should make learned researches about the ancestors of these heroic men, and should show us, in a charming picture, what was Peloponnesian life in the sixteenth century. A little later, in 1833, at a time when one could already foresee the Prussian Kultur-kampf, they were angry that he should paint with an artist's affection the figures of the sovereign pontiffs, whose excesses had caused the Reformation.

The publicist Gustav Freytag undertook, in the name of his fellow-countrymen, to tell Ranke his opinion.

But the latter was unmoved. It is true that, after the publication of his " History of the Popes," he wrote a " History of Germany in the Time of the Reforma-tion," but this was not as a concession to the wishes ot the Prussian patriots: he merely wished to write a " counterpart to his first work."

Yet Ranke recognized that there was something particularly national in the German Reformation, which he called " the act by which the German nation had best shown its deep-rooted unity, since there was a time when Protestantism was the religion of all the Germans." He added: " But this German idea was repelled soon afterwards by the powerful efforts of the opposite party . . . so that the attention of historians has been directed towards the State in which Protestant thought had displayed the greatest political energy. I even had friends who considered the history of Prussia as the second part of the ' History of the Reforma-tion.' " [1]   But he kept aside from all exaggeration.

---

[1] Ranke said that he thought that he had helped to make Luther known to the German people by means of this history (" Zur eigen. Leben.," p. 558). Sybel said of this work : " This history is filled with the enthusiasm of the German patriot for the

At the time when Ranke was completing this work, in 1843, the political horizon in his country was clouded. In addition to the questions of national unity, of Great and Little Germany, there was now another political question even more burning than the others— the question of constitutional freedom. We know already at what conclusion Ranke had arrived on this point. He did not think that the constitutional institutions were a universal panacea. "It is a mistake of our times," he said, "to believe that the happiness and safety of societies is in the wisdom of deliberating assemblies and written constitutions. . . . The true destiny of Prussia is to be and to remain a military monarchy. . . . The true representative of a people is the King. . . . What use is there in rebelling against historical right? The winds of heaven drive the sands hither and thither, but the mountains they leave where they were."

But Ranke thought that the time had come to do something else, and by means of history he wished to prove the truth of his thesis. The history which seemed best suited for that was the history of the French Revolution. The German middle class were at that time most enthusiastic about this event, with which they were only acquainted by means of the extenuating histories of Thiers and Mignet, which were spread throughout Germany in thousands of copies. Ranke was convinced that, by describing this Revolution just as it had actually taken place, the account of it authorized by French historians would

highest manifestation of the German mind. It has a passionate and powerful tone, a startling vivacity and grandeur " (" Gedactnisrede auf L. v. Ranke," p. 12). W. Scherrer said : " This work was the most important from the national point of view " (" Übersicht ").

be destroyed for ever. To do this seemed to him to be a work of national interest, and in 1843 he left for Paris to collect necessary material.

Ranke has told us in his " Autobiography " how, in view of the insufficiency of State papers placed at his disposal, he was obliged to give up his undertaking, and how at the same time chance threw in his way a most valuable account of Prussian affairs in the eighteenth century. This was the letters of Valori, French Ambassador at the Court of Frederick the Great, which contained some very interesting information about the politics of the Prussian King.

" With the permission of my friend Mignet the historian," said Ranke, " I took a copy of this, and provided with this valuable prize I returned to Berlin. . . . This was the beginning of my work ' Nine Books of Prussian History,' in which I sought to explain how the Brandenburg Electorate had become a first-class Power." [1]

To turn from the French Revolution to the history of Prussia was not, in Ranke's opinion, a change of subject, since the one presented, in politics, the positive side of the problem of which the other was the negative.

By showing the normal and regular development of the Prussian State, he arrived at the same result as in describing the French Revolution: he showed the Germans how their unity might be brought about. Again without positively interposing himself in his story, after the manner of Prussian historians, he admits " that he takes an active part in the events which he relates," for without that sympathy, he says, " such a history would not be possible." He recognized even that in this history he has never lost sight of the

---

[1] " Zur eigen. Leben.," pp. 73, 74.

general interests of Germany. "The ideas of Frederick the Great on this subject," said he, "appeared for the first time with the third volume, when Charles VII became Emperor."[1]

But he avoids all exaggeration. Far from seeing, for example, in the Kings of Prussia any extensive schemes or fixed purpose to inaugurate a great German policy, he shows, on the contrary, that the extraordinary state of affairs in Germany at a later period originated in the "altogether Prussian" labours of those Kings. Now that is a most accurate conception, and one which, far from depreciating Prussia, makes her seem greater.

This German conception of Prussian history was confirmed by the war of 1870. At that time Ranke, without becoming intoxicated by victory like a large number of his compatriots, believed that this date marked a new phase in universal history and that it opened to Germany's future infinite prospects. From that time he gave himself up by preference to researches in national history relating to events of the past which had some connection with this war. He wrote the "Origins of the Seven Years War" (1871), "The German Powers and the Confederation of Princes"—history of Germany from 1780-90 (1872), "The Genesis of the Prussian State" (1873), and "The Origin and Beginnings of the Revolutionary Wars, 1791-92" (1875).

In the first of these works, "The Origins of the Seven Years War," Ranke tried to show the close relationship between this war and the Franco-Prussian conflict of 1870. He said in his Preface:

---

[1] Letter to Prince Maxim. of Bavaria, December 26, 1847. Ibid. p. 332.

" After the declaration of war in 1870, days and weeks passed in which it was not possible to concentrate one's attention on anything which was not closely related to this event. While waiting for the result that was to determine the fate of Germany and Europe, the historian's attention was irresistibly directed towards the distant events of the past which brought about this war. One of these events is the war of 1756. Has it not been proved indeed that the war between Prussia and Austria would have ceased had it not been for the participation in it of France? . . . So that while the young men were getting ready around me to take part in this war, I took up, at the moment when the hour for departure had struck, this essay, already begun and laid aside, on that great event which had a certain relationship with the great fight for which every one was getting ready. . . . I can now attempt to offer this writing to the public : it is the tribute I bring to the great events and actions of last year." [1]

But Ranke was satisfied to set out his point of view in his Preface. In the body of the book it never intervenes, and, although France was then Prussia's enemy, he does not take advantage of that, like so many of his country's historians, in order to rail against the "unruly and vain Gaul." He was satisfied to set out facts. It is true that at times these facts have a terrible eloquence.

But Ranke, with all this, was a slave to historical truth. He was incapable of hiding or concealing facts, even though they contradicted his most cherished opinions. Thus it is that, in his "Origin of the Revolutionary Wars," he sided flatly against Sybel,

---

[1] Preface, v–vii ; xxx. 63, 64. " Complete Works."

who wished absolutely to lay the blame of this war on the Girondins. Ranke shows that the Girondins were not responsible for it, but that the Governments of Europe were truly to blame, who by their stupid interference with French affairs over-excited the self-love of the French people and made war inevitable. It is stimulating to notice here that it was the old Prussian Conservative who defended the national interests of a people, while the National-Liberal Sybel thought quite natural those claims of the Kings, drawn up by Kaunitz, to dictate to the French their course of action.[1] But Ranke was a true historian who knew how to sacrifice his personal preferences to truth.

This does not mean that Ranke was absolutely denuded of all the prejudices of Prussian historians. Although there could be nothing less chauvinistic than his type of mind, he willingly believed that Modern Germany was called to take the first place in Europe. The war of 1870 thus had in his eyes a symbolical meaning: it was not merely the victory of one people over another, it was also the victory of one policy over another, of one civilization over

---

[1] Ranke rightly says that at that time a Government was being established in France which was opposed to the political principles which were in vogue in Europe then. He adds: " No one can deny that the French doctrines were fraught with danger for other Governments which rested on principles analogous to those which the French had overthrown. But if it is undeniable that the Revolution was opposed to the historical formation (Gestaltung) of Europe, it is no less true that the setting up of a supreme tribunal to judge on French affairs was in flagrant contradiction with the rights of nations. . . . The whole question at issue was whether a nation has a right to dispose of itself freely or not."

another.[1]   Indeed, it was in order to enunciate this idea that he resolved, at eighty years of age, to write a large universal history whose purpose he thus expounds : " The universal prospect which is now opened to Germany and the world has induced me to devote my last strength to this work." [2]

In his mind, the whole matter was to indicate the place of each race or each people in the work of common civilization. Death stopped him before he could come to modern times. If he had reached it there is no doubt but that, in spite of the leading purpose of the work—to summarize in Modern Germany the civilization of the nineteenth century— he would have done justice to France.   In short, Ranke, in spite of his political notions, was by no means one of those Germans who depreciated the part of France in universal history.   At the time of greatest victory he warned his fellow-countrymen against senseless chauvinism. " There is," he said, " a patriotism which is only manifested in the exclusion of what is foreign and which despises its worth. Such a spirit will only pervert the true national spirit.   Which of us can boast that he has not been influenced by the French mind ? "

Ranke was always a man of taste and breeding.

---

[1] It is in this sense, I think, that we must interpret the words so often quoted of Ranke to Thiers, who, astonished that Germany still went on with the war after the fall of the Empire, said to the Prussian historian : " But against whom are you waging this war ? " " Against Louis XIV," replied Ranke.

[2] Preface to "History of the World." In a lecture given on his ninetieth birthday he said : " As far as I am concerned, I would never have undertaken this history if the political problem represented by those two Great Powers, France and Germany, had not been solved after many vicissitudes and great struggles."

In his own country he never had to ask pardon for excesses of pen. As such he was often a good Prussian who, at all times, defended the age-long policy of the Hohenzollern house. At a time when the Liberal historians cried down certain Kings of Prussia, such as Frederick William II, Frederick William III and Frederick William IV, Ranke put forward his efforts, on the other hand, to have their memory respected.

He only half succeeded as regards the first two. He limits himself, moreover, to pleading extenuating circumstances : he says that events at that time were too powerful, that they dominated men : that Prussia could not at that time take a place in Europe out of proportion to its strength : that the only thing she could do with the means at her disposal was to live and to maintain herself. " The policy of neutrality, which is so condemned," he added, " has this advantage about it, that it allows the development of the arts : the eleven years which elapsed between the Peace of Basel and the battle of Jena were the most fruitful in German literature, the richest in original productions. This was the time of Fichte, Schelling, Voss, Wolf, and the historical school of Göttingen, the period in which appeared the " Roman Elegies," " Hermann and Dorothea," "Wilhelm Meister," the " Bell," " Wallenstein," " William Tell " and the " Maid of Orleans." The literature of that period had the character of being cosmopolitan in ideas : the time was to come when it would lose it, and when patriotic feelings would take hold of all minds."

With regard to Frederick William IV his task was still more difficult. No Prussian King has left behind him so sorry a memory, nor has been so badly treated by historians, who, as a rule, were respectful towards the Hohenzollern. Ranke found excuses for all the acts of this King: if he refused the Imperial crown in 1848, it was because he thought the moment unfavourable: if he shamefully recoiled at Olmütz, it was because Prussia was not yet ready: if his conduct was weak and hesitating in the Crimean War, "his neutrality on the other hand was repaid by the gratitude of the Czar, who did not forget it in 1870." [1]

This was what Nietzsche called "paying court to the powerful." [2] It must be said, however, that Ranke had this indulgence not only for the Kings of Prussia but for all historical personages, whether Loyola or Luther, Wallenstein or Gustavus Adolphus, or Robespierre. One might even say that it was part of his philosophy of history. Ranke was one of the German historians who accepted most completely the sovereignty of facts. He is the antipodes of that historical school which, with Schlosser, made use of the Kantian imperative; in his historical judgments he only regarded time and circumstances.

"I do not know," he said, with regard to Frederick William III, "whether people have any right to speak as they do of mistakes committed, opportunities lost, and culpable omissions. Events rule men: they live their lives under a sort of inevitable necessity: they have on them the seal of fate."

---

[1] Ranke published in 1874 the "Correspondence of Frederick William IV with Baron Bunsen": in 1886 he published in the "Allgemeine deutsche Biographie" a most favourable life of Frederick William IV.

[2] Nietzsche did not like Ranke: he said of him: "He is also in his way the advocate of the right of the most powerful." Elsewhere he called him "the most prudent of those who accept facts."

X

To become truly national, a history should join to those already enumerated another quality : it should have beauty of form. Ranke had this quality to the highest degree. He is one of the great German classics of the nineteenth century. His works are an everlasting treasure in the literature of his country.

At the time when Ranke began to write, in 1824, Germany, had no literary historians : there were still only large octavos crammed with learning for the use of the initiated alone. Elsewhere in Europe were published new and original works. There was some doubt as to whether any such would appear in Germany when Ranke published his " History of the Roman and Germanic Peoples," a book simple, clear, and of great elegance in form. High literary society in Berlin, ready to acclaim the appearance on the horizon of an Augustin Thierry, thought it had found in Ranke what it was waiting for. It welcomed him.

" They count on me to revive history," Ranke wrote to his brother. And indeed he was going to renovate history, but not in the way they expected. He was not going to create master-works whose beauty should consist above all in form: historical interest always took the first place with him : but by the lucid order of his narration, his elegant and clear prose, he was to show the Germans for the first time that " specialized knowledge, no matter how precise in terms, can speak in a language accessible to all, to the greatest advantage of the nation." [1]

He himself, it is true, was but half satisfied.

---

[1] Treitschke, " Deutsche Geschichte," iii. 432.

"What I write," he wrote to his brother, "suffers from too much learning. I should like to write something that could be read by everybody."[1] That was his ambition, and Berlin was about to show him how he might achieve it.

Berlin at that time was scarcely the literary capital of the Germans. It was a city of Philistines, where a primitive simplicity reigned. The Court was first in setting examples of this simplicity. The parsimonious habits of Frederick William III had reduced it to its absolute minimum of officials. "Once a year," said Lord Loftus, who was then Secretary to the British Embassy at Berlin, "the King gave a *déjeuner dansant* to the corps diplomatic, which commenced at 10 a.m. : and as it was generally in the dark days of January, it was necessary to shave by candlelight. At one the dinner was served, and before six the company retired, in order to permit His Majesty to make his nightly appearance at some theatre."[2]

From an intellectual point of view the capital of Prussia left much to be desired. It is true it had the best University in Germany, but in Germany a gathering of professors never made up society. As for what is called "the world," it took no interest whatever in intellectual things. Treitschke the historian, a man who is scarcely suspect of partiality for the nobility, recognized that at that time Prussian aristocracy had need to be taught "that respect to which scholars have a just claim."

The nobility, moreover, rarely appeared in Berlin. Those who did not spend their winter in the country

[1] " Zur eigen. Leben.," p. 166.
[2] " Diplomatic Reminiscences," i. 25.

on their estates went by preference to some provincial capital, Münster, Magdeburg, or Breslau. There
were at Berlin, where, indeed, they had not even
town houses, no well-appointed palaces such as one
sees in Vienna.

The life, again, that was spent there was very
monotonous. If one believes Alexander von Humboldt, who was used to the elegant drawing-rooms of
Paris, a certain courage was needed to live there.
" Berlin," said he in his Berlin dialect, " I am sick of
you : you are, and will remain, a town of bears." [1]
In the matter of society there were a few houses of
intelligent officials like Ancillon, or rich Jewish
bankers like the Mendelssohns and Meyerbeers : or a
few drawing-rooms of amateurs and artists like those
of Rahel and Varnhagen von Ense—a sort of workshop
of over-elaborated wit which mimicked the manners
of the Parisian drawing-rooms at the time of the
Restoration. Everywhere France was imitated as a
model,[2] and Ranke, who, with very German ideas
and tastes, had in the matter of form certain French
qualities—proportion, delicacy, soberness and elegance[3]

---

[1] " Berlin ik her die dick en sat ; du bist en blivst en Baren-
stadt."

[2] Even at the Court of Frederick William III, French was
still the common language. Queen Louisa, in spite of her hatred
of France, liked nothing but French culture. In 1810 her
private secretary was the portrait-painter, Pierre Barthelemy
Fontane, a descendant of the French Huguenot refugees, the
grandfather of Theodore Fontane, the novelist ; she had taken
him into her service " on account of his exquisite French "
(Th. Fontane, " Meine Kinderjahre "). Treitschke notes in his
history the influence of the French spirit upon Berlin literature,
which he calls " a Berlinism strongly imbued with French culture."

[3] He liked—a rare thing in a German—the literature of
the century of Louis XIV. He said, for example, of Pascal's

—recognized what he owed to Berlin society. " Association with men of superior intellect," he said in his " Autobiography," " and the society of distinguished ladies had an effective influence over me which no provincial town of second-rate importance could have had."

Ranke had an intuition for form : all his works are intelligible and pleasant to read. With a penetrating mind, capable of perceiving fine shades, what he excels in describing is the policy of motives, of undercurrents and diplomatic negotiations. No one among the historians of his country has equalled him in understanding political questions. As an explanatory writer he is inimitable. Brilliant like Voltaire, he understands everything and gives us admirably the inner meaning of things. What could be more attractive than the lines with which he opens his " The Ottoman and the Spanish Empires"? " Humble, indeed, is the description the Ottomans give of their own origin. They relate that Othman, the founder of their Empire and name, himself followed the plough with his servants, and that when he wished to break off from work at noon he used to stick up a banner as a signal to call them home. These servants and none besides were his first followers in war, and they were marshalled beneath the same signal. But even he, they add, had in his day a forecasting of his house's future greatness, and in a dream he beheld a tree grow up out of his navel that overshadowed the whole earth." [1]

" Provincial Letters " that they were the masterpiece of argument in modern history : he called Descartes " one of the most original minds of his time." His portrait of Voltaire, well-drawn and intellectual as it is, is one of the most shrewd passages that have been written about him. Goethe himself has not done better.

[1] " The Ottoman and Spanish Empires " (translated by Kelly, 1843), p. 5.

This fragment gives one a good idea of Ranke's style. His narrative moves swiftly and lightly, with sober images scattered by the way. In an elegant description he unfolds to our eyes the young Christian prisoners of the Sultan, "lightly dressed in linen or cloth of Salonichi: they wore caps of Brusa stuff"; [1] elsewhere he pictures for us the sixteenth century at Lesbos: "We see the people tilling their fields and planting their vines, attending to their springs and watercourses and cultivating their gardens." [2]

In his great historical pictures Ranke is not so happy: he lacks relief and colour; he cannot, like Macaulay and Michelet, design in fresco great scenes from the life of peoples. And that is wanting in certain of his works—for example, his "History of the Reformation in Germany," where one might expect to find some great scenes or impressive pictures of the life of the time. [3]   On the other hand his little genre

---

[1] "The Ottoman and Spanish Empires," p. 6.   [2] Ibid. p. 10.

[3] See, for example, in his "History of England," i. 146 (English translation), the description of the marriage of Anne Boleyn: "On the Thursday before Whitsuntide she was escorted from Greenwich by the Mayor and the Trades of London, in splendidly adorned barges with musical instruments playing, till she was greeted by the cannon of the Tower. The Saturday after she went in procession through the City to Westminster. The King had created eighteen Knights of the Order of the Bath. These, in their new decorations, and a great part of the nobility, which felt itself honoured in Anne's elevation, accompanied her : she sat on a splendid seat, supported by and slung between horses : the canopy over her was borne by the Barons of the Cinque Ports : her hair was uncovered, she was charming as always, and (it appears) not without a sense of high good-fortune. On Sunday she was escorted to Westminster Abbey by the Archbishop of Canterbury and six bishops, the Abbot of Westminster and twelve other abbots in full canonicals : she was in purple, her ladies in scarlet, for so old custom required."

scenes and portraits are perfect, when he describes the Court of Ludovic the Moor, Florence at the time of Savonarola, the interior of the Sultan's harem, etc.

Ranke has little colouring, but his rendering of what might be called the moral expression of individuals, things, and groups of human beings—in short, what makes up the atmosphere of an environment—is admirable. Here, for example, is a glimpse at Calvin's Geneva which is very accurate in tone :—

" Geneva still continued to be the great commercial city it had always been . . . but all was order, discipline, and industry. It was still, as it always had been, a principal point of communication for Central Europe, but it was especially so for the refugees on account of religion who assembled here, and, having been instructed in the churches or in the newly erected schools, went forth thence once more into the world . . . it had outstripped even the tendencies of Lutheran reformation itself. . . ." [1]

This is a very well drawn portrait of Calvin the humanist : " He was disgusted with persons who, when they had conned a few positions out of Melancthon's Manual, held themselves to be thoroughly learned divines: for his own part, he was accustomed to study till late at night, and, when he awoke in the morning, to review in quietness and retirement all that he had read : these undisturbed habits of feeling and thinking contributed greatly to his success. He often said that he had no higher wish than to continue these practices throughout life, for he was timid by nature and disposed to avoid strife." [2]

But above all in his master-work, " The Popes of

[1] " History of France " (English translation, 1852), p. 223.
[2] Ibid. p. 212.

Rome," Ranke showed his talent as a portrait-painter and his power of narrative. There is to be found in this work a series of scenes, portraits, views of Rome, interiors of palaces, Cardinals' conferences, all intermingled with reflections on Papal politics, theological considerations and artistic discussions that exhibit the full wealth of his mind.

Ranke did not write his works according to the best classical models. There is a charming *abandon* in his work which relieves us after the historical works written in sections by college professors who know how to make the necessary connections and gradations.

As a subtle analyst of human passions it is in moral portraiture that he has succeeded best. He has shaded his interiors of the mind with the art of a Tolstoi or a George Eliot. He looks at them at all times of their lives, takes them by surprise in their daily habits, with their movements and familiar tricks, which he catches as they pass, and omits no physical peculiarity which might help us to understand their nature better. Thus we learn that Pope Gregory XV was "a small, phlegmatic man . . . feeble, sick, and bent with age":[1] we see Emperor Charles V ill, "his back bent, pale as a corpse, white lips, dragging himself with difficulty about the room, leaning on a stick."[2] Elsewhere we have a picture of the Sultan Amurath III, described when receiving ambassadors; how he would "stare at them with his large lacklustre, melancholy eyes, and perhaps nod his head to them: when he had done this he went back to his garden."[3] Later there is a description of Leo X,

[1] " Popes of Rome " (English translation, 1866), i. 319.
[2] " Complete Works," v. 73.
[3] "Ottoman and Spanish Empires " (English translation), p. 15.

who went out for a walk in Rome "without a surplice
. . . and with boots on his feet . . . to the despair
of his Master of the Ceremonies." [1]

Ranke liked to notice those homely traits which
make the portraiture stand out in relief.   Thus he
tells us of Pope Adrian VI how he brought an old
woman-servant with him from Louvain to look after
his house.   Of Paolo Sarpi he said : " His father was
a man of small stature, dark complexion, and turbulent,
quarrelsome temper." [2]   Of another, Peter Aldobran-
dini, Pope Clement VIII's nephew, he said : " His
person was insignificant, he was marked with small-
pox, he had an asthma and coughed incessantly." [3]

It is by a multitude of small touches, added one
to the other, that Ranke lets us see the inner being
of these great people.   All his figures are painted in
the same style.   Here are a few examples taken from
his " Popes of Rome " : " He [Leo X] had a passionate
love of music. . . . The walls of the palace daily
echoed with the sounds of music : the Pope was
heard to hum the melodies that delighted him. . . .
Leo X was full of kindness and sympathy. . . . ' He
is a good man,' says an observing ambassador to his
Court, ' very bounteous and of a kindly nature ; if
he were not under the influence of his kinsmen he
would avoid all errors.' " [4]   " Adrian VI was of a most
spotless fame ; upright, pious, and industrious, of such
a gravity that nothing more than a faint smile was
ever seen upon his lips, yet full of benevolent, pure
intentions . . . he rose at earliest dawn, said Mass,
and then proceeded in his accustomed order to business and to study, which were only interrupted by

---

[1] " Popes of Rome," i. 48.   [2] Ibid. ii. 235.
[3] Ibid. ii. 219.   [4] Ibid. i. 48.

H

the simplest meals. . . . He loved Flemish art . . .
and of the race of poets [at Rome] he would hear
nothing." [1]   And all the others come to life again
with their individual characteristics.   Clement VII :
" He displayed extraordinary acuteness on all subjects :
penetrated to the very bottom of the most perplexing
circumstances and was singularly easy and adroit in
discourse and argument." [2]   " Paul III was of an easy,
magnificent, liberal nature . . . he weighed every
word with the double consideration of both matter
and form, and uttered them in a soft voice and with
the slowest deliberation." [3]   " Paul IV had already
attained the age of seventy-nine, but his deepset eyes
still gleamed with all the fire of youth : he was extremely tall and thin, he walked quickly and appeared
to be all sinew.   His daily life was subject to no rule
or order : he often slept by day and passed the night
in study. . . . In everything he followed the impulse
of the moment." [4]   All these portraits, and a thousand
others like them, give one the impression that Ranke
knew all the people whose history he wrote.

And yet it is not these descriptive characteristics
which distinguish Ranke as a historian.   He was not
attached to form for its own sake.   His work is not a
succession of scenes, a gallery of portraits.   What he
wished to paint was the great moments of European
politics, and all the detail is only given to add to the
value of the whole.   Again, what preponderates in his
work is general ideas—bird's-eye views.   Diplomatic
negotiations or political discussions have more space in
his writings than anecdotes : everywhere Ranke seeks to
bring out the spirit.   The result is that his language—

---

[1] " Popes of Rome," i. 63.   [2] Ibid. i. 67.
[3] Ibid. i. 164, 166.   [4] Ibid. i. 192.

delicate, direct, and finely shaded—has rather an abstract tone. Ranke in his phraseology belongs to the writers of the eighteenth century : he resembles Montesquieu in that free and easy style that gives his phraseology an appearance of familiarity, he resembles Lessing in his brightness united with grace, and, moreover, in a certain sweetness which never degenerates into insipidity or archness. " You have been able to keep your freshness in your old age like a flower of youth," wrote in Greek verse the Rector of Schulpforta at the time of his eightieth birthday, " and from your lips distils the honey of Nestor." And this expresses it well. Until the end of his life Ranke retained the grace and freshness of youth. At eighty-four years of age he wrote to his old friend ——: " When spring made signs of coming this year I was deeply touched. The spring itself was astonished that my eighty-fourth year again wished to enjoy the flowers and verdure. I said to it: ' Come now, we are old friends, you and I ; let me enjoy your company once more.' It seemed to wish to grant me this, but perhaps it is for the last time." [1]

The man who wrote this in extreme old age was not of that race of which Frederick the Great could say once : " The Germans are a thorough and hardworking people; when they take hold of anything they work at it with a heavy hand." In fine, Leopold von Ranke had two qualities of style which are rare everywhere, but particularly so, it would seem, among his fellow-countrymen—vivacity and grace.[2]

---

[1] " Zur eigen. Leben.," p. 545.

[2] Ranke was an admirable critical writer. His essays in criticism are masterpieces of lucidity. When he discusses political problems, he does it rapidly, without delay or German longwindedness. In his great synthetical summaries he is a marvel of conciseness.

We can understand after this, then, that Ranke has never been popular in his own country. He had neither all the qualities nor perhaps all the ordinary defects of his race. What often distinguishes the German in history is individualism, carried at times as far as eccentricity. Ranke, on the other hand, impartial, just, and deliberate, tried to hold the middle course between opposite opinions, to be the more certain of getting nearer to the truth. This moderation was made a reproach to him, as if it were a lack of originality. Objection was taken, also, to his diction; they said that if it had the clearness of water it had also its insipidity. Heinrich Heine found him too sugared : " Ranke," said he in a bantering fashion—" a very fine talent: mutton nicely cooked with carrots."

The Germans of the South, the Catholics of the school of Böhmer above all, who only liked the decayed strength of old German art, disliked " these importations from the North," as they called them, " that arid and charmless rationalism of Berlin." [1] The bookworms,

---

Above all, in his "Universal History" he succeeded in indicating by striking flashes the general outlines in the history of humanity or in the great historical figures. For example, he says of Saul : " He is the first tragic person in the history of the world " (" Universal History," English translation, 1884, p. 44). Of Solomon he says : " In him are combined the characteristics which, in all ages, have distinguished the great monarchs of the East " (Ibid. p. 56). This extract on Assur gives one a good idea of the tone and general idea of this history : " Assur had no broad foundation for its national life. Its religion was not rooted in the soil, like that of Egypt, nor based upon observation of the sky and stars, like that of Babylon. It was a warlike confederacy of Semitic origin, strengthened by constant struggle with the native inhabitants and gradually subduing every region accessible to its arms " (Ibid. p. 78).

[1] The historian Höfler violently attacked Ranke's " History of the Popes of Rome," as also did Theiner.

so numerous in Germany, thought that his books
were not learned enough, and were not worthy to
be placed upon the shelves of University libraries.[1]
The greater number of them despised these works, saying there was nothing to be learned in them.[2] All were
agreed that Ranke was by no means a true historian,
that he lacked originality and was dull.[3]

Among the politicians and statesmen the reception
was colder still. That prudent and diplomatic manner
of solving historical problems satisfied nobody. The
old Prussian Conservatives would not pardon him
certain favourable remarks about the Liberals. The
Liberals, on the other hand, thought him too reactionary.
The parliamentarians of the school of Gervinus did not
like him so well as the old historian Schlosser, who
was then the representative in Germany of Kantian
morality and the honest democracy. As for the
national historians, they reproached him with being
neither fish nor flesh. Droyson laughed at his pliancy
and his relationship with " the fickle romanticists."
Sybel could not understand his " colourless objectivism."
Treitschke said : " He who looks at history as it really
is, seldom indeed notices that soft sunlight, scarcely
darkened from time to time by the lightest clouds,
which illuminates in Ranke's works an elegant circle
of noble and refined men."[4] Mommsen, on his part,
reproached him for optimism. " You have the truly

---

[1] The historian Rehm, Professor at Marburg University.

[2] Eichhorn on the " History of Germany at the Time of the
Reformation."

[2] Bergenroth, in the *Grenzboten*, on the publication of the
first volume of the " History of England," which was very coldly
received in Germany.

[4] Treitschke, " Zehn Jahre deutscher Kämpfe," Berlin, 1879,
p. 463.

surprising gift," he said to him ironically, "of seeing in every man what makes him look best. You do not paint men as they are, but as they should be." Perhaps: but in the face of these historians, brutal in their attacks, it will be accounted some day to Ranke's honour that he never depreciated human dignity.

Ranke, moreover, can be satisfied that he never had on his side the dilettanti nor the pedantic scholars, nor those historians fired with the Prussian tendency. He had on his side, and—a matter which is of far greater importance—still has on his side the intellectual class : in Germany, the dialecticians, like David Strauss, Julian Schmidt, and Canon Döllinger: in France, Victor Cherbuliez, Albert Sorel, and Gabriel Monod : in England, the historians Freeman, Seeley, Stubbs, Green, and Gardiner, who looked upon him as their master and applied his methods better than any one else.

Ranke also had the approval and admiration of several statesmen of the highest rank. Thiers regarded him as the greatest statesman of the nineteenth century, and Bismarck was not far from sharing that opinion. When he was asked at an interview for his three favourite books, he said, "The Bible, Shakespeare, and Ranke." This is not an idle opinion, coming from this great maker of history.

On the death of the historian, Bismarck wrote to his sons that he had always felt himself in a close communion of ideas with their father. That means that under his modest and peaceful exterior Ranke had a Prussian radicalism by which, one day, even the Iron Chancellor was daunted. People still remember the sensation caused by his letter to Manteuffel, in which he bluntly advised the Imperial Government to annex

Switzerland to destroy a harbour of socialism dangerous to the rest of Europe. Bismarck contented himself with writing on the margin of this letter three great exclamation marks. But he had quickly recognized the ally in Ranke. He knew that in this studious Thuringian who never troubled himself about militant politics he could find a valuable support. King William knew it, too. At a time when the future acclaimers of the Empire conducted a furious campaign in the Prussian Chamber against military reform, Ranke saw through the designs of the Government at once and gave them his approval. One day, indeed, he was summoned to the King's palace. There, in the silence of his study, William explained to him his policy. " He who wishes to govern Germany must conquer it. Gagern's plan is impossible. That Prussia is destined to take the lead in German affairs is what all her history proves : but when and how—that is the question." And the historian could only blindly agree, for that was exactly the policy which, in 1849, he had recommended the King's own brother, the unfortunate Frederick William IV, to take up. Again, on returning to his house that evening, he was able to write in his notebook under the date of June 13, 1860 : " During a half hour I was in the locality of historical political conceptions in the company of a man who knows and can " (welcher verstet und vermag).

Were we not right in saying that Leopold von Ranke was a good and faithful servant of the Prussian Monarchy, above all a disinterested and discreet servant ?

CHAPTER II

THEODORE MOMMSEN

A S early as the year 1835 Tocqueville described the progress of democracy, the gradual development of an equal law, as a providential fact not influenced by human power. And, indeed, what we do see from that time is the transformation of society, less by the effect of revolutionary theories, as has been said, than as the result of new conditions of economic life brought about by the introduction of machinery in industry, by telegraphs and railways. A new world was organized for credit and finance, industry and commerce—canals, sea routes and railroads, ships and ports, manufactures, warehouses and mines—in short, what is called the great industries made an appearance.

This transformation took place later in Germany than elsewhere. It could only be noticed after 1840. "At that moment," said Heinrich von Treitschke, "what took up men's attention was elections, parliamentary debates, the discussions in the various assemblies, and great economic enterprises. They sought distraction in the cafés or in smoking cigars. Family life passed away. Women laid claim no longer to the uncontested control of society life, but sought also to rival man in those activities of life which hitherto had been his monopoly. The newspapers and cheap popular literature awakened in the widest circles a taste for public affairs. The democratic character of the age was revealed in the frock-coat, uniform and comfortable, which all classes of society wore, in the style of beard, the long trousers, and boots, which now appeared in drawing-rooms, where the democratic evening dress disturbed every one, both guests and servants." [1]

It was not only in domestic habits, however, that this change took place, but also in the artistic, intellectual, and scientific life of the nation. Until that time Germany had been pre-eminently the country of philosophy, letters, and historical science. In natural science she had made little mark. Now the Germans turned their attention in this direction and made some of the most remarkable discoveries of the time.

It was in a little laboratory at Giessen that a discovery was made which was to revolutionize the conditions of life: the transformations of organic matter. [2] In physics Dove discovered the law controlling the direction of winds, the basis of a new science, meteorology. The great discovery of Helmholtz, the conservation of energy, was also made at this time. [3]

In philosophy a similar change took place. Germany, which so long had been the nursery of metaphysical systems, produced no more. The only one that now survives is that of Hegel, but how changed it is ! The pupils of that philosopher have so distorted the master's opinions that they cannot now be recog-

---

[1] " Deutsche Geschichte im 19ten Jahrhundert," iv. 5.
[2] Schwann cellular theory, which opened new paths to pathology.   [3] 1847.

nized.   His famous law of contradictories, the keystone
of his system, is no longer anything but an affir-
mation that nothing is true in itself, but only in
relation to what surrounds it, that all knowledge
is relative, and that consequently we are sure of
nothing: so that the philosophy which claimed
to represent the absolute resulted in the deepest
scepticism.[1]

The philosopher's disciples, moreover, turned away
more and more from pure philosophy to take part in
public life.   They renewed the famous contests of the
French Encyclopedists of the eighteenth century.
They could be seen to attempt the assault of all the
fortresses of political and religious orthodoxy.   This
was the time when David Strauss published his celebrated " Life of Jesus," which made such a sensation in
the country[2]: when Büchner, taking up the materialistic
theories of Helvetius and Diderot, declared the in-
destructibility of the atom and of matter[3]: when
Moleschott studied the mechanism of the brain and
made a chemical analysis of thought according to a
theory which Feuerbach summarizes in an untrans-
latable play upon words: " Man is what he eats " (der
Mensch ist was er isst).   It was a German scholar,
Karl Vogt, who, before Darwin, laid down the foundations of transformation in his work " The Ocean and

---

[1] The pupils of Hegel—the Hegelian Left as it is called—said:
" There is no longer a religion but religions, no longer such a
thing as morality but custom: no longer any principles but facts."
Hegel, who was fond of saying that his system was the pillar of
monarchical and religious society, produced some of the most
militant atheists and anarchical theorists of the nineteenth
century.

[2] First edition published in 1835.

[3] " Kraft und Stoff," Frankfort-am-R., 1855,

the Sea," in which he showed that all common phenomena are acts of transmutation and descent, and was
first to give an outline of monistic philosophy which
was developed later in his famous controversy with
R. Wagner of Göttingen and in his celebrated "Physi-
ological Letters," which in sprightliness and spirit can
be compared with Voltaire's.   At the same time another
scholar, Feuerbach, took up the contest of the French
philosophers of the eighteenth century against
Christianity in that strange, subtle book which he called
"Das Wesen des Christentums" ("The Essence of
Christianity ").[1]

This breeze of criticism spread at that time throughout Germany, and in literature was its first stroke made.
That romantic, enthusiastic, and idealistic generation
of the beginning of the century was succeeded by a
positive generation concerned only with facts and concrete reality.   Poetry died.   Romantic literature was
left to women as an inferior class of work.   The only
writer of any talent who deigned to write fiction was
Gustav Freytag, and he did this less from artistic
sentiment than to influence his contemporaries.   A
humorous realist, he wages, in his comedies and stories,
in which he preaches the simplicity of middle-class
life and the taste for truth, relentless war against
romanticism.[2]

---

[1] Leipzig, 1841.

[2] Gustav Freytag began in 1844 with a drama, " The Scholar "
(which was never acted), which he wrote to help on popular
education.   "All political progress," said he, " depends upon the
raising (Steigerung) of popular strength in all spheres of actual
life."   Another play, " Valentine " (1846), had as its object the
ridiculing of life in small German towns at that time.   " The
Journalists " (1852) was also a satire on German life of his time.
In his novel " Debtor and Creditor " (1853), his desire was to

Romanticism was regarded as the enemy by the whole of this realistic generation. In order to combat it, Freytag established at Leipzig, with his friend Julian Schmidt, a review, the *Grenzboten*, whose political tendencies were at the same time purely Prussian.[1]

The two things, moreover, go together in their minds. By declaring war on Young Germany, on feudal and Catholic Romanticism, by cutting out what Julian Schmidt called the "dead parts of German literature," by persecuting with their hatred "the artificial, the affected, the false, morbid delicacy, harmful to national prosperity and fatal to German discipline, morality, and sense of duty, these men meant to work for the triumph of Prussian policy in Germany.[2]

---

point out "that man should take care that the thoughts and desires of the imagination should not have too much influence over his life."

[1] The *Grenzboten* was not exactly founded by G. Freytag and J. Schmidt : it already existed; founded in Belgium by a German refugee from Austria, Kaufmann, it had been transferred to Leipzig, where Freytag in July 1848 took over its editorship and made it a Review of purely Prussian tendencies. Julian Schmidt was already working on it when Freytag joined the staff as co-editor. He held that position until 1861, when he was succeeded by Dr. Moritz Busch, who later became Bismarck's secretary.

[2] Julian Schmidt is the author of a history of German literature from the death of Lessing (3 vols., Berlin, 1866), written from the Protestant and Prussian point of view. An opponent of Catholicism and Romanticism, he could only see in literature of these tendencies " unhealthy growths which had to be torn out by the roots "—the rationalist character of French literature seemed to him less dangerous to Germany than romanticism. In literature he liked none but " healthy people " (gesunde Menschen). His literary conception bears a strong resemblance to that of the French critic, Edmond Scherer.

Gustav Freytag, a true Prussian of positive and solid mind, pitiless towards fantastic notions, was one of the most active propagators of this spirit in Germany. Thanks to him, Leipzig became an enthusiastic centre of Prussian propaganda. Around his paper were gathered from the year 1848 onwards men of varied origin and tendencies, but who were all united by a common love for Hohenzollern institutions.[1]

There, for the first time, before the historians, Freytag extolled the German mission of the Hohenzollern by showing that this mission had begun on the day when, " in order to become a Great Power, the Prussian State had incorporated little by little those States whose death-knell had sounded." He said :—

" In spite of its torn frontiers, its rounding off uncompleted, Prussia is in reality a State with a past, a national consciousness, an idea directing its policy. . . . Unfortunately, this idea extends beyond its actual territory and is as large as the whole of Germany. As for us Prussians, we are willing to be despoiled of our prerogatives to give ourselves up to the good of all : let us abandon all personal feeling for the good of the rest of the Germans, so that together we may honour the German name."[2]

As early as 1848 Freytag foresaw that not parliamen-

---

[1] There was Solomon Hirzel, the famous bookseller, founder of the great house at Leipzig ; Stephani, who later became the town's burgomaster ; Karl Mathy, director of the Kreditanstalt ; Max Jordan, Zarncke, Gutschmidt, and later Treitschke. All these men, who formed a political society, the Maikäfer, met three times a week in a beershop, the Kitzing, and there, while drinking beer, they discussed the future of Germany. " In this little circle of conspirators," said Treitschke, " were formed many political projects which were realized later."

[2] " Politische Aufsätze," Leipzig, 1888, pp. 82, 83.

tary discussions would bring about unity but the good sword of Prussia. "If, in order to bring about this unity," said he, " we must even march against Germans (which God forbid), Prussia will march . . . and perhaps at bottom that is what distinguishes us Prussians from other Germans, for we are ready *to shed our last drop of blood to have our way.* We have an object in view, a great ideal for which we live: our opponents have no such ideal. What should we fear? Are we not a nation of warriors?"[1]

All German Liberals were not at that time of Freytag's opinion. Indeed, there were a very few like him. Democrats by conviction, they were bitter enemies to the ancient regime and the feudal spirit. Moltke, who detested them, said in great joy, on the occasion of the miscarriage of the Frankfort Parliament of 1849: "Democracy has finished its part for the moment: but there will be no doubt other severe struggles: the time of heroes is coming after the time of brawlers and scribblers. . . . For the present, order will be established, and that is a good thing, for, as has been rightly said, order has sometimes produced liberty, but liberty has never produced order."[2]

All German Liberals were not yet won over to this

---

[1] " Politische Aufsätze," p. 86. Freytag said later : " If it has been easy for me, in the struggles that have taken place in my time, to be on the winning side, I owe it not to myself but to my good fortune *in being born a Prussian, Protestant and Silesian,* near the Polish frontier. As a child of that country I learned at an early age to love my *German nationality in opposition to a foreign race:* as a Protestant I attained a knowledge of the liberal sciences more rapidly and without painful struggles : *as a Prussian I was brought up in a State where every one's devotion to his country is the order of the day* " (" Ennerungen aus meinem Leben," Leipzig, 1886).

[2] Moltke, " Correspondence," p. 391 (September 1849).

idea. There were still many of them, even after the check of 1848, who still believed in the peaceful and gradual victories of unarmed democracy and without Cæsar at the end of it. Yet, strange to say, most of them had cast their eyes towards Prussia—an aristocratic and military State, without considering how incompatible were their ideas with the form of the Prussian government.

It is true they had a strange notion of Prussia. They thought that, in order to carry out her mission in Germany, she would be obliged to become democratic and Liberal. Moreover, when the event did not turn out according to their expectation, they did not seem to be unduly disappointed thereat. These Liberals, whose minds had been formed by philosophers, who had taught them that " the world's tribunal was that of history," were quite ready to resign themselves to any accomplished fact. There was, then, no difficulty in convincing them, and there were even some of them who, after Sadowa, acknowledged their mistake and began to love what they had hated up to that moment.

We also see, strangely enough, men who, like Frederick David Strauss, had spent their lives in destroying biblical legends, become hagiographers in their turn and create the Hohenzollern legend.[1]

---

[1] Fr. David Strauss, so prudent a critic when dealing with Jesus Christ, writes without hesitation of Frederick the Great that he conquered Silesia because he wished to liberate the Germans from the yoke of Catholic Austria. He also wrote that Germany had never waged any but " holy wars," whereas the French enterprises (of François I, Louis XIV, and Napoleon) had no other motive than a taste for rapine and robbery (Raublust), and that consequently France in 1870 received her just punishment. Thus he speaks of the war of 1870, " a work of public service performed by Germany on France, which was rotten to the marrow and completely divorced from full moral ties."

But this can only astonish those who consider these men superficially : at bottom the difference was negligible between these democrats, atheists or professing the religion of Darwin or Strauss, and the Prussian military party, those royalists of divine right who believed in Sabaoth, the God of Battles.   Both had the same cult —the religion of force, and both were imbued with the same spirit—the realistic spirit.

Of this spirit Prussia had enough and to spare. Save in literature, which she despised, she had all kinds of realism : political, administrative, military and economic realism.   And as she had, as well, the power of crushing the hated foreigner, all these democrats, after the successes, forgot their old jealousies and joined in noisily celebrating the victories.

This form of realistic spirit of modern Germany was fostered from 1850 on in the German Universities.   The man who best represents it is Mommsen, the historian whom we are now going to consider.

I

Theodore Mommsen is one of the strangest figures in modern Germany.   In him all contrasts are united. He is a great scholar and a man of great imagination : a democrat, and yet no one has contributed to spread the notion of Cæsarism more than he in his " Roman History ": he is an idealist, and yet matter of fact: lastly, he is an enthusiast, and yet few men have so urged the coming generation to regard dreams of idealism as " vanity and idle noise." [1]

---

[1] " As we get on in years," said Moltke, " we become reasonable and throw overboard all enthusiasm as being nothing but vanity and idle noise " (" Correspondence," p. 358).

Born at Garding, in Schleswig, where his father was a pastor, Mommsen grew up in that strange country on the borders of the North Sea, pleasant enough inland, with its meadows and low-roofed farmhouses, but desolate on the coast, where one can see nothing but vast expanses of moors, with swamps and sand-dunes, continually washed by the waves of the grey angry sea, which calls to mind the verses of Heinrich Heine :—

> Before me tumbles the waste of waters ;
> Behind me lies only misery and sorrow.
> And high overhead the clouds are floating,
> Grey, shapeless daughters of air,
> Who draw up the water in buckets of mist
> From the ocean,
> And toilsomely drag it and drag it,
> And again pour it forth to the sea.
> A wearisome, sorrowful task,
> And useless as is my life.[1]

If one had to believe a historian of Taine's school, nothing could be better fitted for causing discouragement and melancholy as the sight of this land. Yet Mommsen presents a most lively type of nature—the happiest and most joyful. This is not uncommon in Germany. With our French ideas, we are easily inclined to imagine that the sad and cold North produces stolid and sullen men, while the South, fresher and brighter, supplies a pleasanter, brighter race. In Germany the contrary to this is often so. It is particularly from the South, from the rich plains of Swabia and the fertile vine-lands of the Moselle and Rhine, that those legendary strong and clumsy Germans have come

---

[1] Heine, " Book of Songs "—" North Sea (wrecked)," English translation (1904), p. 256.

with their immense speculative brains which seemed
to embrace a whole world : there it is that the poets
have sung in sweet, sober verses the true German life
and that the Romanticists extolled the old Imperial
and Catholic Germany. In the North, on the other
hand, in the interminable plains of Pomerania and
Brandenburg, which have never produced almost anything except soldiers and diplomatists, the whole
tendency is towards action.[1] The literary men of that
part are combative, and are soon transformed into
critics. Take, for example, the Berlin Romanticists—
how different are they from those of Heidelberg !
Exaggerated and paradoxical as they are, they are called
Young Germany, just as the Parisians of 1830 are
called Young France of Théophile Gautier, with whom
they are not without some resemblance. One of them
(Gutzkow) extols Nero as the greatest man of antiquity.
Another (Th. Mundt) preaches free love. A third
(Wienbarg) writes "Aesthetische Feldzüge"[2] (Æsthetic
Campaigns) in which he extols the undaunted vigour
of the North Germans. " I like Uhland well enough,
just as I like a fair German from the South, born in the
midst of mountains, of vines in bloom and castles in
ruins; but I only like him at times—at certain moments.

---

[1] Treitschke says that High Germany has supplied all the
poets—Goethe and Schiller, Uhland and Rückert. But, says he,
the revolutions, on the other hand, all come from the North
(" Deutsche Gesch.," iv. 429).

[2] Hamburg, 1834. "He who writes on behalf of Young
Germany," says he, " proclaims thereby that he does not recognize
the aristocracy of ancient days, that he consigns the decrepit
learning of Old Germany to the subterranean caverns of the
Egyptian pyramids, that he declares war on the old Philistines,
and is determined to persecute them relentlessly, even to the last
thread of their classical nightcap."

. . . It is the task of us men of the North to encourage action and effort among these Southern Germans, so prone to sleep, to delude themselves with a thousand dreams."

They are all revolutionary, even that gentle poet Heinrich Laube, who believes that real Romanticism is the theory of Sans-culottism, who takes Robespierre's part, extols " Lafayette and the tricolored flag," and feels in the depth of his heart a profound pity for " those oppressed " Poles.

These æstheticians in spectacles have often, it must be confessed, a rather heavy imagination. But having less of an artistic than of a learned temperament, they are not long in turning towards criticism, and, like the descendants of the French Romanticists, they become, to use Paul Bourget's expression, " the pioneers of an age of exegesis and documents " : they revive the taste for the actual and urge men to action and effort.

Theodore Mommsen is certainly one of this race of men. Readily extravagant and paradoxical, always moving and ready for action, none was fitter than he to shake from their torpor those " Southern Germans always ready to delude themselves with dreams."

With his extraordinarily expressive face full of nervous movement, his eyes sparkling with mischief, his jeering sarcastic lip, Mommsen puts us in mind of Voltaire. He also reminds one of Moltke in his clean-shaved face, with something pitiless and harsh in its cheerfulness. And thus he seems to us in his work : a nature at once ready-witted, petulant, and active, joined to the nature of a positive, practical, matter-of-fact man, quick to unmask sophistry, to burst the bubbles of vanity, to persecute pitilessly idle fancies.

There are in Mommsen two men who do not always

agree with one another, yet who are inseparable—the scholar and the artist. The scholar is undoubtedly one of the most remarkable of the nineteenth century. Mommsen accumulated an enormous amount of learning.

If we consider his work—that work, enormous in extent and in the profundity of the researches involved—which includes, not counting the "Corpus inscriptionem latinarum," which he edited for more than fifty years, a large number of memoirs on subjects of the most varied description: Roman archæology, linguistic science, epigraphy, numismatics, law, mythology: if we consider again the vast amount of information, derived alike from the study of books and men, of which he has shown proof in everything he wrote, speaking with the same authority of a Iapygian inscription, some newly discovered fragments of blind Appius or Cassiodorus or Jordanès, of the state of agriculture among the Carthaginians or the Chinese : if we consider, above all, the noble spirit with which he regarded knowledge—always wishing it to be completely universal, never narrowly national—working hard to ennoble the mind and warning his fellow-countrymen against excessive specialization,[1] which is their peculiar failing—if we consider all this, Theodore Mommsen is one of the finest examples of German learning of the nineteenth

---

[1] " We should specialize in some particular branch, but not lock ourselves up in it," he said in a lecture on Leibniz delivered at the Berlin Academy of Science ; " through that branch, indeed, we ought to gain a knowledge of everything. . . . How small and despicable is the world in the eyes of those who only see in it Greek and Latin writers, layers of earth, or mathematical problems." See also the fine letter he wrote to his pupils on the occasion of his eightieth birthday (*Frankfurter Zeitung*).

century, in its nobleness, its greatness and disinterestedness.

But beside this there is in Mommsen the most animated, most fanciful artist one could imagine. And this is something that seems strange enough by the side of such profound learning. This man, whom one would readily imagine to have the characteristics of a serious and rather severe scholar, is in truth a man of passion and impulse—not one, it is true, who quivers, like Michelet, for all noble and great causes, or who is filled with sympathy and compassion for all that has lived and suffered on earth, but an intellectual enthusiast who is fired by everything that has played a brilliant part in the world, by everything that has been distinguished by its force and genius.

This artist might never have been published but for a chance circumstance. About 1850, a Berlin publisher was looking for collaborators for a series of historical manuals. He approached Mommsen to write a history of Rome. He might have made a mistake. Mommsen, indeed, was the first scholar in Roman affairs, but as a rule scholars are less fitted than others to write books for the general public. But chance willed that Mommsen was a great writer. Indeed, as a writer, he had passed his apprenticeship in a class of writing that best prepares one for vivid writing—journalism.

This is another characteristic to take note of in this scholar. Mommsen did not belong to the old race of German professors who lived only for their study. He had a passion for public affairs. A native of Schleswig-Holstein, he had been educated in Kiel University, which did so much to spread throughout the duchies the ideas of a German Fatherland.

Mommsen was deeply patriotic. He was angry with
people for considering that any of his fellow-citizens
had any Danish blood in their veins. "There are
some fools," he said, "who insist that Schleswig and
Holstein are not German countries."

At the same time Mommsen was a Liberal. Born,
like Niebuhr, in Dithmarschen, that glorious republic of
peasants "who had for more than three hundred years
maintained their independence against the Danes, and
who after their subjection still retained for themselves
valuable rights," [1] he was always distinguished by the
fire of his democratic sentiments.

During the revolution of 1848 he took a prominent
part in the political movement. Although he did not
sit in the Frankfort Parliament, he was one of the most
vigorous upholders of the nation's right. It was in
these circumstances that he became a journalist. For
several months he edited at Redensborg a Liberal
paper—*Schleswig-Holstein Journal*—in which he upheld the principles of Liberal politics.

After the failure of the Frankfort Parliament he
still took part in politics. In 1851, at Leipzig, where
he was Professor of Roman Law at the University, he
was dismissed with two of his colleagues, the philologists Haupt and Jahn, for having taken part in that
Liberal movement which was called the May disturbances.[2] Expelled from Germany, he went to
Zurich, where for two years he was Professor of
Roman Law at the University.

This exile, however, was only temporary. The
Prussian Government did not bear him any malice

[1] Treitschke, "Deutsche Gesch.," iii. 589.
[2] See Sybel, "Die Begründung des deutschen Reiches," ii.
99, 100.

for his Liberal opposition. In 1854 it recalled him to Breslau University. The reason was that Mommsen, while very Liberal in spirit, was also very Prussian in sentiment. It is true he did not like Frederick William IV's politics. He had a horror of the courtiers around that pious Conservative King, those Junkers, "those prejudiced old men," as he called them, whose obstinacy passes among the simple-minded as conservative energy. But to him this was not Prussia : she was to be found in the enlightened traditions of Frederick the Great.

He saw that, in order to preserve its existence, Prussia would be obliged to return to these traditions when, in order to bring about German unity, she would have to make an appeal to the national German sentiment. He shared the confidence of that Liberal who said to Victor Cherbuliez in 1866 : " The Hohenzollern will show the world that a Prussian king can join boldness of opinion and that generosity of character which trusts liberty and takes pleasure in difficulties, with the military virtues, with the feeling of duty, and with the diligence of his ancestors." [1] .

But the difference between Mommsen and the rest of the National Liberals is that he remained faithful to the ideal of his youth. He was able to resist all the temptations of victory. Both after 1866 and 1870 he never gave up his Liberal ideas. What he wanted was a great, strong, enlightened Germany—a Germany that would light up the world by the brilliance of its science. " The events of these late years," said he, " have convinced scholars themselves that the Government had good reason for giving up its attention

[1] " L'Allemagne politique depuis la paix de Prague," Paris, 1870.

exclusively for several years to political interests : but now that work is finished, and we must return to science once more."[1]

So, from the moment he saw that the Imperial policy was following an anti-Liberal path, he became one of its opponents. He was never a partisan of the laws of exception. Bismarck could never drag him into his confessional struggle. When the odious anti-Semitical campaign broke out, which carried with it many an old National Liberal, Mommsen eloquently branded these racial and religious struggles, which take us back to the sorriest days of the Middle Ages. Far from believing, like the narrow and jealous nationalists, that Jews made an obstacle to the formation of a powerful nation, he proved, on the contrary, that, by their modern spirit directed altogether towards progress, they were more fit than others to drive away what was still " too Teutonic and too particularistic in German habits and customs."[2]

But it was especially in the struggle against Bismarck that Mommsen gave evidence of his Liberal ideas. This struggle is traditional in Germany. Mommsen was a member of the Imperial Reichstag in the first years of the Empire. He sat, if not among the avowed

---

[1] He thought, indeed, that German science since 1860 was no longer what it had been. " It is worn out," he said. " Those aspirations, so ardent, of late years have been arrested in their course. Seeds full of promise have been withered. Our Government should have no more pressing need than that of encouraging and strengthening the sources of German greatness. Our task is difficult, but we can and will develop ' German science.' "

[2] " I am of the opinion," said he, " that Providence knows better than Stöcker why the German metal, in order to take up its proper form, needs a certain percentage of Jews " (" Auch ein Wort über unser Judenthum "), Berlin, 1880.

Progressives, at least among the true National Liberals, who, like Lasker, Bamberger, and Virchow, never came to any terms with the reactionaries. Once, indeed, Mommsen in a public meeting attacked violently the dishonest policy of Bismarck,[1] "who speculates at all times on public credulity." Bismarck, who, as a rule, attached no importance to such speeches, felt himself hurt to the quick by the Professor's words, and brought him before the courts. Mommsen took on his own defence.[2] "I made no personal attack: I discussed opinions and facts: I consider I have the right to oppose every system that seems to me contrary to the people's interests. He who represents one of these systems might think himself aimed at if he wished. I did not mean one person more than another. If Prince von Bismarck feels himself insulted, there are thousands of others who are with him." And the old Professor was acquitted.

And yet, strange to say, we cannot see this love of liberty anywhere in his "Roman History." He condemns therein, if you will, absolutism. He says, for example :—

"The least perfect political constitution, provided it allows a little play to the free decision of the majority, is better than the best absolutism, It is susceptible to progress and consequently lives. Absolutism is therefore a dead thing."

But what stands out most distinctly in this work is an undisguised defence of Cæsarism. Mommsen excused himself for having made this defence. He wished to draw a distinction between Julius Cæsar's coup d'état and all other coups d'état. "Such were

[1] Meeting of the Tempelhof, September 1881.
[2] "Schwindelpolitik."

the circumstances at Rome," said he, "that the dictator-ship was necessary. . . . To wish to make a comparison between Napoleon's coups d'état and this action of Julius Cæsar is absurd." He adds, "In all other cases it has only been parody and usurpation. It was because there was no parliamentarianism at Rome that 'this *tyrannis* was a necessity."[1] It is possible, but it is no less true, that Mommsen, by the enthusiasm with which he glorifies this act of Julius Cæsar, helped more than any one else to make Bismarck's policy possible, or, at least, to excuse it. That, as we shall see, was a trick played on the politician by the artist after playing so many on the scholar. But before we look into that, let us first say something about his "History of Rome."

II

Mommsen's "History of Rome" is two things: it is in the first place the most illuminating summary, the most exact and vivid of the conclusions arrived at by historical science on Roman affairs: next it is an extraordinarily partial judgment on Roman politics. And these two things, each having an absolute character, are as opposed one to the other as much as it is possible for things to be opposed.

Knowledge with Mommsen is as objective as his judgments are subjective. In all the latter we can feel the influence of the ideas of the time. We find every-where the National Liberal of 1848, with his wrath and rancour, his complaints and hopes.

---

[1] "History of Rome," *passim*. "The dictatorship," he said, "was a necessity in a country and at a time when the repre-sentative system had not rendered useless the saviours of society."

From these two points of view—which are in truth the two aspects of Mommsen's mind, the scholar and the politician—it is best to examine this work.

In the scientific exposition of the " History of Rome " we do not know which to admire most—the enormous knowledge of the author or the art with which it is used in the work.

It was an enormous enterprise to summarize all the works on this subject since Niebuhr. Mommsen himself had contributed towards this by the large number of memoirs he had written on particular points of Roman law, archæology, and history. Now all this is assimilated in a marvellous manner into a historical narrative which is one of the master-pieces of historical writing. The " History of Rome " is an extraordinary work in its condensation, for there exists no other which contains in such narrow limits (three volumes in octavo) so many and such good things. Mommsen tells his story in such an attractive fashion that from the very first lines you are carried away with it. His great pictures of the first migrations of the peoples of Italy, of the beginnings of Rome, of. the Etruscans, of the rule of the Hellenes in Italy: his chapters on Roman institutions, law, religion, the army, and art : on economic life, agriculture, industry, and commerce : on the internal development at home of Roman policy : on the Celts and Carthage : on the various Roman revolutions from the Gracchi to Julius Cæsar : on the Greek East, Macedonia, on the conquest of Gaul : all this makes up an admirable whole.

As a painter of great historical pictures I can see among contemporary historians only one man who can be compared with Mommsen: that is Ernest Renan: the same broad touch, the same sense of proportions, the same art of making one see and understand, of making things live again by means of characteristic details which impress themselves on one's mind.[1]

Like all the German historians sprung from Niebuhr, Mommsen attached great importance to the development of the individual life of peoples. Rome seemed to him particularly appropriate for making this understood. He set himself the task of teaching his contemporaries how to state and solve the national question, for that State was, he said, the example of the process by which the independence and unity of the States composing an Empire leads to the independence and unity of a nation, by which they bring about, or should bring about, the completion of their progress.

But what an abundance of developments he adds to this idea. From the time when Niebuhr applied it for the first time, all the advances in the biological sciences had come to the aid of the historical sciences, and Mommsen, like Taine, availed himself in his history of all these discoveries. To discover the origin of certain peculiarities in the Roman temperament he examines the physical conditions of the land,[2] and he sets out to describe to us " the plains of Latium, which must have been in primeval times the scene of the

---

[1] Mommsen himself said, " To reconstruct detail everywhere is not possible. It is better to pay attention to the important outlines."

[2] Mommsen was far from sharing the opinion of the materialistic historians of the school of Buckle and Taine, who believed that all the characteristics of a people, even their moral traits, could be explained by physical causes—the soil, air, and food. He recognized that there is something spontaneous and living in the human mind, which could not be explained by physical causes. When speaking of Polybius, he reproaches that historian with having disregarded the moral forces of humanity and with having a merely mechanical conception of the world.

grandest conflicts of nature," [1] and then with the help of
prehistorical investigation, of general ethnology, of the
comparative study of the Italian dialects, he shows us
what sort of people were the primitive peoples of Italy,
especially the Latin people, who mark "the stage at
which Italian civilization commenced, the starting-
point of the national history."

It was to the study of the "primitive cell" of the
Roman people, as he calls it, that he gave his whole
attention, since it is owing to her qualities that Rome
dominated first Italy and then the whole world.
Mommsen follows up the psychology of the Roman
people from its sources, and seeks to show the reasons for
the superiority of this people over the other peoples of
ancient history.   The Italian, said he, "surrendered his
own personal will for the sake of freedom, and learned
to obey his father that he might know how to obey the
State.   Amidst this subjection individual development
might be marred . . . the Italian gained in their stead
a feeling of fatherland and of patriotism such as the
Greek never knew, and alone among all the civilized
nations of antiquity succeeded in working out . . . a
national unity which at last placed in his hands the
mastery not only over the divided Hellenic stock, but
over the whole known world." [2]

Beside this feeling of duty, Mommsen also finds as
an explanation of the later success of Rome the keen
intelligence of the race, its common sense, which made
it a political people par excellence : it had to a marked
degree the notion of what could be done—in its laws,
ignorant of their wise simplicity ; in its religion, simple
too, but quite spiritual, and never attempting to set up

---

[1] " History of Rome " (English translation, 1908), i. 41.
[2] Ibid. i. 37.

images of divinity, a religion without a temple, which was scarcely more than a moral law drawn up by the priests and as democratic in form as the Greek religion was aristocratic.

Having thus determined the psychology of the Roman people, Mommsen follows up all the manifestations of it in its life and explains the whole of its history according to these ideas. In this we recognize the method which Taine employed in his great critical works, especially the "History of English Literature." The disadvantage of this method is that history assumes a sort of concatenation which becomes so necessary and rigorous that everything seems to be mechanical. "Events follow so naturally from each other," says M. Gaston Boisser, "and with such logical relation, that we run the risk, if we are not careful, of assigning too great a share to calculations and contrivance and of suppressing all that has happened by chance. That wonderful series of conquests, beginning at the gates of Rome and spreading to the furthermost confines of the civilized earth, seems then to us to be the realization of a plan conceived on the very first day and which had been continually followed up. The supposition would be that the Senate of Romulus—a meeting of several shepherds holding council in a field—dreamed of a conquest of the world, and set about at once to carry out their project."[1] No criticism more penetrating than this could be made of Mommsen's work.

Mommsen's conception of the history of Rome was taken purely from a political point of view. It is true he attaches a great deal of importance to all the manifestations of national life—his chapters on agri-

---

[1] Preface to the "Histoire romaine" by Michelet, pub. C. Levy, 1898 (*Revue des Deux Mondes*, April 1, 1898).

culture, industries, and commerce at Rome, on national economy, on Latin art and literature, are among the best we have—but politics still remains in his eyes the most important manifestation of the life of a people, for this it is which determines and conditions all the others.[1]

There are two ways of studying political history. The first of these—that of Tocqueville—is concerned with institutions, and really has less to do with events than with their meaning, the causes to which they must be attributed, and their consequences.   It may be said that this method is the only scientific one, as the author has but one object—to suffer himself to be taught by facts without trying to express his sympathy with or antipathy for any particular political form.

The second of these ways, and the most common one, consists of passing judgment on historical facts according to a certain political, social, or religious standard.   Thus we have history from the Liberal and Conservative point of view: the history of the Individualist and the Socialist, the history of the Protestant and the Catholic.

For a long while the Germans avoided this form of history, which particularly flourished in the first half of the nineteenth century among the English and French.   Niebuhr and Ranke, the forerunners of the national history, limited themselves, as we have seen, to the impartial relation of facts without taking sides with any political form.   But from the year 1850 we find a new school of historians growing up.   The result of the Revolution of 1848 was the formation of pro-

---

[1] He almost apologizes, on entering upon the chapters on art and literature, for having given them so important a place ("History of Rome," i. 284).

fessors who had dabbled in politics and had sat at the Frankfort Parliament. When they came back to academic life, they brought into their lecture-rooms the interests of the outside world, and in dealing with the political questions of the past they infused into them a little of the personal feeling which they had for the affairs of their own country.

Chronologically Mommsen was the first of these historians. Roman history to him is something real and actual. He enters fully into the political struggles which tore asunder the Empire. He sided with the national monarchists against the republican aristocrats with an intensity of feeling which leaves a Macaulay's or a Thiers' subjectivism far in the rear.

Yet in writing his history Mommsen did not think he was partizan: he thought his judgments were in conformity with the experience of the past. But in reality these judgments, if they are drawn to a great extent from his conception of historical life, are also very often due to his patriotic feelings, to the political circumstances in the midst of which he lived, and we might also say to his subjective impressions as an imaginative and artistic man. And it is under this fourfold aspect that we are now to examine his judgments.

Mommsen's philosophy of history is that of the struggle for life: internal struggles for the formation of political unity, external struggles to affirm the nation's greatness: the whole history of Rome consists to him of a series of immense struggles.[1]

At first these struggles were of a mercantile and strategic character. Latium, an agricultural and com-

---

[1] This valiant branch of the Italic stock, which he called the most warlike of all, did not cease to make war, both civil and foreign (" History of Rome," i., Book I, chap. vii.).

mercial area, surrounded by hostile tribes, carried on the intercourse of war. "The whole future development of the Roman State was bound up in this."

Then follow internal struggles : political struggles between patricians, plebeians, and those who had no citizen-rights, the first trying to lessen individual power for the advantage of the central power, the plebeians trying to win equality of power with the patricians, and those without citizen-rights and strangers struggling to obtain equal rights with the citizens.

On these political struggles were grafted social ones, which, though quite distinct from them, were often involved in them ; for they crossed and recrossed each other so as to form the very framework of Roman history : these were the struggles between the capitalists and great landed proprietors on the one hand and the middle class on the other.

While relating these struggles, Mommsen shows us with masterly description the expansion of Rome by conquest, as the result of that law of history by virtue of which, says he, " a nation which has become a State tries to annex its neighbours of less political power."

Mommsen returns over and over again to this law of the historical life of nations, which he considers as inevitable as the law of gravity. The object of history, says he, must be civilization. And, in order to triumph, civilization demands " the suppression of races less capable of, or less advanced in, culture [civilization] by nations of a higher standing." [1] War therefore becomes the great machine which elaborates progress, and the prosperity of a country exacts that struggles should become wars and pillage conquest,

[1] "History of Rome," i. 9.

K

in order that the political power of the State might begin to be organized.

It must be recognized that this is the philosophy of history which suited a people who rushed into three wars, one after the other, in order to establish their preponderance, first in Germany and then in Europe and the world. Mommsen doubtless could not foresee these wars when he wrote his work in 1854, but he justified them beforehand by showing that politics cannot go on without wars, and that these wars have a moulding force which is not to be found in revolutions.

In stating this Mommsen did not say, like Hegel, that there is a moral idea at the bottom of every war, and that force and virtue are synonymous terms. He never troubled himself about morals. He simply stated a historical law, which was that the strong oppressed the weak "in the mighty vortex of the world's history, which inexorably crushes all peoples that are not as hard and as flexible as steel." [1]

Thenceforward history becomes the tribunal of the world, and success is the only criterion of the value of politics. If the Celts were conquered by the Romans it "was no accidental destruction . . . but a self-incurred and in some measure historically necessary catastrophe." [2]

One may feel some surprise to see such doctrines defended in the country of the Kantian Imperative and the great modern apostles of moral conscience. But the Germany of 1850 was no longer the Germany of Fichte and Kant. She had gone to the school of practical philosophers, who showed her that conditions are always changing, and that the value of right is only

---

[1] "History of Rome," v. 99.   [2] Ibid. v. 98.

relative, and consequently only depends upon the force
which upholds it: that if this force be wanting, then it
is but just that the weak should be sacrificed: and that
if in the final crash the innocent are taken and the
cunning guilty escape unscathed, there is nothing to
be troubled about: it is a law of the world, and all
our protests will not alter it.

This practical philosophy, which Bismarck expressed
one day when he said, "Even if he has poor arguments
at his disposal, that man is always right if he has the
majority of bayonets on his side," is really the philosophy to be found in Mommsen's "History of Rome."
This work is nothing but the glorification of force, even
when it has been used against what is right. To
Mommsen the vanquished is always wrong. He sides
with Julius Cæsar, that deceitful and cunning man,
against what he calls the honest mediocrities of the
senate. But even that is not enough, he must needs
season his remarks with sarcasm. Nothing pleased
him better than to ridicule the virtue of these honest
but dense people.

"They congratulated each other on the heroic
courage which they had displayed; the declaration
of Bibulus that he would die rather than yield, the
peroration which Cato continued to deliver when
in the hands of the lictors, were great patriotic
feats." [1]

Julius Cæsar, on the other hand, is a perfect man
because he was an unconscionable prig. "On each day
when Cæsar appeared before the people, his colleague
Bibulus instituted the well-known political observations
of the weather which interrupted all public business
(p. 208). Cæsar did not trouble himself about the

---

[1] "History of Rome," iv. 511.

skies, but continued to prosecute his terrestrial occupation." [1]

The constant object of Mommsen's contempt is the honest citizen who struggled to save what he thought was the liberty of his country, to prevent its downfall, or at least to delay it.[2] He could not understand Cicero's scruples of conscience, and he makes him a ridiculous poltroon, "one of those dull fellows who are always talking gospel and for whom hell has no use." Mommsen readily poses as a man detached from the "middle-class prejudices in the accepted code of morals." He attacks all those who did not see in Cæsar's deceitfulness the mark of genius, and who added to their want of intelligence the tedium of their stupid speeches.

That was the principal lesson he wished to teach the Germans of his time. Too long had the kindly German been regarded as a simple being devoid of malice. Mommsen wanted no more of it. "We are not simple," said he, in a fashion humorous enough in itself, "and we don't wish to be so at any price."

Mommsen's prayer has been granted. No one can accuse that nation of simplicity which produced Bismarck. The unfortunate part is that intelligence

---

[1] "History of Rome," iv. 511.

[2] The historian Freeman says rightly : "One mourns to see in such a scholar's historic judgment only the morals of Macaulay's Avaux ; one mourns to see in him the politics of an œcumenical Jingo falling down and worshipping brute force wherever he can find it" ("Methods of Historical Study," 1886, p. 291). See also Lord Acton : "It is important to understand along what lines of reasoning men so eminent, so quick to inquire into every new thing, have adhered to maxims which it has cost the world much effort to reverse" ("German Schools of History," *English Historical Review*, i. 34).

has not always concealed this Machiavellian policy
among the Germans. In the Reichstag, not long
ago, every time a protesting member—Danish or
Polish—made any demands on behalf of his fellow-
countrymen, loud bursts of laughter were heard on
all sides.

"Can one blame the Prussians," said Victor Cher-
luliez on this point, "for that sort of harshness and
brutality which is in them, that taste for encroaching
which alarms and annoys its neighbour, that un-
generous treatment of small nations?"[1]

That lack of generosity towards the small is one
of the characteristics of Mommsen in his "History of
Rome." He is full of haughtiness when dealing with
the peoples who were overcome by the Romans. All
this typically German superior feeling is revealed in
certain descriptions of his. What contemptuous
sarcasm, for example, is that with which he charac-
terizes the Celts : he compares them with the modern
Irish :—

" . . . Every feature reappears ; the laziness in
the culture of the fields : the delight in tippling
and brawling : the language full of comparisons and
hyperboles, of allusions and quaint turns . . . the
curiosity—no trader was allowed to pass before he had
told in the open street what he knew or did not know
in the shape of news ; . . . the childlike piety which
sees in the priest a father and asks for his counsel in all
things . . . at the same time the utter incapacity to
preserve a self-reliant courage equally remote from
presumption and from pusillanimity. . . . It is and
remains at all times and all places the same indolent
and poetical, irresolute and fervid, inquisitive, credulous,

---

[1] "L'Allemagne politique," p. 107.

amiable, clever, but—in a political point of view—
thoroughly useless nation."[1]

If the Irishman is thus maltreated, a little farther
on it is the Frenchman's turn : The Celts are an
intelligent people, it is true, but fickle : wonderfully
gifted from a literary point of view, but devoid of any
moral or political understanding : good soldiers but
bad citizens : destructive warriors, these Celts have
overthrown many States without being able to
build one up for themselves, nor even a powerful
civilization.[2]

Mommsen did not like the French.   In 1870 he
hailed the war as a war of deliverance which at last
would extricate his people from that "stupid imitation
of the French."   In a letter addressed to the Italians
to prevent them from allying themselves with the
French, he spoke with the tone of a prophet of the
impending fall of modern Babylon, of the decay of
French literature, "as impure as the waters of the
Seine."   The Emperor Napoleon III, whose good
offices Mommsen had not despised when he needed
them for his historical researches, is spoken of as "a
swindler, whose Court was nothing but a gang of
adventurers who wished to degrade the world to the
level of the *demi-monde*."   And celebrating the return
of Alsace to the German Fatherland the historian
exclaims : "Bitter indeed to see a French flag waving
over that masterpiece of German work, Strassburg
Cathedral.   When the German student, in the German
University of Strassburg, read the sweet story of
Goethe's love, that exquisite idyl of Sesenheim, the
dear Alsatian village, he shut the volume and asked

[1] " History of Rome," v. 99.
[2] Ibid. i. 27–32.

his heart what manner of men his forefathers could
have been, who abandoned to the foreigner this sacred
field of the German muse—to men who cared neither
for its buds nor for its blossom, whose whole aim was
to extirpate German manners, German religion, and
our German tongue." [1]

Mommsen is an ardent German patriot, and this is
shown in every line of his " History." By the side of
the German race all other people are contemptible.
One might have expected that he wrote the " History
of Rome " because he had a keen admiration for the
Latin people. But in truth he liked them but little.
If he recognized all that made them great, their strong
character and the powerful discipline of their education,
whose " wisdom was as simple as it was profound," he
did not like their genius ; he thought it at once too
judicious and too rhetorical, lacking poetry and depth
of sentiment : " Poetry is impassioned language and its
modulation is melody. While in this sense no people
is without poetry and music, some nations have
received a pre-eminent endowment of poetic gifts.
The Italian nation, however, was not and is not
one of these. The Italian is deficient in the passion
of the heart, in the longing to idealize what is human.
. . . His acuteness of perception and his graceful
versatility enabled him to excel in irony and in the
vein of tale-telling which we find in Horace and

---

[1] " Letter to the People of Italy." Mommsen for a long while
refused to attach any importance to the work of French scholars
from a scientific point of view. Speaking of spurious inscriptions,
he cries in a victorious tone : " It is not sufficient to say that they
come from a French source." In his " Roman Provinces," published in 1885, he took no notice of foreign works or quoted them
sarcastically. Since then, however, Mommsen has done justice to
the remarkable works of the new French schools.

Boccaccio, in the humorous pleasantries of love and song which are presented in Catullus, and in the good popular songs of Naples, above all in the lower comedy and in farce. In rhetoric and histrionic art especially no other nation equalled or equals the Italians. . . . The very highest literary works that have been successfully produced in Italy, divine poems like Dante's ' Commedia,' and historical treatises such as those of Sallust and Machiavelli, of Tacitus and Colletta, are pervaded by a passion more rhetorical than spontaneous. Even in music '. . . really creative talent has been far less conspicuous than the accomplishment which speedily assumes the character of virtuosoship. . . . The field of the inward in art . . . is not that which has fallen to the Italian as his special province; the power of beauty, to have its full effect upon him, must be placed not ideally before his mind, but sensuously before his eyes. Accordingly, he is thoroughly at home in architecture, painting, and sculpture; in these he was during the epoch of ancient culture the best disciple of the Hellenes, and in modern times he has become the master of all nations." [1]

Mommsen's peremptory and haughty mode of treatment is a part both of his mind and feelings. He is as systematic as Taine. In writing history his object is to prove certain notions of his, and consequently he omits all facts that would destroy or weaken these notions. He means the Roman people to remain at all costs what he set out by laying down that they were. The lack of genius among the Romans for anything except politics is a dogma to him which history is entrusted to prove, and thus it is that from one deduction to another he arrives at this epigram-

---

[1] " History of Rome," i. 284.

matic formula which sums up his idea: Rome produced but one man of genius—Julius Cæsar.

Against this Roman people, mighty in politics and war, Mommsen sets other peoples who seem to him more accomplished: the Greeks and the Germans. " The Greeks and the Germans alone possess a fountain of song that wells up spontaneously: from the golden vase of the Muses only a few drops have fallen on the green soil of Italy." [1] Powerful art, depth of thought and feeling, original learning, these are the heritages of the Hellenic and German races. In his mind, Mommsen constantly contrasts them with the Latin race. The German race, above all, assumes in his eyes a symbolical value. When he criticizes the Latin temperament we feel that he is secretly praising the German temperament. He notes, not without pride, that the only parts of Gaul which energetically and successfully resisted the Romans were those parts whose inhabitants had German blood in their veins. [2]

Thus it is throughout the whole of his work, so that the Roman " History " becomes, in a manner of speaking, an apology for the German race.

His audience and readers made no mistakes about it. A short while after the publication of this work other works began to appear, which, taking their inspiration from his lessons, used the psychology of races for the glorification of their country. A new science was instituted, *Völkerpsychologie*, by which professors of history and geography, ethnographists and schoolmasters explained the superiority of the German race over all others. *Deutschland vor Allem und über Alles in der Welt.* Thus it is that we could read in

---

[1] " History of Rome," i. 297.
[2] Ibid. v. 99.

the German geography text-books for use in schools: "Germany is in truth the heart of Europe, and as the duty of the heart is to circulate through the limbs a blood which will renew the parts that are growing old and strengthen the young ones, so Germany's mission in history is to renew the youth of this old continent of Europe by the diffusion of German blood through its worn-out limbs." In this text-book the young Germans are taught that everything that is good in France is due to the German race: then not only are the Flemings, the Normans, the Burgundians Germans, but also the people of Champagne with their striking figures, fair hair, and blue eyes: the people of Languedoc, descendants of the conquering Visigoths, and those of Provence, deeply imbued with Gothic and Burgundian blood, should be regarded as belonging to the German race: that the only part that is really French is the Ile de France, "the stuffing of the French pie, a fermenting mass of rottenness which has slowly succeeded in raising and corrupting the rest." [1]

The punishment of these German scholars has been the finding of persons more stupid even than themselves who have made a caricature of their teaching. Falling on ill-prepared or ill-balanced brains, this teaching has brought forth strange flowers. Several specimens could be seen in the immense literature which the war of 1870 brought forth. There are thousands of witnesses of that event who saw therein the confirmation of all the lessons which had been taught them in school, and who have shown, in their "Recollections of the War," which burst forth nowadays on the other side of the Rhine like weeds, how much

[1] A. Hummel, "Handbuch der Erdkunde," 1876.

the German race was superior to the others, and how richly the French deserved to be thrashed by the Germans—the judges of Europe.

It would be absurd, of course, to hold Mommsen responsible for all these lucubrations, but is he not in some measure responsible for that state of mind ? Has he not helped, at least, to make it possible by his lessons on the psychology of the Romans and the Gauls ? [1]

---

[1] Nothing is more significant in this respect than certain of these lucubrations which contain actual phrases from Mommsen. A soldier fighting in France writes daily his impressions to his father. The latter, a Saxon schoolmaster, a typical Teuton, both enthusiast and realist, a guzzler and a bit of a drunkard, of a dreadfully brutal positivism, sends his son woollen stockings and sausages and practical advice how to " improve his French and miss no opportunity of perfecting it," all this intermingled with curses on Sodom and lyrical effusions on the purity of the German race and the Germans' mission in the world. "German calmness, firmness, intelligence, discipline, and conscience gives us a superiority over the talkative and conceited French." "Your hatred of France is right. Have no pity for the nation." "The German nation far surpasses the French in morality." The comparison of Turcos and French : " The Turco," said this gallant schoolmaster, " is still lower than woman. . . . You are the admiration of the whole world. . . . The little ragamuffins in the streets of London, the negro children on the coasts of Africa, the redskins of North America know that now. The German warrior is the greatest in the world. How happy am I to see thus realized the prophecy I made twenty years ago to my pupils : ' United Germany will be the terror of the earth, but she will also be its blessing and a model for all.' " And this little sentence : " The German scarcely loves the French, but he willingly drinks their wines " (*300 Tage im Sattel : Erlebnisse eines sächsichen Artilleristen, 1870-71*, Dresden, 1892).

In another place, in the letters of a colonel of Uhlans, we find some even more conspicuous Mommsen : " The French character," says this psychologist in uniform, " is the result of two great heritages of the past : one from the Gauls or Celts, and the other

The same thing happened with politics. By the lessons to be drawn from his work Mommsen brought about just the opposite to what he wished to do.

His conception of Roman history, in the first place, was strongly influenced by the events which took place in his country after 1848. The great notion of his history was that, with the Romans, democracy and royalty were the same thing. This notion is due, no doubt, to the analogy he saw between democratic Germany and the Rome of Julius Cæsar.

In the earliest ages we can understand that these two terms were synonymous, and Mommsen shows, in an admirable fashion, that the Roman State, constituted on the model of a family, formed a sort of huge family with a chief—the king. The Roman community "was composed of free and equal husbandmen, and could not boast of a nobility by the grace of God."[1] The king was only a delegate of the power of the people; he was consequently only one of them: so that monarchy and democracy are, in their origin, identical.

But where Mommsen falls into error is when he thinks that the political struggles at Rome after the abolition of royalty had no other object than to return to this original state of democratic monarchy. In his eyes, the revolutions from the Gracchi to Julius Cæsar had this one meaning alone.

---

from the conquerors of the land. . . . With the Gauls their glory was the glory of arms—a peculiarity of the Roman also, who always regarded himself as the master of the world. Among the French this love of glory has reached its highest point of expression. The French cannot get used to the idea of a people superior to themselves," etc. (Moritz von Berg, *Ulanenbriefe von der 1 Armee*, Bielefeld, 1894).

[1] " History of Rome," i. 81.

This conception of Roman history, which consisted in contrasting Roman liberty under Julius Cæsar with the aristocratic Republic, which only represented the interest of certain classes, was strengthened in Mommsen's mind by the consideration of what has just happened in his own country. He had seen that Liberalism was powerless to create the unity of Germany. Its result had been anarchy on all sides and the disillusionment of his fellow-countrymen. His conviction was that the sword alone could settle the difference, and that that was Prussia's mission. In his opinion, the King of Prussia had to do what Julius Cæsar had done in Rome. Hence the fervour with which he defends this dictator. All his wrath as a Prussian democrat bursts out in this book. He gives one the impression at all moments of making some allusion to the affairs of his own country.

The Roman aristocrats are to him "Junkers," " prejudiced Conservatives," " a camarilla of defenders of the throne and altar." When he speaks of Pompey's cowardice, who shamefully put his sword in its sheath when the time came to advance, we can feel in his words all the patriot's indignation at Frederick William IV's shameful retreat at Olmütz.[1]

Similarly when he attacks the democrats, those orators of street-corners and clubs, "those longbeards

---

[1] His allusions to the narrow and prejudiced character of the Prussian nobility are frequent in this work :—
" The exclusion of the plebeians from all public magistracies and public priesthoods . . . and the maintenance, with perverse obstinacy, of the legal impossibility of marriage between old burgesses and plebeians, further impressed on the patriciate from the outset the stamp of an exclusive and wrongly privileged aristocracy" ("History of Rome," i. 334. See also his remarks on " Roman Aristocracy," Ibid. *passim*).

who make speeches in their bass voices to crowds of peasants," one might fancy himself in the midst of one of those democratic assemblies and " the greybeards of 1848."

When he comes to Julius Cæsar, Mommsen becomes lyrical: here at last is the saviour of society, the man of genius who is to organize democratic Rome.

If Mommsen has such a lively admiration for Julius Cæsar, it is because he finds in him one of the rare examples of humanity who was perfect. He enumerates his qualities: an incredible activity which allowed him to undertake all things with ease without ever feeling the weight of the most difficult affairs: a mind always clear and alert, remarkable for the distinctness of the orders he gave : a matchless memory, a wonderfully well-balanced mind: a sense of the realities of life which amounted to genius : a passion for every task he undertook and yet always restrained by reason: the curiosity of his mind so continually awake that in the midst of the camp he still found time to study the inflexions of substantives and the metre of Latin verse.

Mommsen does not know what to admire most in Cæsar, the statesman or the general—the inventor of "national strategy." He says, " If we still after so many centuries bow in reverence before what Cæsar willed and did, it is not because he desired and gained a crown (to do which is, abstractly, as little of a great thing as the crown itself), but because his mighty ideal—of a free commonwealth under one ruler—never forsook him, and preserved him when monarch from sinking into vulgar royalty." [1]

That is a statement which seems exaggerated to us,

---

[1] " History of Rome," iv. 507.

but Mommsen emphasizes it by giving Julius Cæsar
the highest place among human geniuses. Among the
moderns there are only two men who can approach
him at once as statesmen and *soldiers, Cromwell and
Frederick the Great.* But still what a difference!—
" little as the Puritan hero seems to resemble the
dissolute Roman." And he adds : " The most remarkable peculiarity of his action as a statesman was
its perfect harmony . . . however much occasion his
disagreeable relations with the Senate gave for it, he
never resorted to outrages such as that of the
18th Brumaire . . . He is, in fine, perhaps the only
one of those mighty men who has preserved to the
end of his career the statesman's tact of discrimina-
ting between the possible and the impossible . . . he
thought not of unbounded plans of world-conquest, but
merely of carrying into effect a well-considered regulation of the frontiers." [1]

Carried away by his enthusiasm, Mommsen becomes
prophetical and declares what the Empire would have
been if Cæsar had lived. " He would not have been
a vulgar despot, he would not have fallen into the beaten
track." This is all very fine, but is it true ?

When we read this defence of Julius Cæsar, a
defence of such exaggerated enthusiasm, we soon discover that it was not merely the analogy between the
states of affairs in Germany and Rome that so aroused
Mommsen. There is a deeper, more inward cause
than that—one in the very nature of the historian.

In a celebrated passage in his " Pensées," Pascal draws
a distinction between three kinds of greatness : the
greatness of the flesh, the greatness of the mind, and
the greatness of goodness : " that is, between the earthly

---

[1] " History of Rome," v. 310–13.

genius who fought great battles which strike the eye, the leaders of art and science who filled the world with their fame and lustre, and the saints whose greatness consists in charity." It is not necessary to have read much of Mommsen to see which class he admires. He is for the earthly greatness. One word which comes most frequently from his pen, and which seems to betray his secret preferences, is "passion." Whenever he comes across the great personalities of men of action who have done something great in the world, his artist's soul is stirred and his imagination aroused. That is the kind of beauty which he understands. He does not form his opinions as a historian but as a poet. Energetic and passionate natures fill him with enthusiasm and he speaks of them as Shakespeare would. He does not hesitate in his choice between honest but moderate men like Pompey and perverse but violent and hot-headed natures like Catilina : he prefers Catilina.[1]

But Mommsen, in his conception as an artist of the great heroes, does not go so far as Friedrich Nietzsche, who, in his admiration of all natural forces, of the display of all human energies, arrives at last at the morality of the princes and artists of the pagan Renaissance. No. Mommsen wanted the actions of great men to be directed towards higher goals. He did not separate beauty from morality. In his " History " he branded the luxury of manners, the effeminate character of the educated classes and of those society people which went hand in hand with the politics of inconsistent, arrogant, and short-sighted demagogues. He

[1] " Catilina, who before the beginning of the battle had sent back his horse and those of all his officers, showed on this day that nature had destined him for no ordinary things, and that he knew at once how to command as a general and how to fight as a soldier " (" History of Rome," iv. 485).

despised the elegant dilettanti who, towards the end of the Republic, already foreshadowed the decline of Rome—those like Metellus and Lucullus, who, in warfare, were less studious to extend the frontiers of the Empire than to add to the list of game and delicate fish which they might bring back to Rome.

But if Mommsen's conception of life is not that of lovers of the beautiful, one might easily thereby be led to a wrong conclusion. The best proof of this is that the author of the "History of Rome" has found enthusiastic admirers among them. Would it be too much to declare that he prepared the way for Nietzsche, and made such a person possible in his country? At any rate, no one has done more than Mommsen in bringing about the reaction against the Christian conception of human life.[1] His ideal, at least the one which he reveals in his "History of Rome," is identical with the one put forward by Machiavelli in his "Discourse" on Titus Livy: "Our religion rewards the humane and meditative virtues rather than the active ones. It sets the supreme happiness in humility, abjection, in contempt for human affairs, while pagan faith made the highest good to be magnanimity, physical strength, and all those qualities that make men redoubtable. If our religion demands any strength of mind, it is that which enables us to suffer the ills of life rather than that which performs great actions."

His whole defence of Julius Cæsar ends with that conclusion: that is why, in spite of his oft-repeated

---

[1] That is one of the reasons, it seems, why he never wrote a continuation of his "History of Rome." The historical problem of the *Origin of Christianity* caused him difficulties.

protestations of having wished to deify the great heroes, to create the men with a divine mission and resuscitate saviours of society, Mommsen was, in Germany, one of the most ardent apostles of the theory that "might is better than right." By praising, as he has done, the energy and skill displayed in order to attain the goal of dominion, he spread in Germany the idea of Cæsarism, whose historical rôle seems to him to be to lead, by any and every means, the human flocks to civilization. In this sense we may say that his most direct disciple is Nietzsche, who, driving this theory to its logical conclusions, hailed in Machiavelli's Prince "the greatest example of a leader of men."

III

Few historical works have had a more resounding success than Mommsen's "History of Rome." When it appeared, in 1854, the effect was immense and re-echoed far throughout the nation. The Universities, it is true, were not pleased with it. The historian, in his work, overthrew all accepted opinions and treated with an absolute lack of respect men whom they had been wont to venerate. Cicero, for example, was treated therein as a coward, a journalist in the worst sense of the term, a conceited invalid, a compiler, nothing but an advocate and not a good one, and a short-sighted egotist. Even Cicero's work "does not count among Latin literature . . . but any one who seeks classical productions in works so written can only be advised to study in literary matters a becoming silence." [1]

But what helped to make him inferior as a scientific

[1] "History of Rome," v. 504-10.

historian was his greatest force as a historian of narrative. The Germans had hitherto no man of talent who knew how to relate events with such vigour. Mommsen had accomplished a miracle : that of making Roman history an actual and living thing. Under his pen, manners, customs, private life, place and men come to life again. " The ' History of Rome,' " said Treitschke with justice, " is one of the finest things ever written in our language, and there should be no young man or soldier who would not be delighted with his descriptions of Hannibal and Cæsar." [1] And indeed Mommsen's portraits are marvellous. What could be finer, for example, than that of Sulla ?—

" Physically and mentally of sanguine temperament, blue-eyed, fair, of a complexion singularly white but blushing with every passionate emotion — though otherwise a handsome man with piercing eyes—he seemed hardly destined to be of more moment to the state than his ancestors. . . . He desired from life nothing but serene enjoyment. Reared in the refinement of such cultivated luxury as was at that time naturalized even in the less wealthy senatorial families of Rome, he quickly possessed himself of all the fullness of sensuous and intellectual enjoyments which the combination of Hellenic polish and Roman wealth could secure. He was welcome as a pleasant companion in the aristocratic salon and as a good comrade in the camp : his acquaintances, high and low, found in him a sympathizing friend and a ready helper in time of need, who gave his gold with far more pleasure to his embarrassed comrade than to his wealthy creditor. Passionate was his homage to the

[1] Th. Schiemann, " H. v. Treitschke," Munich, 1896, p. 227.

wine-cup, still more passionate to women. . . . Yet amidst these jovial Bacchanalia he lost neither bodily nor mental vigour : in the rural leisure of his last years he was still zealously devoted to the chase, and the circumstance that brought the writings of Aristotle from conquered Athens to Rome testified at least to his interest in more serious reading. The specific peculiarities of Roman character rather repelled him. Sulla had nothing of the blunt hauteur which the grandees of Rome were fond of displaying in presence of the Greeks, or of the pomposity of narrow-minded great men. . . . He was wont to say that every improvised enterprise turned out better with him than those which were systematically planned. . . . His contemporaries said of him that he was half lion, half fox, and that the fox in him was more dangerous than the lion . . . but so far as concerns the total absence of political selfishness—although, it is true, in this respect only—Sulla deserved to be named side by side with Washington. . . . He [the statesman] will place the deliverer of Rome and the accomplisher of Italian unity below, but yet in the same class with, Cromwell." [1]

Among the talents which Mommsen possesses as a historian, there is one in which he has not been surpassed in his own country—the plastic art. Under his pen everything takes colour and shape. With two strokes of the brush a place arises before our eyes. He shows us, for example, Trasimene and its pass— " a narrow defile between two steep mountain walls, closed at its outlet by a high hill and at its entrance by the Trasimene Lake " ; [2] elsewhere he describes to

[1] " History of Rome," iv. 139–48.
[2] Ibid. iv. 278.

us "the north-east dense forests, attaching themselves
to the heart of the Ardennes, stretched almost without
interruption from the German Ocean to the Rhine:
and on the plains of Flanders and Lorraine, now so
fertile, the Menapian and Treverian shepherd then
fed his half-wild swine in the impenetrable oak
forest." [1]

Mommsen has a picturesque style even in expressing
abstract things. Thus in five lines he describes to us
Pompey's return: "After the illegal condemnation
of the adherents of Catilina, after the unparalleled
acts of violence against the tribune of the people
Metellus, Pompeius might wage war at once as
defender of the two palladia of Roman public freedom—the right of appeal and the inviolability of the
tribunate of the people—against the aristocracy, and
as champion of the party of order against the
Catilinian band. It seemed almost impossible that
Pompeius should neglect this opportunity, and with
his eyes open put himself a second time into the
painful position, in which the dismissal of his army
in 684/70 had placed him, and from which only the
Gabinian law had released him. But near as seemed
the opportunity of placing the white chaplet around
his brow, and much as his own soul longed after it,
when the question of action presented itself, his heart
and his hand once more failed him." [2] Elsewhere he
says of certain intrigues which followed each other
without success : "They burst in the air like soap-
bubbles." Cicero with his pompous speeches is a
general who attacks with great noise pasteboard
fortresses.

[1] "History of Rome," v. 14.
[2] Ibid. iv. 499.

Mommsen always excels in making the past seem real by borrowing his images from the physical world or from familiar historical events. We know what advantage Ernest Renan derived from this process in his "Origins of Christianity" and in his "History of Israel." Mommsen, too, has some wonderful finds : for example, he will describe Alexandrinism as a hot-house literature, Lucretius' "De Natura Rerum," a poetic wilderness, the critics of the Vedas, "literary botanists ": Theodorus of Mitylene the first "Maire de palais": Labienus, "a Marshal of Napoleon": Salonica with the Pompeian refugees, "a new Coblentz": Sulla, "a Don Juan": Cato, "a Sancho Panza." He said, "The Romans had the same opinion of the vestals as the Italians of the 'Decameron' had of the nuns." Fabius, "a man advanced in years, of a deliberation and firmness which to not a few seemed procrastination and obstinacy," reminds him of a Prussian general, for "he looked to a methodical prosecution of the war as—next to sacrifices and prayer—the means of saving the State." [1]

There is no doubt something arbitrary in this process. When Mommsen speaks, for example, of Roman meetings and clubs, drawing-rooms, Celtic pence, Junkers, the "high finance of the capital," of sbirros, ultras, the Volkspartei, lansquenets, marshals, Prince Ariovistus, we might think that he carries local colour too far. By trying to modernize things, he ends in parodying them. And what makes this fault worse is that Mommsen does it with too large a number of foreign phrases. To give more colour to a phrase he has recourse to French words when he cannot find a German one. These are scattered throughout his prose:

---

[1] "History of Rome," ii. 281.

he says, Blasirtheit, bornirt, chicaniren, die chicanöse Opposition, peroriren, haranguiren. German writers like David Strauss, trained in the school of Lessing and the prose-writers of the eighteenth century, find Mommsen's language execrable. No doubt it lacks elegance and purity, but, on the other hand, how living and expressive it is![1]

The public has found Mommsen right. When his "History of Rome" appeared, they were tired of well-trimmed academic styles. This was the time when Taine said in France : "The best style is that one which gets itself a hearing." And Mommsen had this art in a very high degree. He wished, above all, to give his work the character of reality. He uses no rhetoric. His hard phrases, with keen and decisive periods, conjure things up before us with all the appearance of life. There is in his style a certain picturesque brutality which is a sign of the times and which his contemporaries liked best in him.

In truth, a change was taking place in the literary habits of Germany. Realism, which was making its appearance throughout Europe, was there also winning over the new generation. The Germans had not, in literature, emulators of Gogol, Flaubert, and Taine, but they had historians of a powerful realism, and Mommsen is in the first rank of these.

At that time three works filled German youth with enthusiasm : Goethe's "Faust," Schopenhauer's "The World as Will and Idea," and Mommsen's

---

[1] Take, for example, a very fine description of Republican Rome : "Imagine London with the former slave population of New Orleans, with the police of Constantinople, the political troubles of Paris in 1848, and you will have a sufficiently exact picture of the magnificent Republican city whose fall Cicero and his contemporaries deplore in their complaining letters."

" History of Rome." There is no difficulty in understanding what in these three works won the fancy of that generation, tired of dreams, positive, and attracted only by reality. Goethe's " Faust " taught that philosophy at which the poet, after having tried so many things, had finally arrived and which he expressed in these words : " Action consoles us for everything."

" The World as Will and Idea," a book of practical metaphysics based upon experience, which only stated facts, offered, no doubt, an unlovely kind of philosophy, unhappy often but real, and which in its nihilistic madness drove one to action : this philosophy seasoned with biting and brutal spirit, clever at unmasking sophistry and pointing out without compunction the weak spots in life, was certainly the one which would be appreciated by that disabused generation, cured of all its illusions and therefore ready to throw itself entirely into the struggle for life.

Schopenhauer, the apostle of the new philosophy, had long awaited his hour. For thirty years copies of the first edition of his work had lain piled up in the back of the bookshops. And suddenly, in a night, in 1844, the whole edition was sold out. Schopenhauer became the most read, the most liked and most commented on. At last he had found his public.[1]

It is the same with Mommsen. It is because he

---

[1] Schopenhauer's influence on the writers of the new German Empire was very great. Not only are writers like Nietzsche and Max Nordau and Düring descendants of his, but even writers like Treitschke, who have opposed his philosophy, have expressed his ideas in almost identical terms. Treitschke's prejudices against women, for example, are pure Schopenhauer. The irony best liked by the Germans, that of Bismarck and Treitschke, has the same flavour as Schopenhauer's.

was under the influence of the preoccupations and
passions of his age that he was able to write so
living and attractive a work.   He felt better than
any one else what the nation needed and the qualities
it was necessary to infuse into it.   By making war on
dangerous illusions, by pitilessly attacking with sarcasm dreamers and schemers, in ridiculing the honest
and well-intentioned souls who acted according to
"schoolmasters' rules," as he said, by repeating in
every variety of tone " Our age is one of iron," he
prepared the generation of his time for future struggles.

The " History of Rome " was an act, perhaps one of
the most significant, of that strange period between
1850 and 1870.   Mommsen in that work revealed
himself altogether, and it was a little on this account
that he took such a hold on his contemporaries.
Instead of a book full of cold and lifeless learning,
in which only scholars could take an interest, he
wrote a passionate history in which the people found
all their sorrows and hopes.[1]

But this book had no sequel.   Although he had
stopped on the threshold of the Empire, Mommsen
never continued the work.   Thirty years later, in 1885,
it is true, he published a new volume, the " Roman
Provinces," but the qualities which made the charm of
the " History of Rome " were not present in it.   It was
a scholar who had written that book : it was temperate
in its judgments, it contrasted with its predecessor

---

[1] Mommsen recognized later that his book was extremely
partial, and he wanted to modify certain judgments.   But he
did not do so.   " The idea which stopped him," said Julian
Schmidt, " was that the work should be regarded as a work
of art which would be spoiled by alteration.   He preferred,
therefore, to leave it as it was " (J. Schmidt, *Deutsche Rundschau*, vol. 44, p. 66).

in its calmness and scientific serenity, but by the
side of it, how dull and unstriking it seems! The
human interest which added so to the value of
the "History of Rome" was not to be found in it.
Mommsen knew this. When he brought forth this
new-born he begged indulgence for it. "It should
be read," he said, "as it was written—with self-
effacement." The historian—I was going to say the
poet—was right. In 1885 the old man could not
bring back the enthusiasm of his young days: the
great ray of sunlight of 1848 had ceased to shine.

CHAPTER III

HEINRICH VON SYBEL

A GERMAN publicist of great ability—Karl Hilde-brand—wrote in 1874: "History in Germany, in spite of the impartiality on which its writers pride themselves, is, above and before all, national and Protestant." The professors may have as many illusions as they wish about their objectivity, their "scientific incorruptibility," on the "uprightness of their conscience" and the "infallibility of their method ; whether they wish or know it or not, they have served national and Protestant interests. They have made history to suit their fancy. Among its facts, they have chosen those which supported their point of view. They have soon forgotten the science learned on the benches of the University: the national and Protestant tendency alone has remained."

These lines apply to no one better than to Heinrich von Sybel, who was, in Germany, the representative *par excellence* of the national and Protestant tendency. He used, moreover, no concealment about it. Historical science in its results ended for him in the same conclusions as his political and religious ideas. He defended these ideas with the utmost passion.

Up to the present the national historians we have

dealt with did not interpose themselves in their histories to defend a personal point of view in politics. Niebuhr and Leopold von Ranke were satisfied to make known the historical development of the peoples they were dealing with, leaving their readers themselves to draw the political lessons which their point of view deduced. Mommsen had gone a step further than this. Finding at Rome a situation of affairs which bore some comparison with the situation in Germany after 1848, he had described it with a fervour which had never before been displayed by the historians of his country. In Sybel we shall find a historian who subordinates everything to his own ideas and for whom every circumstance of the past serves as a pretext to prove the excellence of the Hohenzollern institutions and the truth of the principles of National Liberal politics. He developed these ideas particularly in his " History of Europe during the French Revolution " and in his no less considerable work on the " Origins of the New German Empire."[1]

I

To describe Heinrich von Sybel's psychology is to describe that of the National Liberals, of whose tendencies and spirit he is, perhaps, the best representative in Germany.

A National Liberal was a man for whom nationality did not consist in the characteristics of race and

---

[1] "Geschichte der Revolutionzeit," 5 Bände, Düsseldorf, 1853–71. There is an English translation by Walter C. Perry under the title of " History of the French Revolution " (London, 2 vols., 1867). The other work is " Die Begründung des deutschen Reiches," 7 Bände, Munich, 1889–96.

language. To these had to be added certain political ideas and particular religious beliefs. To be national in Germany about the year 1850, it was necessary to be Protestant, if not in faith, at least in spirit, and to be Prussian in political ideas. As for the liberalism of the men of this party, it had nothing in common with that of Canning, Cavour or Laboulaye, who loved liberty for itself, while this party could only conceive liberty surrounded by certain institutions whose model was to be found in Prussia.

Certain peculiarities of character, life, and education must have been present to create this type, which drew its numbers particularly from the enlightened middle-class, among those pursuing liberal occupations, professors, publicists, and men of letters. Heinrich von Sybel is one of the Germans who have best realized these conditions.

A positive and sturdy temperament, destitute of imagination and penetration, with dogmatic brain, rather domineering in his doctrinairism, but active and sane, Heinrich von Sybel by his ancestry belonged to both the currents which joined to form this party—the middle-class and aristocratic spirit. On his father's side he belonged to a noble West-phalian family which had many officials, lawyers, and pastors to its credit : on the side of his mother, who descended from a family of manufacturers and merchants of Elberfeld, he was one of the middle class.

This double aristocratic and middle-class character was the basis of Sybel's nature ; externally this great broad-shouldered man, agreeable, pleasant, companion-able, a great hard-worker, knowing how to enjoy life, his frankness intermingled with middle-class pompous dignity, resembled a self-made man from the

United States.[1] In his ideas and tastes, on the other hand, he belonged to the aristocratic class of Prussian officials of whom Baron Stein was an example. To this were added several peculiarities which were due to his nature and to the circumstances in the midst of which he lived.

Sybel was a Rhine Protestant. This qualification, which does not mean much to us nowadays, had, about 1840, a particular significance. The people of the Rhine, in a general way, were more Liberal than the other Germans of the North. The French domination, which had taken a firmer root there than elsewhere, had left there a desire for liberty which was found in all the politicians. I know, of course, that for many of these Germans this French liberty, which they called State liberty as opposed to municipal liberty, was not liberty at all. They attached little importance, too, to political equality, which, since the time of the French domination, had abolished class distinctions in this part of the country and put all citizens under one denomination.

Sybel was one of those people. As a Rhenish Protestant he felt, like all his fellow-Protestants, attracted towards Prussia, whose strongest support they had been from 1815, while the Catholic majority still kept its sympathy for French ideas. And this seemed natural. Overwhelmed in the midst of a Catholic population hostile to all their ideas, these Protestants regarded Prussia as the bulwark of their faith. But the strangest thing of all is that, brought up in a country where public liberty had penetrated into their customs,

---

[1] Obituary article in the *Neue Freie Presse*, August 6, 1895. See also P. Fredericq, " L'Enseign. de l'hist. dans les Universités allemandes."

they made extraordinary efforts to show that Prussia, a military and feudal State, alone was able to save their liberty. Like many German Protestants, they were inclined to confuse the religious, intellectual and economic liberties which actually existed in Prussia with the political liberties of which that State had none.

The little town of Düsseldorf, where Sybel was born in 1817, was just one of those centres of Protestant culture where a mind such as his could be developed best. In this town, which had been a centre of art ever since the Palatine Elector Charles Theodore had founded a Drawing Academy there, where Cornelius, Schadow and Bendemann had been professors, one might meet there at that time musicians like Felix Mendelssohn, men of letters like Karl Immermann, who was managing director of the theatre, where were staged German and foreign plays—Shakespeare, Calderon, Goethe and Schiller. The house of Sybel's father (a distinguished lawyer) was one of the meeting-places of this artistic society. The historian said later on in life: " I acknowledge all I owe to this admirable environment." He might have added that this centre of Protestant art was at the same time a centre of Prussian influence, which in its mind and tendencies was totally different from the other artistic centres of the Rhine country, whose culture was exclusively Catholic.

We can understand, then, that it was among the Protestants of the Rhine country that this German liberalism had its origin—a liberalism which has been called National Liberalism and which has the triple character of being Prussian in spirit, anti-clerical, and anti-French. Its first leaders were men of the Rhine: Hansemann, von der Heydt, Sybel the elder, Kamp-hausen, Mevissen—who all helped to form the mind of

Heinrich von Sybel, the future theorist of the party. Indeed, from 1840 on he placed at the service of their cause a talent, as publicist and historian, of the first rank. It was he who spread their ideas throughout the whole of Germany by means of his works and took the first steps in the formation of the great party of the Empire—the National Liberal party.[1]

II

When he made his first appearance in political life, about 1840, Heinrich von Sybel was a young historian who had just finished his studies at Berlin University, where his mind had been formed by two masters: Ranke, the historian, and Savigny, the jurist.

The first of these, Ranke, had initiated him in the critical method and Savigny had taught him his philosophy of history : two sciences, two truths, in his eyes, which by their united power would serve to supply the proof in a scientific fashion of a certain number of political problems.

In the historico-political system of Sybel, which at bottom is only an exaggeration of Ranke's system, historical criticism is an element of the first rank. As political judgment, indeed, depends upon the knowledge of historical facts, it is necessary, above all, to establish the truth of these facts in an irrefutable manner.

---

[1] "The National Liberal ideas," Schmoller, the economist, said rightly, " were a combination of the old feudal ideas of the Prussian aristocracy with the ideas of the Rhenish Liberals. Sybel was the scientific champion of this moderate Rhenish constitutionalism, with a bias at once middle-class and aristocratic (Kaufmännisch-aristokratische Farbe)." He might have added : " A most Protestant bias in opposition to the equalitarian liberalism of the Rhenish Catholics."

Under Ranke's direction, Sybel had become a critic of the first rank. Endowed with a clear-thinking, lucid, and vigorous mind, he had no equal, in his own country, in the art of classifying authorities, in his manner of establishing the authenticity of sources and searching out the truth in the midst of contradictory evidence. His critical essays on Jordanès, on the " History of the First Crusade," on "The Origin of Kingship in Germany," are masterpieces of precision, lucidity, and common sense.

But to Sybel history was not scientific through the exactitude of researches alone, but also through the number of moral, social, and political truths it could establish. That, at least, was what the jurist Savigny had taught him when he showed him that all societies, from the beginning of the world, continually evolved in the same direction and fashion, and concluded therefrom that the number of political experiences that humanity has undergone could be collected under certain types : that as these experiences repeat themselves under analogous forms at all periods of history, it is sufficient to examine the past to have the key to all the political problems of the day.[1]

With this theory of the historical school of law

---

[1] " A true historian," said he, " should unite in himself three conditions : he ought to be an investigator endowed with a critical sense, a man endowed with a sense of politics, and an artist capable of expression.

" In the matter of research," said he, " the historian's duty is to set aside all personal feeling.

" In order to understand the basic meaning of events, the subjective point of view must always be the most useful."

" Finally, as to the artistic point of view, it will always be the " artist's personality" which will set its seal on the story " (" Historische Zeitschrift," vol. 56, p. 484, article on G. Waitz).

M

Sybel did not become, like Niebuhr and Ranke, merely a defender of the theory of nationalities, and like Mommsen a partizan of the struggle for historical life: he attempted further to explain by this means all the great events of history and contemporary politics.

Now to what results did this philosophy of history together with textual criticism lead? To prove in the first place that if the French Revolution failed it was because its political principles were wrong: because the present age could not accommodate itself to the communistic theories which were at its root nor to the Napoleonic universal empire which was its consequence: that the organization of States on a national basis is the great historical fact of the nineteenth century: that Germany would succeed in this, and that to achieve it she had to exclude from her mind everything that tended to destroy national life, viz., Catholicism and the anti-German policy of the Hapsburgs. Once the Hapsburgs were removed the Hohenzollern would be able to assume the leadership of the movement. "Thus it is," says the critic Julian Schmidt naïvely, "that the author's political opinions ended with the same conclusions as science."

This conviction had in Sybel's eyes great importance. It allowed him to state his opinions as indisputable truths. And he did not fail to do so. From his earliest works he openly expresses his opinions as a Protestant, a Nationalist and Liberal.

In a work on Jordanès (1837), which was his thesis for his doctor's degree, he could see, even at that early period, in that historian the apostle of the national idea in opposition to the dream of Cæsarian and Catholic universal dominion. Another little work "The History of the First Crusade" (1841), gave him an opportunity of dissipating the halo of romantic legends, of waging war

" against the monks and their lying fashion of writing history," and of showing us what conception he (Sybel) had of religion. " We have seen," he said, " what caused the Crusades to fail : not Zenki's impetuosity, Noureddin's firmness, or Saladin's joyous valour. In the great streams of history, none hopelessly sink but those who destroy themselves. It was the heat of religious excitement which called the Crusades into existence and then irresistibly hurled them to perdition. We have seen how over-excitement, thirst for the miraculous, and contempt for the world rendered any regular and consecutive plan of conquest in the East impossible from the very beginning. The Crusaders despised all earthly resources of the mind, and thus their mystical transports led them into every other miserable passion. . . . Men in modern times . . . no longer see, as in the Middle Ages, an inveterate hostility between heaven and earth, or expect religious perfection from the renunciation but from the right use of earthly things. Thus it is that this age, apparently so lukewarm in religion, has succeeded in attaining an object which the zeal of Urban and the power of the Baldwins in vain strove to effect." [1]

---

[1] " The History and Literature of the Crusades," translated from the German by Lady Duff Gordon (1861), pp. 125-6. Sybel frequently returned to that idea. " Nowadays," he said in another essay on the Crusades, " there is no more opposition, as in the Middle Ages, between heaven and earth : religious perfection is not expected from mortification, but from the right use of earthly things." Again : " But now we say, with St. Bernard, ' It is better to struggle against the sinful lusts of the heart than to conquer Jerusalem ' " (" Kleine historische Schriften," ii. 103). " In the Middle Ages," he said elsewhere, " people turned with disdain from science and art. . . . The fatherland, the State, civic duty, were all, owing to the prevalent tendency, without charm or value : they were of the earth, earthy and swallowed up in sin.

In a third work, "The Origin of Kingship in Germany," a work nevertheless of purely scientific character, Sybel endeavours to show, in contradiction of the Catholic historians, who, in their hatred of Protestant Germany, tried to sever every connection between the past and present, that kingship in Germany evolved quite spontaneously and did not undergo any influence from the Roman State in its development.

This thesis, which gratified Sybel's national point of view and which he endeavoured to uphold by ethnological, economic and social considerations, was far from receiving the support of the scholars of the country. Even in the camp of Prussian historians the great mediæval scholar Waitz opposed it successfully, thanks to his deeper knowledge of the subject and its sources, to his sense of judgment, and even to his historian's eyes.[1]

With this polemical incisive spirit Sybel would seem to be of such a kind as to succeed rather in pamphlets than in history. He was, indeed, a wonderful writer

---

They had no notion then of that simple human sentiment which considered that he who acts and works also serves God, and which could with a joyful and calm face imbue itself with the eternal presence of God. That was not enough for them then. They wished to take hold of God with their senses."

[1] Treitschke the historian, who on a number of points is as partial as Sybel, recognizes that the latter often allows himself to be carried away by his passion of patriotism. This is what he says of Sybel's "Origin of Kingship in Germany" : "Sybel has that tendency of all philosophical brains to construct history and to gather together under one heading whole historical periods without always succeeding in a very happy fashion ; he sometimes rashly attributes to the Middle Ages tendencies of the eighteenth and nineteenth centuries. This is the defect of his work, which contains no false facts but many erroneous judgments " (Schiemann, " Treitschke," p. 229).

of occasional pamphlets. At all the critical moments of Prussian politics he wrote them. His first work of the kind was an anti-Catholic pamphlet, "The Holy Coat of Trèves," published 1844.

During that year the Rhenish Catholics, as if to work their revenge on the Kulturkampf, had exhibited at Trèves "the seamless Holy Coat of Our Lord," as they called it, which was kept in the Chapter House of the Cathedral. "For seven weeks," says Treitschke, in his "History," "thousands of pilgrims came to Trèves: in all the towns and villages in the beautiful Moselle country the church bells rang when a company of pilgrims passed with banners displayed: the innkeepers and the sellers of religious relics in the episcopal town made fortunes. Ardent prayers resounded throughout the Cathedral: 'Holy Coat, pray for us.'" [1]

When Sybel heard this "he danced with rage at this insult offered to the common sense and honesty of the German people," and in a satirical pamphlet, written in Voltaire's style, he determined to kill once for all "the Holy Coat of Trèves and all the Holy Coats in the world." [2]

Sybel played an important part in his country's confessional struggles. Ultramontanism had no enemy more vigilant than he. In 1847 he published a pamphlet, "The Political Parties in the Rhine Provinces," in which he wrote: "To be Ultramontane and a German patriot are two things which preclude each other: we cannot serve two masters at once, the Pope and the King: we must make our choice between them."

---

[1] Treitschke, "Deutsche Geschichte im 19ten Jahrh.," v. 335-6.
[2] The pamphlet was written in collaboration with an Oriental scholar of Bonn University, Otto Gildemeister.

When he wrote this pamphlet in 1847 Sybel was already a man well in the public eye in Germany. A professor at the University of Marburg, he had taken an active part in the political life of the nation. Prussian and Liberal, he sat, in the first place, in the Hessian Chamber while waiting to become a member of the Prussian Chamber. Sybel was not one of those Liberals who believed that liberty was enough to constitute German unity. He knew that, without Prussia, this unity could never be brought about, but he also believed that, in order to make its mission in Germany popular and efficacious, Prussia should take its place at the head of the Liberal movement. " The position of Prussia in Germany," he wrote, "and in regard to the rest of Europe is such that she needs in an equal measure two things which unfortunately often preclude each other : strong unity and strong liberty. To live and eventually to become greater she needs a powerful sovereign and a public opinion : she must possess military power and at the same time parliamentary institutions. To elaborate such a problem fifteen years are few, and if the task still awaits, to-day, a complete and lasting solution, we may yet say that the notion of liberty has not for one moment left the attention of the Prussian Government. It is indestructible : it is in our blood : it belongs irrevocably to the air which we breathe." [1]

Stating this opinion still more exactly, Sybel added : " One thing is certain, and that is that those who place obstacles in the way of the Pan-German efforts of Prussia render a service not to the cause of liberty and parliamentary constitutionalism, but to the feudal parties and legitimists in Germany and Europe. Offer

[1] " Kleine historische Schriften," ii. 389.

up your prayers for liberty, ask the Prussian Government not to falter in the German cause."

What Sybel meant by liberty is not exactly what is commonly signified by that word in France or in England. He said this, later, at the beginning of his " History of the Formation of the German Empire ": " I do not desire liberty in the ordinary sense of the word, liberty which is nothing but a weakening of the central power to the advantage of individual rights: my liberty is a strengthening of the power of the State by the patriotic co-operation of the people in all the duties of the State." At bottom the fundamental principle of his politics was not liberty but national individuality, which is often quite opposed to political liberty. " They will recover," said Tocqueville, "from that mania for nationalities which eclipses for the moment their passion for political liberty." And Tocqueville was right. Sybel, who, later, was to set at such little account the essential liberties, while he had a strong government, undertook, from 1850, to demonstrate the truth of Tocqueville's statement in the struggle which he made against the ideas of the French Revolution.

From the year 1848, his attention attracted by the power of these ideas in Germany, Sybel determined to oppose them by showing what, " in practice, the theories of radical democracy and the dogma of popular sovereignty, which was the result of the French Revolution, brought them to."

His first intention was only to write a short essay, a pamphlet [1] in a lively style. But, as often happens,

---

[1] " I had determined," he said, " to write a short essay or a pamphlet to explain to the people into what misery the French Revolution had plunged the lower classes owing to its communistic tendencies " (" Pariser Studien," p. 303).

the pamphlet grew to a volume, and then volumes followed one after the other. For twenty years, with an indefatigable patience which no research wearied, Sybel buried himself in his subject ; he read everything that had been published : general works, memoirs, and correspondence. When the printed sources were exhausted, he had recourse to unpublished sources— State papers and archival documents. At a time when, in Paris, Frenchmen had difficulty in obtaining permission to examine the archives, he was allowed access, by a special favour of Napoleon III, to the most precious documents of the Ministries of War, Home, and Foreign Affairs. When all this information had been collected in Paris, he completed it by further research in London, Brussels, the Hague, and Berlin.

In writing this history, Sybel had but one idea— but one passion : to dissipate for ever the halo of heroism which was attached to the French Revolution.

" As the Revolution," he said, " began with the struggle of a feudal monarchy and under the cry of liberty and equality, we have become accustomed for a long time to consider revolutionary and liberal movements of an equal importance : and while blaming all revolutionary excesses, we have become used to describe the tendencies of the parties of that time as more or less liberal according to how much or little they advanced along revolutionary paths." [1]

Sybel thought that by placing the performances of the actors in this great drama, so transfigured by the French historians of the Restoration, in their proper light ; by displaying the secret intentions of these men as they are to be found in the State papers, and by showing the real motives which led them to act, he

---

[1] " Hist. of French Revolution," iv,

would reduce them to their true proportions. The pity
is that Sybel had his own ideas on this subject.
They had been made to seem giants, he wished to
make them pigmies : and both pretensions were equally
absurd.

Sybel was pursuing another object side by side with
this one. The Liberal middle class in Germany did not
like Prussia. They had many prejudices against that
State, which they called the land of militarism and
bureaucracy. Sybel wished to overcome these prejudices.
And his work was also intended to serve this object.
The first thing was to show by history that Prussia
had a mission to fulfil in Germany, one which, moreover, she had never lost sight of even in the most
troubled periods of her history, as, for example, the
period of the Revolution. It was also necessary to
prove that this liberty, which the Liberals were seeking
so far away in France, could be given to them by
Prussia, for her institutions were the most Liberal in
Germany. And thereupon Sybel, drawing a parallel
between Prussia and England and the United States,
said :—

*" In these three States it was the party most animated
by ideas of national unity, of independence and devotion, which took command of affairs.* In Prussia this
command fell to the King and his servants, while the
higher classes remained aside through unfriendliness or
indifference, and the mass of the people were completely
ignorant of politics."

But this is not all. Sybel, by his history, wished to
prove a third thing to the German people : viz. that
Austria should be kept out of the future German
Confederation because she had nothing German in her.
" The Jesuitic spirit of the House of Hapsburg," he
said, " has completely destroyed in her the principle of

true German life ": this he endeavoured to show during the whole of the revolutionary period.

Thus it was that he set up in Germany, in 1853, that enormous instrument of war in five compact volumes, which was assuredly a scientific work of the highest standard by reason of the large number of new facts which it brought to light, but which was a long historical pamphlet, intended to adjust the judgment of those German people who did not yet believe in the Hohenzollern mission.[1]

Sybel was bound to succeed. Science always over-awes the German people, and his science was enormous. Benjamin Constant said : " I have forty thousand facts and they change at will." Sybel had found more than forty thousand in the bundles of paper which he had taken from the archives. His good faith, it is true, cannot be doubted : but he was an impassioned man pursuing a theory, and involuntarily he went straight to the testimonies which sided with his bias. " Untruth," says a German proverb, " is often not in what one says but in what one keeps back." Sybel once again will show this to us.

III

Let us recognize at once, before we criticize this work, that it is one of the masterpieces of historio-graphy of the nineteenth century. Sybel in the first place brought to light again many points of this period of history by publishing new revelations. We may even say that he was the first to go to actual sources.

---

[1] The historian Erick Marcks says, in an excellent notice he published on Sybel, that this history is the work " which con-tributed most to the political education of the nation, which was so difficult (muhselig)."

Before his time, the history of the Revolution had been written, so to speak, a priori. Mignet in his large sketch had related it according to the testimony of eye-witnesses who were still alive at the time of the Restoration. Thiers, too, was satisfied to question survivors of that time. Edgar Quinet, who came a little later (1846), had a written basis to work upon : the memoirs of Baudot, a member of the National Convention : but that was all. The only one to draw upon the archives at Paris was Michelet, who wrote the first part of his history in the Central Depôt, where he was the chief of the historical section.[1] After December 2, 1853, when he retired to the provinces, he also examined the archives at Nantes and the valuable archives of La Vendée. And in spite of his bias, the enthusiasm with which he grasped at facts to brandish them like conquering darts, we must recognize that these facts exist and that he gave them to us. " That I should be attacked as to the meaning of these facts," he says in the Preface to his " French Revolution," " is well enough. But it should be acknowledged in the first place that he owes to me those facts with which he wishes to attack me."

Sybel has increased to marvellous extent the knowledge of these new facts of the Revolution, and he has subjected to a most vigorous examination all those facts which we already knew. He had perhaps an advantage over French historians in that he was the dupe of nothing. He knew nothing of the respect attached to

---

[1] He consulted with good result the manuscript proceedings of the Assemblies, garbled and mutilated nearly always by the *Moniteur* : the accounts of the federations which came from towns and villages : the registers of the commune of the Committees of Public Safety and General Security. Many of these documents have disappeared, burnt during the Commune.

certain legends.   No consideration whatever would
stop him in his examination.[1]   And we must acknowledge, too, that his keen-eyed hatred has at times served
him an excellent turn.   After his examination everything seems to leave him renovated : events, men, and
institutions.   His affectation is more than is really
necessary in order to show how much he disagrees
with most historians who have preceded him.   But after
making all reserve as to his opinions, which most often
are questionable and to which we will return later, we
must acknowledge that this history is the completest
picture existing of European life at the end of the
eighteenth century, for he did not deal alone with the
history of the French Revolution, but with that of all
Europe of the period : for Sybel is one of those historians
who believe that an event cannot reveal to us all its
secrets unless light be thrown upon it by the other
contemporary events.

Sybel's history is purely political : but at the same
time it is an economic and social study.   And as he
makes no distinction, unlike all the historians of that
tendency whom we have studied, between politics and
national life, he is consequently led to attach great
importance to all the manifestations of that life : to
rural government, to finance, industry, commerce,
taxation, and the army.   These chapters, which are
perhaps the best in the book, give us the completest
picture of the Ancien Régime (it must not be forgotten that Taine came more than twenty years after
Sybel) and of private individual life at the time of
the Revolution, in all its phases.

" A stranger," he said in his Preface, " is on that account all
the less exposed to the danger of adhering through attachment
to some darling error, to incorrect or even now sometimes
dangerous views."

The importance he attached to the economic life of ancient France had for its first result the modification of the very idea that one had of the Revolution. Before Sybel this event had been studied almost only politically : the parliamentary struggles filled almost entirely the works of historians who, explaining the progress of the Revolution by means of these struggles, were led, when excusing the excesses of which it became guilty, to distinguish between 1789 and 1793, between that fine enterprise—the taking of the Bastille—and the bloody horrors of the Reign of Terror. Sybel shows that in reality this distinction could not exist.

" These first years," he said, " have often been called the finest period of the French Revolution : but in truth they were to the year 1793 what the seed is to the harvest." And he gave a proof of this, or rather, by setting out the history of the economic life of the nation, he proved that this Revolution had above all a social character, that it was in reality a transference of property, a new division of riches. He expresses it in this way : " The greatest omission in all the previous histories of the Revolution is to have maintained a profound silence in the matter of the economic facts concerning it, so that the commonplace has long obtained currency that the last century aimed at a political revolution, while this one aimed at a social one, and that the first instigator of this revolution in France was Babœuf. To-day it is no longer so : our sight is keener, and we recognize that the most extreme communists had their model in the Jacobin chapter of the Revolution. . . . But this history is still a long way from being explained according to that theory." [1]

---

[1] " Oekonomische Verhältnisse," Book II, chap. iv.

But once in possession of this idea, instead of proceeding calmly to its demonstration, Sybel, when studying the details of the Revolution, shows a peculiarly partial mind. He is just neither to events nor to men : as to the former, in that he continually attempts to diminish their importance, and as to the latter, in that he invariably portrays them in the most unfavourable light.

Sybel exhibits this partiality in the first place by diminishing the range of influence of the French Revolution. Now, without wishing to regard that event as being absolutely unique, as certain historians still wish to do, we are forced to recognize that it is the most important fact of modern history and that its character was never local and accidental, but universal. Even Sybel cannot but agree to this to a certain extent. "What happened at Versailles," he said, "had the merit of giving peoples and rulers a great lesson as to the directing of their policy." Later, when the Revolution spread its influence throughout Europe, he admits that the effects of this propaganda were far from being all evil.

"It is true, no doubt, that in this case, as in every other, a good cause is furthered by every occurrence, and that in this sense freedom was furthered by the French Revolution. A century would probably have passed over half Europe before the mouldering rubbish of feudalism could have been removed by peaceful means."[1]

But this is all he grants, and with what bad grace ! Moreover, what he offers with one hand he takes back with the other one. Scarcely has he granted this than he seeks to lessen its significance.

---

[1] "French Revolution" (English translation, W. C. Perry, 1867), ii. 198.

The Revolution, in the first place, is to him nothing more than one of the forms of the end of the old regime, and as such it should be placed on the same footing as the other manifestations of the same thing, which are the fall of Poland and the destruction of the Holy Roman Empire.

"These three events," he said, "hang together: their accidental externals may be various, but their basis is common. Everywhere in Paris, Warsaw and the German Empire, it is the crumbling of the Middle Ages : everywhere a new policy triumphs—the modern military monarchy—which levels and centralizes."

But if Sybel shows prejudice in wishing that these events should not result expressly one from the other, and that France should not be the originator of the great movement which transformed modern history, he shows still more in the efforts he puts forward to set these events on the same level, by giving them an equal importance.

Next to the significance of the Revolution it is the incidents which he disparages. We must evidently not ask Sybel for an enthusiastic account of the "great revolutionary days." He has given them but little space, excusing himself on the ground that he wished to write a history particularly of the institutions.[1] But in the few words which he gives them he does not conceal his disdain. He speaks sarcastically of the infatuation of an entire people who "think that liberty is founded by enthusiasm." Clearly Sybel is not one of those men who,

---

[1] "I have attempted," he said, "to throw light on certain aspects of events left in the shade hitherto. I will devote my attention particularly to the financial and economic situation of the French Republic, as well as to the relations of France with the other States of Europe."

like Michelet, vibrate to all the outbursts of a people's magnanimity. Having a methodical and practical disposition, he is rather inclined to mistrust popular enthusiasm. On the other hand, when he comes to the history of the Republic he lends a willing ear to all its horrors : he emphasizes with evident satisfaction all the dark and tragic aspects of that period. He very soon comes to see nothing but these aspects of the Revolution. Everything that could increase one's impression of crime and scoundrelism he readily takes hold of. It has been said that if Taine saw in the Revolution [1] nothing but scoundrels, it was because he sought his information principally in the police reports. Sybel must have done the same, for he mentions scarcely anything but the excesses and acts of violence.

Indeed, a strange thing happens, and that is that he, who pretended to be nothing more than a historian of institutions, who in the Preface of his work announced his intention to study the society of the revolutionary period, what it was and what it had done, by determining its influence over modern society, he, I say, through his detestation of this event, ends by attaching value only to what is accidental. When he is speaking of crime, the smallest incidents accumulate beneath his pen, but when the time comes to demonstrate the permanent and solid results of the Convention, the historian passes them by.

This bias plays bad turns on Sybel too. It causes him frequently to contradict himself. When describing the old regime, he shows eloquently by the unhappy condition of France that the Revolution

---

[1] Vols. ii., iii. and iv. of the " Origines de la France contemporaine."

was necessary. But when he comes to the Revolution itself, he expresses regret for the old regime and finds that " it was not so bad, and that it would have been sufficient to improve the institutions by making some reforms in details," so that all would have been for the best in the best of worlds.

This hatred of the Revolution has many causes with Sybel, but the first and strongest of them is in his turn of mind.

With respect to the French Revolution it has always been possible to divide people into two classes : the first of which is as excessive in its admiration as the second is in its hatred.

These two classes of people are really two classes of minds, and we might say that they share the world between them : the idealists and the realists. The idealists are not all poets, as were the first admirers of the Revolution—Klopstock, Schiller, and Wordsworth—but also philosophers and politicians who, with Fox, Fichte, Kant and Herder, repeated to the next generation the noble words of Herder : " The seed falls into the earth : for a long while it seems dead, when suddenly it pushes up its tiny shoot, thrusts aside the hard earth which covers it, struggles with the hostile clay, and at last becomes a plant bearing flowers and fruit."

We can readily acknowledge that all the great hopes dreamed by these noble minds have not been realized, that the Revolution fell short of its promise, that it did not reconcile all classes of society in a brotherly love, that it did not put an end to injustice nor to dogmatism nor to wars on this earth. This is true, but are the aspirations of the Revolution less noble on that account ? Might they not elsewhere, in other circumstances, transform society ? Who can set humanity's

194 MODERN GERMANY AND HER HISTORIANS

course? They speak of the bankruptcy of the French Revolution as if it were over. It still continues. The leaven which it put into society is still active. From this point of view it is not an exaggeration to say that it resembles Christianity, which after eighteen centuries is far from having realized on earth its ideal of humanity. Yet who can say that it has not moulded our race and introduced more justice and love into the world? Progress is achieved but slowly. It is only little by little that society will be imbued with the ideal of the Revolution. We are at present only at the dawn of this movement. " Modern Europe," said Frederic Harrison rightly, " regards 1789 as a date which marks in humanity the greatest evolution which the world has known since Christianity."

But in opposition to the idealists who dream as above, the pessimistic realists form a compact battalion. We know their leaders : they are Burke, Mallet-Dupan and Taine. Sybel, by the tendencies of his genius, belongs altogether to this group. Burke was one of his first admirations, and remained, I think, the strongest. He said of Burke's " Letter on the French Revolution " : " It is my political gospel." He praised the depth of thought and penetration of the man who, from October, 1790, foretold that " this Revolution would end in military absolute power." After this, how could one doubt the truth of the political principles of such a prophet? Then, outdoing the English critic, Sybel utters a sharper criticism than Burke's of the rights of man—he calls them "trivialities unworthy of an intelligent man," concerning which he writes seven pages of bitter and prejudiced argument addressed to " those simpletons who imagine that a State is founded or a revolution accomplished by means of hopes and enthusiasm."

" Nothing," says he, " is more painful, more tiresome, or more humiliating to read than these discussions in which they tried to decree by a majority of votes what the words 'right' and 'liberty' meant. . . . They destroyed with untiring zeal the last traces of tradition in order to build up the State according to the laws of nature."

But when we go to the bottom of things we see that such deep passion was not aroused only to refute political ideas which displeased him. There was a more intimate and secret reason : fear. It was possible to say with justice of Burke's pamphlet: " Never was a work more arrogantly and passionately national than the attack he made on the French Revolution : all the pride, jealousy, and animosity of England found their expression therein : the bitterness about the American War, the pride of being alone worthy of a free government, the antipathy of Protestant strictness against Gallic licence, turn this powerful invective into a sort of manifesto of British patriotism." [1] Now a similar criticism might be written of Sybel's " History of the French Revolution." Under cover of putting the French Revolution on its trial, he really does it to the French mind and French history.

Sybel did not like France. It is true he acknowledges in the French people great qualities—the solid virtues of the middle class, the æsthetic sense, the intelligence and hard-working spirit of the people, who succeed wonderfully in all arts [2]—but he did

---

[1] A. Sorel, " L'Europe et la Revolution " (2nd edit. 1889), ii. 145–6.

[2] " The greater part of the middle class in Paris "—he said in an interesting pamphlet published a little after 1870 under the title of " What can we learn from France ? "—" is distinguished for its

not think that in politics the nation had done anything lasting or at least worthy of imitation by
the Germans.[1] The reason he gives for it is that
the average Frenchman is incapable of managing his
affairs himself and that he has great need of the
assistance of the State. " While the nature of the
Anglo-Saxon race is expressed in the word ' self-
government,' the Frenchman's nature finds its expression in a continual effort towards centralization."
The failure of the French Revolution, in his mind,
has no other cause. " To explain the Revolution," he
said, " we must always return to this question :
How is it possible that the enthusiasm of 1789, which
aspired so strongly after liberty, ended, after six years,
in such a murderous result ? No doubt the incapacity of the leaders in the first half of the
Revolution, the mob's lack of experience in the
management of political affairs, and the raising of
public passion for the foreign war, contributed to it.

---

diligence, activity, and modest tastes. That is a thing which must
not be forgotten when we read in the newspapers accounts of
scandals, when we look at the books, when we see the theatres
and restaurants. In those you find no allusion to that healthy
private family life and that continuous hard work . . . just
because among all the working people who make up the majority
of the citizens of France there are no scandals to attract the public
taste " (p. 6).

[1] In an interesting essay he compares the Frenchman with the
Pole : " Like him," he says, " he is turbulent, unstable, and fickle :
his impressions are very lively. He has great mobility of feeling,
which makes him a refined artist, enjoying æsthetic and sensuous
pleasures, etc. In the matter of religion, like the Pole he
ignores what is the individual and inner feeling of the German.
To him religion consists of a number of external practices which
one can perform without interfering with one's natural frivolity,
fanaticism, or intolerance " (*Deutsche Rundschau*, i. 17).

But the principal fault was the complete absence of any understanding of the two fundamental ideas of the revolution : liberty and equality."

When defining liberty to us, Sybel shows us that the French people are not capable of it. " True liberty," said he, " is the right (Befugniss) of man to develop all the moral dispositions of his nature according to his free will. True equality consists in acknowledging that this liberty exists for all men who have a right to equal protection and to an equal position in the sight of the law. Hence is derived the true and eternal democratic idea which claims to fix the political right of individuals, not in the old feudal manner according to the blind chance of birth, but according to what he has done, giving preference to the capable and well-informed patriot, though he should come from the humblest cottage, over the selfish or ignorant descendant of nobility. An open career for talent and merit, that is the meaning of liberty and equality."

You will stop in surprise and say : " How can you say that the French Revolution did not establish that principle ! It was precisely the French Revolution that introduced it into Europe." Sybel would answer this objection by a distinction. " The French," he says, " have completely failed in the first of the tasks they set themselves, which was to set up liberty in their country, and they have only half succeeded in the second, which was to establish equality among the citizens."

Thereupon he exposes to us what he calls the false notion of equality among the French. " The French," he says, " assert that men are born equal in rights, and that it is the State's task to realize that equality by exacting for every one a right of equal suffrage, a right of eligibility to, and an equal share in, political power. This assertion should lead them speedily to the claim which is its logical consequence : the right of equal possession, of equal enjoyment, and also of equal work. And we know how near Robespierre and Hébert came to the realization of this idea. Therein is the cause of the check sustained by the Revolution, the reason for all the coups de force, the origin of the instability of all its works, whether in the nineteenth or eighteenth century."

What strikes one most in this extract is the assurance with which he sets these facts out. It is clear that to Sybel these are irrefutable truths. He does not satisfy himself with stating them, he must also explain them, and naturally he does so through "the psychology of the Frenchman."

In examining the Gallic type, Sybel cannot find in it any of the characteristics which make up the true democrat ; "not the desire to obey the established law nor respect for the State nor for individuals."

"Every one," he says, "speaks of his rights, and no one asks himself what are his duties towards himself and towards his fellow-citizens, or what efforts he should put forward to enable the State to satisfy the wishes of all."

What, then, is the remedy for this evil ? Sybel has no hesitation. They need a man. If the nation had been capable of choosing one freely who would have been acceptable to all, it would have been all well, but as she was not capable, it was the man who imposed himself on the nation—Napoleon, who thus became the necessary saviour.

Sybel belonged to that class of historians who believe in the necessity for great men. The example of countries like England, America, or Switzerland, where admirable political tasks have been performed by collective assemblies in which there were no men of genius, but only upright, honest, and well-intentioned minds, is not very convincing in his eyes. " I maintain with Treitschke," he wrote in one of his letters, " that it is the strong men who make history. The mass do nothing: they feel very pressing needs. Educated men catch a glimpse of the ideal of the future, but only confusedly. To realize it a man is needed—a strong man, who not only, like the others, recognizes the ideal of the times, but who finds in himself true means of attaining his object. Thus it was with Bismarck and German unity. When and where will social reform find its Bismarck ? It seems to me to be now at the point at which the German movement for unity was in 1844: a praiseworthy effort, obscure exaggerations, and false experiences." [1]

For the French Revolution Bonaparte was the man. Through the failure of the nation he became the " saviour," that is, the man " powerful enough to unify by controlling them the positive acquisitions of this revolution, in order to assure for the people the prevalence and enjoyment (Behagen) of civil existence and to throw open at once to the active forces of the country careers of glory."

" There is no occasion to look for the origin of the coup d'Etat in the rascality or duplicity of the military chief," he says elsewhere. " . . . It was the consequence of the state of affairs. . . . In September 1797 the fate of the Republic was in all respects sealed. The attempt of the 18th Fructidor had shown once more that on the basis of radical ideas a true State was not possible, equally so under the form of the Constitution of 1795 as with the prescriptions of the Consti-

---

[1] Quoted by Erich Marcks, " Study of Sybel,"

tution of 1791. It could be foreseen that with such theories the condition of all sound political life, a respect for law, would never be attained. Politics degenerated into a continuous oscillation between anarchy and the coup d'Etat, until at last a superman arose strong enough to silence the others, and, by destroying all liberty, capable of putting a stop to the misuse made of it."

Sybel thinks that, if the Revolution at its beginning had found this man, Bonaparte would not have been necessary ; but there was no such man. The only one who rose above the ordinary level, Mirabeau, had but "a tainted glory." The dissolute life he had led had destroyed in him all moral strength. He had, it is true, some pre-eminent statesmanlike qualities: a sovereign intelligence which rules events and can direct them : will united with the enthusiasm of conviction. But, a slave of his past and his life, he could not take up the place which was his by right, and by the fate that weighed him down he was "reduced to the intrigues of a Court in difficulties which still hoped to save itself by expedients."

After the death of Mirabeau, in Sybel's opinion, the reign of mediocrity began : the Assembly was subjected to all the fluctuations of the popular will. The mob ruled. The Commune, with its fanatics who were supported by the mob, was mistress of the Assembly and controlled a whole nation according to its own will.

Among those men who from that time governed the policy of France, Sybel only distinguishes two categories: the pedants and the rascals.

The pedants, well-intentioned simpletons, votaries of the pure idea, narrow-minded men, were in his eyes very dangerous, for they had faith and could be carried by fanaticism to the worst extremities. The others, the rascals, only saw in the Revolution a position of affairs which they could turn to their own advantage. These were the majority. Indeed, it would not be necessary to give Sybel much encouragement to make him declare that all the revolutionary leaders were more or less of this quality, for to him a simple revolutionist most often had a criminal within him. But what is certain is that he was not afraid of bold generalizations. He would say, for example : " For the French, fraternity was nothing but a pretext for attacking, out of a taste for plunder, the neighbouring peoples." Elsewhere : " The cry of liberty everywhere was nothing more than the signal for despotism and war." And again this : " No one felt the least attachment for the existing state of things. While dreaming of most wonderful Utopias, they were accustomed to exploit the present state of affairs to their private advantage." And finally this : " Liberty to the men of the Revolution was the licence to do what seemed best to them, the absence of any hindering government, and the possibility of satisfying their own covetousness."

With all this, what becomes of the spirit or devotion to the native land which sent the volunteers away to the frontiers ? Sybel did not believe in any such spirit. Soldiers and officers to him were nothing but common looters. The generals were " unable to bridle the greediness of their officers and their commissaries or the gross lack of discipline among the soldiers (die Soldatesca)."

When reading things like this you ask yourself whether you dream. What, then, are all the officers adventurers and the revolutionary armies " undisciplined gangs that had no taste for anything but rapine and plunder " ? Then you will think of other testimonies—

of that of Stendhal, who went through the first Italian campaign and who was unceasing in his praise of the disinterestedness of the soldiers and their leaders. You will recall, too, the fine words of Tocqueville : "I have long studied history, and yet I have never seen a revolution in which men were found of such sincere patriotism, such self-sacrifice, and such magnanimity."

Which of the two was right, Sybel or Tocqueville? By piercing a little beneath the surface of his work you will not be long in making up your mind : you will perceive at last that this impeccable historian, who has read everything, seen everything, checked everything, has peculiar likings for witnesses who support his point of view. He who is so hard when dealing not with Terrorists, but with Liberals like Lafayette, Duport, Barnave and Lameth, is full of condescension for the absolute monarchs of Europe, " who," he said, " while the revolutionists destroyed every obstacle that stood in their way, were solicitous of the prosperity and *wishes* of their people." Where did he see that?

Elsewhere Sybel undertakes to vouch for the sincerity of Marie-Antoinette. He states that she was ready to make a "reasonable trial of constitutional monarchy on condition that the King's safety should be guaranteed and that he should have the necessary power to restore order " : he says again that if she wished to fly, it was because she wished " to place herself at the head of the Catholic movement in La Vendée or Provence " (Varennes, however, is not in the south or west of France) : he knows, moreover, that in the event of victory, the new constitution " would have established the fall of the feudal system and of the privileges of birth, the unity of government and freedom in trade and industry." What evidence does he bring forward to support this? None. He believes it, and that is sufficient.[1]

Of the captivity and death of the little Dauphin in the Temple he makes a tragical history, of which the principal features and details are taken from Beauchesne, whose pathetic romance he accepts in full. A witness for the prosecution always has a chance with him of being heard, especially if his testimony demonstrates the natural ferocity of the revolutionists. Thus in the case of the Reign of Terror—the least certain part of his history—he follows *literatim* the more than suspicious evidence of Mortimer Ternaux. Elsewhere he invokes the authority of M. Ponjoulat.

We might let this partiality of Sybel pass were it not emphasized by the tone in which his account is written. Facts do not suffice him to show his sympathies or antipathies; these malevolent opinions must also be expressed in acrimonious terms. He cannot, for example, mention Lafayette's name without such epithets as "intolerable coxcomb, conceited and incapable fellow, humbug and poltroon," running to his pen. If he mentions any inherent weakness of the French temperament, he never fails to add as an antithesis "la grande nation." There are in his work several little ironical pictures which are an ornament to it. This, for example, is the way in which he describes the famous scene of the Convention which preceded the expulsion of the twenty-seven Girondins:—

"Barère then made a last attempt and suddenly proposed that the Convention should break up in a body with the president at their head in order to test their freedom. A unanimous shout of assent was

---

[1] He recognizes well enough that these are only suppositions. "Nothing is certain," he says.

raised at the proposal, and the deputies began to move, with the exception of about a hundred Montagnards, who remained in their seats with irresolute curiosity. The others got as far as the main entrance of the palace, where Henriot, slightly intoxicated, was stationed in front of a battery of democratic gunners. He answered the address of the president with brutal ribaldry, and after the exchange of a few words drove the crowd of men, who called themselves the representatives of France, back into the palace, by the word of command 'Aux canons'! Wherever the Convention tried their fortune in the garden they fared no better : and they soon allowed themselves to be led back into the hall by Marat, who, surrounded by a troop of gamins, marched triumphantly along." [1]

There is another thing in the "History of the French Revolution" which reveals even better perhaps the partiality of Sybel, and that is the constant efforts he puts forward to demonstrate that his country owes nothing to France.

One of the common characteristics of all historians of Prussian tendency is the belief that Prussia, long before the Revolution, had brought about for herself and by herself all the good resulting from that Revolution in the realization of the principles of social justice and equality and in the evolution of modern society. Sybel is not wanting in this: he points out the solid bulwark of German liberty in the Prussian institutions.

In another place, he will not have it that Germans in other parts of the country were indebted to France for anything. We know, for example, that the French were received with enthusiasm by the people in the Rhenish provinces. Sybel will hear nothing of this:

---

[1] "Hist. French Revol." (English translation), iii. 82, 83.

" There," he said, " the people trembled with a powerless rage. There it was that were scattered in Germany
the first seeds of the national spirit : then, in thousands
of irritated minds, there grew the conviction that no
German citizen could enjoy his life in safety at his
own fireside if the whole nation were not united in a
powerful German State."

Sybel confuses quite plainly two dates : 1793 and
1807.

But it is particularly in the account of the origin
of the wars of the Revolution that this national self-
love bursts out.   Sybel's patriotism could not suffer
that the Allies, of which Prussia was one, should be responsible for the war.   He must, at all costs, throw the
fault upon the Girondins.   He recognized well enough
that after March 12th Frederick William II desired
the war " to punish the Jacobins, to save chivalrously
Louis XVI and the émigrés, and finally to add to his
dominions a huge Polish province " ; but it is no less true
in his eyes that it was the Gironde " which began this
war to overthrow the constitutional monarchy of 1791,
Louis XVI and the Feuillants."   As for the Emperor
Leopold II, he is assured that he " only sought to
defend that constitution—the last bulwark which still
protected them from the establishment of the Republic
—from the attacks of the Jacobins."

Not for a single moment did Sybel ask himself by
what right did the Emperor Leopold and the King of
Prussia arrogate to themselves the claim to interfere
in French affairs.

He finds it quite natural that these monarchs
should make demonstrations on the frontiers of this
country, which, he says, they had no intention to
violate, in order to create fear in the minds of the
people. He approves of their desire " that France

should become a monarchy wisely controlled and not the battlefield of savage disturbances ": he justifies them finally for wishing " to give the French Government the necessary power to wipe out the revolutionary propaganda which threatened Europe."

And if the Girondins took offence at all this, if their rather jealous patriotism revolted against such pretensions and was alarmed at the intrigues of Marie-Antoinette with the émigrés, Sybel finds in that another reason for attacking them :—

" In this state of affairs it was ridiculous in the Parisian patriots to affect anxiety about the machinations of the émigrés. The latter numbered about 4,000 men, living partly in Coblenz, partly in Worms and Ettenheim. What could this handful of men undertake without the help of Austria, against a people who, in spite of their differences, could bring against them, as was proved in June, no less than 4,000,000 armed citizens ? " [1]

But the point was not that. The question simply

---

[1] " Hist. French Revolution" (English translation), i. 380. Nothing proves better the set purpose of Sybel against France than the Preface which appeared in the fifth volume of his history, published in 1871. France conquered seemed no longer a menace to his country. " Since 1870," he said, " we Germans regard the changes in French policy with greater calmness than since the time of our morcellement. The danger of war is removed by the defeat of Napoleon. The danger of the invasion of French ideas (1789, 1830, 1848) is also lessened. The progress of our State is quite different from that of France after 1789. Our Empire is the result of the principle of nationalities, quite irreconcilable with the false ideas of equality of the French Revolution. These ideas denied any right to individual existence, whether that of a people or that of an individual. The supposed universal liberation of the Girondins, the universal conquests of Napoleon, were nothing but the logical application of that basic principle which, in France itself, stifled the free develop-

was whether it was possible that a people who had just shown their spirit of independence and their desire to manage their own affairs would tolerate that strangers should interfere in their politics. Sybel takes good care not to answer this question, and yet no one was better qualified than he to do so, since, in his own country, he was one of the men who asserted with the greatest vigour the principle of national independence. But when dealing with the affairs of France, Sybel is no longer of that opinion.

But it is not only towards France in regard to Prussia that Sybel shows he has two sets of weights and measures, but also towards the other parts of Germany in regard to the Hohenzollern and particularly towards Austria. Sybel was one of the bitterest opponents in his own country of Austrian policy. From 1848 he preached the formation of Little Germany under Prussian hegemony with the exclusion of Austria. In his Prefaces and pamphlets he uniformly treated the Austrians as " idiots and uncultured people " who did not deserve to be attached to the great German fatherland. In his history the expres-

---

ment of individuals. The principle of nationalities, on the other hand, rests on ideas absolutely opposed to that one—namely, that personal liberty cannot exist save under the protection of a government whose chiefs speak the language of the people, share their ideas, and feel the beatings of their heart. . . . As its basis—respect for the individual : the complete accord of liberty and power is the result of the principle of nationalities. Is it too much to prophesy that Germany will remove from the State that false equality and licence which she knows shelter under those two despotic excrescences, the Church and dictatorial radicalism, of which the Commune and the Jesuits are the most striking examples—excrescences which impede the realization of a free State ? " (" History of the French Revolution," iv. Preface, viii. and ix., 1871).

sions are not so coarse, but he does not express this idea the less for that, and he tries to justify it. He does this in two ways : first in sketching the philosophy of the history of each State : and then in showing the part which each of them played during the revolutionary period.[1]

Sybel begins by stating that in every modern State " the advances in civilization had for their basis the principle of independence in art and science."

He had no difficulty in showing us that Prussia, in Germany, has best realized these conditions, while Austria is farthest removed from doing so. It all comes back, in his opinion, to the question of religion. " By embracing Protestantism," he said, " the Elector of Brandenburg became by that very fact the defender of independent Germany : Austria, on the other hand, by destroying the work of the Reformation in her territory, and by entrusting the education of the people to the Jesuits, definitely alienated herself from the true German spirit."

" The Jesuit's education," said Sybel, " incomparable when directed to training all men for a specific purpose, begins precisely with the negation of all individuality and all free disposal of oneself. The most certain sign by which one could recognize Austrian nationality at

---

[1] In the first editions of the " History of the French Revolution " Sybel openly attacked Austria in his Prefaces. Later he removed the more violent expressions, but in Vienna his attacks were not forgotten. Few Prussians—among those who were called in Vienna "the architects of Kleindeutsche Geschichte "—were detested as much as Sybel on the banks of the Danube. On his death the *Neue Freie Presse* said that Sybel had only himself to blame for this hatred. "Who sows the wind must reap the whirlwind." See in Sybel's "Kleine hist. Schriften," ii. 8, his violent attacks on the Austrian historian Vivenot.

that time was its failure to participate in the progress which was made in the rest of Germany."

Therein Sybel sees the origin of the struggle between Prussia—the truly free German State, " which was able during the last century to defend, with good conscience and devotion, the true interests of the Empire within and without—and Austria—the State which, knowing that the constitution had lost all influence, turned aside without scruple from her duty of submission to the laws of the Empire whenever the interests of her reigning House demanded it."

Sybel does not attribute this superiority of the Prussian State to Protestant thought alone, but to the work of the Prussian kings as well. " It is thanks to these kings," he said, " that the State has become great, energetic, resisting, powerfully formed, governed by one will alone, but by one which is able, under all circumstances, to consider the good of the whole nation and that of individuals too. On this solid basis the greatest and most glorious of these kings proclaimed by his own authority as king the two elementary rights of liberty (a rare thing then in Europe)— liberty of conscience and independence of justice."

Sybel does not carry this monarchist sentiment so far as to hold that a King of Prussia, merely because he was King of Prussia, was of necessity a great king: he grants that there were ordinary ones: but there is one thing at least which he would discover in all of them, and that is a regard for the greatness of their House, together with a feeling of their mission in Germany.

In his work he shows this in a most unexpected manner with regard to Frederick William II. If this monarch abandoned the Coalition and concluded peace separately at Bâle, in Sybel's eyes he did not betray

o

thereby German interests. On the contrary, German
interests demanded it. " If at this moment," he said,
" his intentions were wrongly interpreted in Germany,
it was because the people did not know the secret
motives of Viennese politics and its absolute indifference to German interests."

A few years later it was Austria's turn to conclude
the peace of Campo Formio with France. This time
Sybel shows less magnanimity. There is scarcely
enough water in the Danube to wash away the
Austrians' crime of disloyalty. By giving up German
territory to France in return for the cession to Austria
of Venetia, he considers the Austrians to have given " a
new proof of their selfish policy, marked by complete
indifference to German interests."

Arguments are never wanting to Sybel when it is
necessary to wash Prussian policy clean from all
suspicion of duplicity. He shows this particularly
with regard to the second Partition of Poland.

Shutting his eyes and affecting to deplore " this
catastrophe, greater than anything the world had ever
seen since the destruction of Jerusalem," he finds
authoritative reasons for proving that the determination
to annex a Polish province was certainly, for the
King of Prussia, the only one which " would not
lead to a public calamity and which was compatible
with the duty of the Prussian Government." [1]

Sybel recognizes plainly enough that Poland was
guilty of no offence against Prussia, that Prussia
was aggressive towards that country " in the com-

---

[1] The same Sybel, explaining the aggression of Frederick II
against Maria Theresa, says : " If the King of Prussia took Silesia,
it was because he wished to regenerate Germany and replace
the old constitution by a solid and lasting confederation."

pletest sense of the word and without the shadow
of a right." But he excuses this by saying "that
in the midst of the crisis caused by the French
Revolution, which suddenly brought into question
all existing rights, the sentiment of self-protection was
paramount": that, moreover, Poland deserved her
fate, "the justice of history demanding that we
should not be silent concerning the faults by which·
a nation has herself brought about her ruin," and
that finally everything should give way to this consideration, that "a million of Germans were thus
released from a foreign yoke which was hateful to
them, and that thereby the first of all the truly
German States won a considerable extension of
territory."

This last reason, at bottom, is the real one for
Sybel. Why, then, call up others? He who wishes
to prove too much ends by proving nothing. By
wishing on every occasion to prove his fellow-countrymen innocent, to show them as white as snow, Sybel
shakes his credit as a historian. It is with him as
with Taine. When we see the author of the "Origines
de la France contemporaine" borrow from a menagerie
of wild animals the most vituperative epithets to
bestow on the Revolutionists, we say involuntarily,
with the common sense of the popular saying,
"You are getting angry, so you must be wrong."
The expressions with Sybel are less coarse than with
Taine, but calmness is equally absent from his work.
We must pay our respect to his knowledge, and are
ready to profit by all that is good and even excellent
in it, but we must take his work with a great deal
of caution: we only accept it, so to speak, as part
of the assets.

IV

With the qualities with which he was endowed, it would seem that Sybel should have been called to fulfil some important political part in his country. He was indeed to take up militant politics, but it was not till later, in 1861, at the time when he was elected to the Prussian Chamber. At the time when he was writing the first part of his " History of the French Revolution," political life in Germany was completely dead. No great question filled every one's mind. There was not even a place from which a man might give out his ideas. The rare Parliaments of individual States were only concerned with questions of local interest. The Press, on the other hand, was not, as in France and England, a powerful instrument : a journalist's career in Germany led to nothing : it did not even give him influence or honour. In view of this dearth of public platforms, it is quite natural that University chairs should become the means of certain professors to express their ideas.

After 1848 there were a certain number, the remnants of the Parliaments of Frankfort, Erfurth and Gotha, who taught in the German Universities. Bismarck always laughed a good deal at these parliamentary professors, who thought by their speeches to bring about German unity. In default of anything else, they brought back from their experience of public affairs a taste for present-day problems and the power of dealing with them in a practical way. When they returned to private life and resumed their University chairs, they turned these into parliamentary platforms. This was true particularly in regard to the teaching of history. While preserving their sound learning, they paid more attention to form and began more rhetorical lectures, which indeed were not unlike those of the French historians of the Restoration, Michelet and Guizot. It is true that it was not love of humanity or liberty which inspired them. They preached to the Germans the excellence of the Hohenzollern institutions. They took their seats in the most diverse Universities. Between 1850 and 1870 they were by turn, or at the same time, at Berlin, Kiel, Jena, Bonn, Heidelberg, and even at Munich [1] and at Freiburg in Brisgau.[2] Among all these men three particularly distinguished themselves : Häusser, Droysen, and Sybel.

Häusser was, in the opinion of those who had heard him, the most eloquent professor in Germany during the nineteenth century. His lectures at Heidelberg University attracted an immense crowd of students; these came from all parts to hear him, as much for what he said as for the manner in which he said it. He was a Liberal, and, a strange thing for a southern Liberal, a decided partisan of Prussia. It is true he was attached less to what Prussia was at that moment in politics than to the spirit which she represented and to the mission which he saw she had in Germany. He also said that this mission was essentially Liberal.[3] An ardent patriot, filled with the part which Germany united and strong would play in the world, he placed all his eloquence at the

---

[1] Sybel (1856–61).   [2] Treitschke (1864–6).

[3] Häusser founded in 1847 at Heidelberg a paper, the *Deutsche Zeitung*, in which all the Liberals of that time wrote : Dahlmann, Beseler, Gervinus. His belief was particularly strong in the value of the moral conquests of Prussia in Germany. In 1864 he protested against the annexation of the duchies, which, he said, would weaken the moral prestige which Prussia needed in regard to the rest of Germany.

service of that idea. By stimulating, moreover, the patriotic feeling of his audience, he prepared them for accepting Prussian hegemony, which, in his eyes, alone could realize that unity. Thanks to him, Heidelberg became in the South an advanced stronghold of the Prussian idea.[1]

Häusser realized all the qualities of the national historians. Like them, he was, above all, a man of action, filled with the notion that it is through history that the political problems of the age are solved. He said that the historians' place in Germany was to become "the educators and leaders of the nation." He said also that the historical value of a work depends less upon its wealth of information or beauty of form than upon the advantage the nation can derive from it. "We must cultivate the historical sense of the nation and by initiating her into our method enable her to solve the problems of the moment." He made an attempt at this himself by writing a "History of Germany from the Death of Frederick the Great until the Treaties of 1815,"[2] which is the first pleading in favour of Prussia coming from a South German and a Liberal.

Yet Häusser is not a true historian of the New Germany. Or rather, something further was wanted in him to have truly been one : form. His work is truly a remarkable one. It is lucid, well arranged, but it lacks genius, or even originality. It had

---

[1] The historian who took his place at Heidelberg was Treitschke (1867). Treitschke, no less eloquent, but more narrowly Prussian still, was at that time a Liberal.

[2] "Gesch. Deutsch. seit dem Tode Friedr. des Grossen," Berlin, 1854–5, 7 vols. Treitschke calls this history "a jewel of German historiography in the nineteenth century," but Treitschke was speaking of ideas, not form.

influence through the ideas it spread, but it has not
remained a real enrichment of German literature of the
nineteenth century. To-day it is almost forgotten.
Droysen underwent the same disfavour as Häusser.
His influence was greater as a professor than as a
historian. As a historian, he is the author of a huge
" History of Prussian Politics," [1] a work typical of the.
German scholar, a true Benedictine's work, stuffed
with knowledge, meticulous and exact ad nauseam, but,
on that very account, untractable and unsuitable for
general reading. Add to this a most involved diction,
trained by Böckh, the philologist, and Hegel, the philosopher, who gave him—one his method of research,
and the other his ideas.[2] Droysen has at once the
heavy style of the philologist who desires to express
everything and the elusive style, bristling with abstractions, of the metaphysician. Those who wish to
see what point of abstruseness German prose can

---

[1] " Geschichte der preussis. Politik," Berlin, 1855–76, 12 vols.

[2] Droysen was the representative par excellence of Hegelianism
in history. In his first works, the " History of Alexander " and
the " History of Hellenism," he attempts to apply directly the
theories of his master by showing in Alexander " the bearer of
Greek civilization throughout the world." Most Prussian in sentiment, he saw in Prussia a sort of Macedonia, destined to do for
Germany—civilized (gesittet) but politically powerless—what
Macedonia had done for Greece. " The Greeks by themselves,"
said he, " were not able to realize their national unity : neither
Athens, nor Sparta, nor Thebes was able to place itself at the
head of the movement. They were continually in a state of
rivalry one with the other. The idea of the " city state " dominated their minds. They did not consider the greatness of Greece.
To them Greece was nothing. It was necessary for a barbarian to
see this, to synthetize their civilization and spread it throughout
the world." " What result," he adds, " had Demosthenes' victory
but the continuation of a deplorable state of affairs ? "

reach, I would advise to read a little work by Droysen, "The Science of History," a veritable Chinese
head-racker written in German gibberish.

But this strange writer was, as often happens, an
incomparable professor. From this point of view he
resembled his master Böckh, the philologist, who wrote
thorny works but delivered clear lectures. When he
was once asked the reason for this, he replied, " It
is because I set down my knowledge in my books, but
in my lectures I express my ideas." Droysen, similarly, was a poor writer but an eloquent speaker.
" He would begin in an undertone," said Professor
Frédéricq, "like the great preachers, in order to get
the completest silence. You might have heard a
pin drop. Bending over his little blue note-book
and darting at his audience penetrating glances
which seemed to pierce the glasses of his spectacles,
he spoke of falsifications of history. It was in
his lecture on historical instruction and method that
he had the appearance of being deeply vexed at
the falsities published under the name of history, and
his habitual expression of nervous displeasure added
still more to the energy and pitiless passion with
which he unfolded his subject, speaking with closely
pressed lips and frequently uttering sighs of anger
and contempt. Each moment a successful joke, always
biting and keen, would send a quiet smile across the
benches. Now he would fix some characteristic of
a historical personage, now he would laugh at the
expense of some contemporary scholar—of Schliemann,
for example—or of one of his colleagues of higher
education whom he would mention by name. The
subject would be treated with the greatest originality,
with an abundance of characteristic examples, a mischievous sprightliness which seemed only to be concealed

beneath a manner of speaking that was frigidly comic.
The lecture would be ended with a Homeric outburst
of laughter, raised by some anecdote related by Droysen with irresistible humour.   Never was I so diverted
at a University lecture. . . . But rarely too have I
heard things so serious and full of matter." [1]

As a propagator of Prussian ideas, which he set
forth by turn at the Universities of Kiel, Jena,[2] and
Berlin, Droysen, according to the words of his
biographer, Max Duncker,[3] was " able to inspire the
middle class with a love for the Hohenzollern army and
institutions, created by the Kings of Prussia for the
welfare of all Germans." [4]

Droysen was, in fact, a good and true Prussian,
who had faith in Prussia alone, and who never
became enthusiastic, like his colleagues, about liberty
alone.

He had been trained quite young according to
these ideas by his father, the chaplain of a Prussian
regiment during the War of Independence, who
did not cease to repeat to his. son as a memento
mori : " Remember the evil which the Gauls did us."
Droysen, who had all the qualities of a true Prussian
—obstinacy, a practical and vigilant mind without
a shadow of superficiality, never leaving go of an
idea whose usefulness [5] he once recognized—attached

---

[1] P. Frédéricq, " De l'enseignement supérieur de l'histoire,"
Revue de l'Instruction publique en Belgique, 1882, vol. xxv.

[2] At Jena Droysen founded a historical seminary specially
destined for the study of Prussian history.

[3] " Abhandlungen aus der neueren Geschichte," " Droysen,"
pp. 350–90.

[4] For this he wrote his " Life of York," one of the heroes of the
War of Independence.

[5] Seeing all these qualities in him, his father, like Thomas

himself indissolubly to the fortunes of the State which best represented these qualities. He remained narrowly Prussian, and nothing but Prussian, like Gustav Freytag. With Treitschke, he became the truest apostle of Imperialism.[1]

Quite different from this was Sybel's part as a professor. In his teaching, the author of the " History of the French Revolution " did not distinguish between Liberalism and Prussian politics. A political writer of the first order, an indefatigable debater and dialectician, he tried to convince rather by the close network of his arguments than by the pathos or brilliance of his eloquence. Above all, he was a powerful opposition speaker, whose best opportunity occurred at the time of the struggle of 1861 and 1862 between the Liberals and the Prussian Government.

He made his first appearance in the little Hessian University of Marburg, but, fully occupied at that time

Diafoirus' father, augured well for his son's sagacity. " In the matter of patience, obstinacy, and orderliness he leaves nothing to be desired," he said.

[1] Another professor of the same tendency is Max Duncker, who in turn lectured at Halle, Tübingen, and Berlin before being made Superintendent of the Prussian Archives. He it was, speaking of the mission of the history professors in the Universities, said to Sybel, when the latter was going to Munich : " The outposts are more important than the home guards." A Liberal of the same class as Dahlmann, he wished to prepare by his lessons for " the advent of the truly national German Constitutional State." With Gustav Freytag, he was a constant friend of the Crown Prince, the future Emperor Frederic III. His works are " H. von Gagern," 1850 ; " Vier Monate ausw. Politik," 1851 ; " Feudalität und Aristokratie," 1858 ; " Gesch. des Althernthums (1852–1857) aus des Zeit Fried. des Grossen " (1876). This last is his best work, very accurate in its statements and moderate in its form.

with his scientific works, he gave no signs whatever of the orator that was within him. At Munich, where he became a professor in 1856, he had a more numerous public, but there he found, as he said, that the soil was harder to work. From the moment he wished to begin his teaching in the National Liberal sense he was attacked with the utmost violence by the old Bavarians and by the Catholic party. Each day saw some new pamphlet issued against him. The "Almanach de Munich," very widely read among the Bavarian population, ended its wishes for 1860 with the words : " You will soon see that the true light is not the light of the North, and with me you will offer up this prayer to God : Lead us not into temptation, but deliver us from Sybel. Amen." [1]

For four years these attacks were renewed with the same violence, so much so that Sybel, who had never felt himself at Munich but as " a missionary in a foreign country," left that town at the first opportunity. In 1861 Professor Dahlmann's chair had fallen vacant at Bonn, and Sybel took it up next.

At Bonn, Sybel's real political career began. " When coming back to Bonn," wrote Gustav Freytag to him, " you doubtless did not count upon a peaceful, smoothly

---

[1] King Maximilian knew his Liberal sentiments, his hatred for Ultramontanism, and his admiration for Prussia. He had long hesitated before calling him to Munich University. It was only after an interview with the historian, in which the latter stated his ideas, that he decided to let him come. " In that interview," said Sybel, " I explained to him how in 1848 I had gradually become a ' Gothaer,' and how to-day quite different questions and tendencies seemed to me to govern the world. I concluded by saying that I was what I had been before—a moderate Whig, a partisan of monarchy in the personal sense of the word" (Varrentrapp, " Biographische Einleitung," p. 83).

flowing life : the struggles at Munich will scarcely be
more disheartening than those which await you here.
But we are not placed on this earth for rest. To see
you on the first battlefield of Germany is to me, as to a
number of brave people, the essential thing."

Freytag was right. A period of fierce struggles was
now beginning for Sybel. The State on which he had
based all his hopes and of which he had said a short
while before : " The position of Prussia in Germany,
and even in Europe, is such that she needs two things
to an equal extent—two things which seem to exclude
each other—a powerful unity and a powerful liberty :. . .
liberty above all, for it has ineradicably penetrated the
flesh and blood of our State : it belongs to the air we
breathe : it has given life, strength, and prosperity
to the State of Prussia "—this State, I say, betrayed
the trust he had placed in it by declaring war on the
representatives of the nation with regard to the
military credits which they had refused to vote.

Sybel took an active part in this struggle. He had
just been made member for a district of Elberfeld and
sat in the Prussian Chamber. With professors Gneist
and Virchow he was one of the most ardent opponents
of the Government's obstinacy. In a violent speech
he went so far as to foretell a great revolution and
cast all the responsibility for it on those " blind rulers
who remain deaf to the just complaints of their
subjects."

Sybel, like all the Liberal professors, had not foreseen
Sadowa. Even on the eve of that battle he could only
see in Bismarck a sort of Polignac, who only sought to
make war to rid himself of internal difficulties, and who
already discounted the victories in order to put down
public liberties. But when the victory came about his
eyes were opened. Filled with admiration, he under-

stood that this country squire whom he had taken for a reckless fellow was a most discreet politician whose calculated hardihood was full of prudence, a player sure of his power, bold and successful. From that time on he no longer persisted in his error. He made his *mea culpa*. He trifled no longer with the military credits. " To keep what she has taken," he said, " Prussia needs a strong army. She needs it also to assure the peace of Europe. Germany should be invincible in the world." [1]

From that moment onwards we may say that Sybel's liberalism was very ragged. The historian still protests his attachment to liberty. Some years afterwards, at the unveiling of a statue of Baron Stein at Nassau (end of 1872), he said :—

"Yes, the Prussian people deserved to be called to liberty, for they learned in a school of unexampled misfortune that liberty, far from being the subversion of egotism, signifies work useful to all, political duty, and patriotic efforts. May these ideas remain alive in every one's heart, for the greatest good of the people's rights and the power of the State."

Yes, Sybel still said that, but the time was not long in coming when, completely won over to Bismarck's policy, he would say exactly the opposite.

After all, this strange, sudden change could only surprise those who knew Sybel superficially. In reality he had always been more Prussian than Liberal. He had displayed more eloquence in demanding the rights of the Hohenzollern than those of liberty. To be assured of this it is only necessary to glance at the " Historical and Political Essays " which he published from 1847 to 1871.

---

[1] Letter quoted by Varrentrapp, p. 126.

As a publicist Sybel would deserve a separate study, so great was his output during the Empire's years of preparation. No week passed without his publishing a pamphlet, without his writing a newspaper article or a notice in a review. He even founded a historical journal for the needs of his cause, the *Historische Zeitschrift*, "with the purpose," as he said, "of spreading throughout the nation the true historical method" and of "inculcating in the Germans sound political principles." "The more false knowledge," he said, "can do us harm in the present state of our affairs, the more desirable is it to give true knowledge an organ and to lead the crowd to a proper recognition of the value historical science has for our national life. I do not think that within our sphere of influence there is a task more urgent than this." [1]

The *Historische Zeitschrift*, which is still to-day the first scientific historical review in Germany, has played a very great part in the development of national life. Founded at Munich in 1857, it was addressed not to specialists, but to the general public. "Our arguments," wrote Sybel to the historian Waitz, to whom he was stating his ideas, "are not for our learned confrères who are in agreement with us on this question. Still less are they for the triflers in literature, for neither you nor I can hope to improve them. What we desire is to awaken among our educated people the knowledge of the true technique of history. . . . When we speak of the Ultramontane historians, is it not our duty to

---

[1] These essays, and others published until his death (1895), were collected in three volumes by the publisher Cotta at Stuttgart, under the title "Kleine historische Schriften."

explain their lack of scientific spirit. . . . Our object
is to serve not the Church, but science." [1]

In what way he expected to serve science is
thus explained by Sybel in the Preface of his new
review: The observer endowed with a historical
sense notices that the life of peoples is manifested,
under the dominion of moral laws, as a natural and
individual development, which spontaneously produces
from within itself forms of State and of civilization
which cannot arbitrarily be obliterated or hastened,
nor can they be submitted to regulation from without. This conception therefore excludes :—

Feudality, which would wish to introduce dead
elements into the forward march of progress in order
to attempt to revive them.

Radicalism, which puts subjective arbitration in the
place of organic evolution.

Ultramontanism, which places national and spiritual
development under the authority of an external Church.

That was what Sybel called founding " an independent organ of purely scientific character which would
not be the mouthpiece of any party."

In reality it was the organ of a purely Protestant
and national conception of history. I know, of course,
that Sybel held that this conception would end with
the same results as science. He said so, but he was
scarcely in a condition to prove it. Has it been
proved? His collaborators, it is true, were the first
historians in Germany: Mommsen, Strauss, Zeller,
Häusser, Droysen, Dahlmann, Bernhardi, Waitz,
Giesebrecht and Loebell. We might even concede, too,
that, in the matter of the rigour of their critical method
and their science, these men were superior to the

_____

[1] Letter of May, 1857, quoted by Varrentrapp, p. 87.

Catholic historians of Great Germany, but they do not represent the less, on that account, a tendency equally narrow as the others. To enter this house it was necessary to show a clean slate, and that did not always involve a diploma of scientific honesty, as, for example, in the case of Palacky, a Tcheck Protestant historian, whose great merit in Sybel's eyes was his enmity towards Catholic and feudal Austria, who published an article the texts of which he was convicted of altering. When the Austrian historian Höfler, who caught him red-handed, offered to prove this in the review, Sybel refused.[1]

By saying that he did not found a review for a few dozen specialists, but "to swell the current of the national movement," Sybel showed by that very fact in what spirit he was going to direct the enterprise.

Until that time Germany had no literary reviews similar to those of England and France. It was perhaps this gap that Sybel wished to fill. His intention was to place the great questions of history within the public reach. To do this it was necessary to avoid too much technicality in the discussion, but to limit oneself to the great facts, results, and ideas. No one has done more than Sybel to turn historical study in this direction. He gave the first examples. As a disputant, Sybel is admirable: he

---

[1] The same happened later in the case of the famous quarrel between Treitschke and Baumgarten. The review openly took Treitschke's side, although scientific truth was on the other side. The historian H. Baumgarten (1825-93) was a National Liberal historian, a partisan of Prussian hegemony, but never gave up his Liberal convictions. See, with regard to his contest with Treitschke, "H. Baumgarten, ein Lebensbild," by Erich Marcks, Munich, 1893.

has a quick, nervous style of discussion, a sharp, acrid manner, a biting wit and the gift of sarcasm. The tone of his articles is always lively and keen. With all this he is a skilful dialectician and fertile in resources. No one understands better than he how to find his opponent's weak spot. To defend his causes he often displays the ability of a most artful lawyer. His marvellous learning stands him in good stead. History to him is a huge arsenal from which he may help himself to arms wherewith to defend all causes, whether it be to show that since the thirteenth century "the small Danish nation, powerful, cautious and warlike, continually attempted to attain a position disproportionate to its means . . . until the day when Germany, collecting her forces, drove her back to her just and natural conditions,"[1] or to prove with new arguments the theory he had developed in his "History of the French Revolution"— namely, that Austria was not fit to aspire to govern the German people because, during the Revolutionary Wars, she had betrayed German interests by signing the Treaty of Campo-Formio.

And it must be acknowledged that Sybel wrote this sort of article with undoubted superiority. Those who wish to see the richness of resource he has, I recommend to read that most interesting study he devoted to the historian Vivenot.

The Viennese historian Vivenot had attacked Sybel with great vigour respecting the part he makes Austria play during the revolutionary period. Some years afterwards he published a monograph on Duke Albert of Saxe-Teschen—a Field-Marshal of the Empire, who

---

[1] "Rechts- und Machtverhältnisse Deutschland und Danemark im 18ten Jahr." ("Kleine hist. Schrift.," ii. 108).

P

commanded the Upper Rhine Army from April 1794 till March 1795. Now in this work, the author, although an officer of the Austrian Army, gives a most confused account of the military operations of that time. You should see how Sybel dresses him down. "When a layman," he says, "examines the detailed history of an army and its leader, he takes care in the first place to find exact and precise information about the strength and composition of that army, since to him, as a layman, the complete understanding of the actions of leaders and of their mistakes would seem to depend particularly on those circumstances: and the more so when the author of the book is an officer, an Imperial and Royal Captain (K.K. Hauptmann), and when, moreover, he is in possession of all the documents on the war in the Imperial and Royal Archives. But whether the military flight of Herr von Vivenot rises too high or his style of writing falls too low, the fact remains that it is a particularly difficult task to find anything among the information he gives us, and I confess, for my part, that, after having studied to a certain extent the military history of all the nations of Europe during the revolutionary period, I never found anything to be compared with this." [1]

Thereupon follow several sarcastic pieces of advice on the way to write history, on the art of choosing and classifying documents and the manner of making use of them. "Now," he said, "if he has any regard for his literary reputation he will do another thing: he will give up writing history, himself, until he has acquired, by a study extending over many years, the rudimentary information necessary to a historian: he

---

[1] "Kleine hist. Schrift.," ii. 332.

will limit himself . . . to collecting documents. But even for the elaboration of such a work he will not trust his own intelligence: if he is wise, in the future he will send nothing to press without first having submitted the proofs to some one who really understands history. There is no lack of them at Vienna, even among those who are least suspected of sympathy with Prussia.

"When dealing with so unskilful an enemy, the least one can do, to fight him fairly, is to furnish him with the means of finding efficacious weapons and to show him the way in which his feeble hands may use them."

All Sybel's critical articles are written in this lively, clear, and cutting style. They are on all subjects, from the Political and Social State of the Early Christians to Napoleon III, from Socialism, Communism, and the Emancipation of Women to Clerical Policy in the Nineteenth Century. In all these Sybel proves himself to be the same alert and vigorous disputant.

It can readily be understood that he had great success in Germany. Since Lessing, that lively and brilliant manner of approaching and discussing questions had not been known. But the question may also be asked whether these articles were in place in a historical review which claimed to be purely scientific.

After 1870 Sybel's passion slackened down a little. Not that his talent as a historian was on the decrease, but, having won the game, he could rest after his struggles. Never were victories greeted with such enthusiasm as were those of Prussia by Sybel. "How happy am I," he wrote at the beginning of the war, " to see these great days in which the nation has risen

at a single pound to the height of her destiny. " [1]   On
the news of the surrender of Paris his joy knew no
bounds : " When I read this news, the tears ran down
my cheeks. ' What have we done, O Lord,' I cried,
' to see such great and powerful things ? ' How can
we live henceforward ? *What has been for twenty
years* the object of all our desires and efforts has been
accomplished in a most magnificent way. How can
one at my age take up a new cause for the short
space left for one to live ? "

There could now be no question of any opposition
to the Government. For several years Sybel had
been converted to Bismarck's policy,[2] together with
the most of the National Liberal party chiefs. Of
the old Liberals of note there were only four left
faithful to the ideal of their youth : Mommsen, Hoenel,
Rickert, and Virchow. Sybel, moreover, now grown
old, was clearly tired of the struggle. The last time
he took part in the political passages of arms was in
1874, at the time of the Kulturkampf, of which he was
one of the most ardent supporters in the Reichstag.
He was at that time completely won over to Bismarck,
who had just vanquished Germany for the second
time by giving the death-blow to the Liberal party
(1881). Sybel did not raise a protest. Appointed five
years before to the charge of the Archives at Berlin,

---

[1] Letter to Baumgarten, August 4, 1870.

[2] In 1867 he wrote : " The Liberals who desire a change in the
person of the Foreign Minister, as a condition of their acceptance,
are guilty of a gross error. The enemy would soon take care
to teach them that. Let them learn at Vienna or Frankfort if
there is any event that would be received with greater joy than
the recall of that bold man of genius who after fifty years of
neglect made the Prussian name respected and feared throughout
the world " (Varrentrapp, p. 125).

he took no more part in politics, but devoted his remaining strength to the writing of the " History of the Foundation of the New German Empire," a great work which was only to be interrupted by his death.[1]

This is the way he explains the origin of this work: " Having described in my 'History of the French Revolution (1789–1800)' the disintegration of the Holy German Empire, no desire took such a hold on my heart, after the great events of 1806 and 1870, as the desire to describe the resurrection of the German Empire."

The writing of that work was in Sybel's mind the accomplishment of a national act, for he thought thus to work towards securing the great results of the war of 1870.[2] Indeed, he saw a close connection between the events of 1789 and those of this war. In the first of his works—the " History of the French Revolution "—he had stated the negative side of the vital political problem of the nineteenth century. By writing now the history of Prussia's work in Germany, he thought he was going to state the positive side. Having criticized, it was now necessary to construct. The question was whether Sybel would succeed in his second task as well as he did in his first. An inquiry into his " History of the Foundation of the German Empire " will now show us that.

V

As a historian, Sybel had revealed, in his "History of the French Revolution," qualities of the highest

---

[1] " Die Begründung des Deutschen Reich durch Wilhelm I vornehmlich nach den preussischen Staatsakten," 7 vols., Munich and Leipzig (1889–95).

[2] Quoted by Varrentrapp, p. 130.

order. Tireless in research, active in discussion, his mind always alert, he was unequalled as a critic. And he did not show his superiority alone in collecting State papers and in classifying and analysing them, in determining which were authentic sources of information, and in throwing light on points where there was contradictory evidence, but also in his criticism of the ideas and great political events, in the analysis of negotiations and in the discussion of affairs.

But his talents ended at that. He had not the art of bringing historical characters to life again: he gives us an idea of what they did, but not of what they were, and in spite of his knowledge of the undercurrents of politics, of the secrets of diplomacy, he never succeeded in giving us a living picture of the great movement he wished to describe.

We have seen already that this defect was due to a certain gap in Sybel's mind: his lack of psychological feeling. Interested particularly in the play of diplomatic contrivances and giving his attention to the solution of the great political problems which are comprised in the actions of these statesmen, he is rather inclined to forget that it is these men with their passions and interests who make history. In no part of his " History of the French Revolution " has he succeeded in giving us an idea of the complexity of human nature. To him, one might say, man is nothing but a brain. Events seem to follow from the pure logic of situations. The characters are conceived as if they were unconditioned.

Sybel, who reproaches the revolutionists in so vehement a manner for having founded their arguments on abstractions, at bottom does this very

thing himself. When entering upon the history, he
has his ideas on each type of character, and consequently his mind made up, as is usually done,
but instead of regarding these ideas as provisional
and being ready to modify them according to what
he finds out, he looks for nothing among the facts
but what will confirm his point of view. Now the
characters, with very rare exceptions—and this is
also true about the logicians of the Revolution—are
never constant to themselves. They depend upon a
thousand circumstances which modify them. And
to describe them with truthfulness they must be taken
by surprise at all times of their lives. A man may
assert a thing very sincerely to-day and yet to-
morrow act in a sense diametrically opposed to it.
Through the lack of an intellect supple enough to
enter the recesses of the minds of men, Sybel is
never able to penetrate those characters which have
many shades. And this is particularly true when he
describes women. We have seen it already with
regard to Marie-Antoinette. To understand a nature
as variable and fantastic as hers, he would have needed
the penetration and suppleness of Sainte-Beuve, accustomed to all variations of that delicate perception
capable of seizing the most elusive changes of the
heart. Sybel, who forms logical opinions according
to conditions, fails entirely. In all the Queen's false-
hoods, in her double-dealing and subterfuges, he sees
further proofs of the purity of her intentions. Even
in the case of the notorious letter to Count Mercy,
which he quotes: " I must throw them off their guard
in order to deceive them the better later on," he finds
explanations which lessen the guilt. " She was persuaded," said he, " that all that Barnave and his
followers offered her did not guarantee her safety for

the future." How does he know ? What proof does
he offer that this is what Marie-Antoinette really
thought ? None but his personal conviction, or rather
his bias.

Bias is, in truth, Sybel's greatest enemy. It is this
which misleads him and deceives his judgment, which
prevents him from seeing clearly and from distinguish-
ing things. If he *will not allow at any price* that Marie-
Antoinette should have committed any errors, it is
because he wishes the responsibility for the war to fall
upon the Girondins. And he does not do this inten-
tionally, but from a sort of natural infirmity, the
abundant proofs of which we are now going to see in
that page of contemporary history in which he himself
took a certain part.

We might think that, when writing the history, not of
a period ancient already and one for which he had never
felt the least enthusiasm, but of an event in which he
was closely concerned and the realization of which had
been the great event of his life, Sybel would give us a
living piece of work. Had he not known personally
the greater number of the actors of this great period ?
Had he not been in the confidence of highly-placed
men [1] who had been able to inform him as to
the undercurrents of Prussian politics, without which,
he writes himself, such a work could not have been
written ? Did he not hold, also, in his capacity as
Director of the Archives, the secrets with regard to all
these events ? Yet in spite of this he was not able to
give us a living picture of the political life of Germany
during that second half of the century. He remains
the same critical and diplomatic historian that we
already know. The finest parts of his " History " are the

[1] " Bismarck," Vorwort, p. xii.

expositions of great problems : for example, the question
of Schleswig-Holstein, a masterpiece of lucidity and
intelligence, at least in so far as we set aside the author's
personal opinions, in which he shows his Prussian prejudice: his accounts of the campaigns in Denmark and
Austria, of a clearness and simplicity worthy of all
praise : his exposition of the origins of the war of 1870,
in which he shows the same critical stability, the same
sagacity as ever, particularly in that part where he
annihilates the lying assertions of Gramont. But all
that which would give charm to the book is wanting.
You would look in vain not only for a fairly vivid
picture of German life of that period, but even for an
interesting characteristic of Prussian politics in what is
human and consequently living in it. He has not
understood its true spirit nor its inner life. What he
needed for such a work was a certain warmth of feeling,
a little enthusiasm. Now Sybel has not that warmth
of feeling, and his enthusiasm, moderate as it is, is
purely intellectual. So it is that he has succeeded
in creating an exact and true piece of work, if we have
regard to its facts, but one destitute of that higher
human truth.

"In no part of this book," said Sybel in his Preface,
"have I attempted to conceal my Prussian and
National-Liberal opinions." And this seems natural, or
at least it conforms with his philosophy of history, for
Sybel is one of those historians who only judge the
value of a policy by its results.

Prussia having succeeded in bringing about German
unity, everything in German history during the nineteenth century should be judged in relation to the
Prussian policy.

We can easily see in what conclusions this idea,
logically deduced, must end; the two instruments

which brought about German unity were Prussian administration and the army : the first, by means of the Zollverein, had prepared that predominance of Prussia in Germany which the second had brought about on the field of battle.

German unity had not been able to be accomplished until the day when Frederick the Great had a true successor. This successor is King William, who in 1848 had described the situation : " This affair will not be decided in Gagern's way, but by force of arms : when and how, is the secret of the future."

This is the idea which Sybel tries to illustrate in his " History." He recognizes that " in order to live " Prussia should progress, that " to stand still was death to her," that her life was staked on the establishment of her power in Germany, and that German civilization urgently demanded this. With regard to the Schleswig-Holstein question he recognizes that, at bottom, to Prussia it is but a question of interest—" the question of life or death for her commerce." [1] In the same way he explains the origin of the Austro-Prussian War as being due less to the arbitrary result of personal passion than to the inevitable conflict between ancient rights acquired during centuries and pressing national needs growing continually stronger." " The state of discomfort which resulted from it was intolerable, and it was only a formidable crisis which could lead to a permanent cure. It was for the well-being of Germany that this cure was accomplished." [2]

He acknowledges, too, that the war of 1870 was inevitable (that war which, in his correspondence, he confesses he awaited for twenty years !), because at

---

[1] " Die Begründ.," iii. 30, iv. 81.
[2] Ibid., Preface.

bottom it was nothing but one of those necessary struggles of historical life " between a young State wishing to make for itself a place in the sun and an old nation which was struggling to keep up its position."

After that, you would expect Sybel, faithful to his philosophy of history, to describe in a straight-forward manner this work of conquest, justifying the Prussian wars, as Mommsen had done in his " History of Rome," by Darwin's law of the survival of the fittest.

Now this is not so. When it comes to going to the logical consequences of his theory he draws back. It is repugnant to him to have to confess that his country may have had recourse to reprehensible means to achieve her ends. And so when he approaches the causes of these three wars, he en-deavours to cast the blame in turn upon the Danes, the Austrians, and the French.

When Frederick the Great entered Silesia, he said cynically: " I take in the first place: I can always find pedants enough to prove my rights." [1]

---

[1] Bismarck said also : " The most indifferent arguments are good when one has a majority of bayonets." But, on the other hand, the Kings of Prussia have always taken great care to pre-serve appearances. When Frederick William III, with the connivance of France, invaded Nüremberg, Upper Bavaria, Sybel tells us that the King did not decide on this step until he had made profound researches in his archives, where some title-deeds extended back in part to the fifteenth century, against the neigh-bouring dynasties, the Knights of the Empire and the city of Nüremberg. It was only after this that he undertook the campaign." Sybel adds in astonishment : " There followed between Vienna and Berlin recriminations and reproaches which could not have been sharper had a state of war existed between them."

There has never been a lack of these pedants in Germany, especially among her historians, and Sybel now offers us a good example.

Sybel has shown himself already, in his "History of the French Revolution," to be a most expert casuist in the art of passing what is white for black and vice versa.[1] But that is nothing in comparison with the efforts he puts forward to show that Prussian policy—let us say, if you will, Bismarck's policy—was always irreproachable in the matter of correctness and loyalty.

The public in Germany, however, was of another opinion. When Sybel's work was announced, its curiosity was aroused to a great extent. They expected sensational revelations and they were glad. The people, who have an instinct for justice and can be roused to enthusiasm for great and noble causes, is also full of indulgence for rogues when they are lucky. In its attitude towards these men it is like the child who applauds tbe misdoings of Guignol in thrashing the policeman.

Bismarck, the most skilful among the skilful, adding to his skilfulness a cynical boastfulness, fills them with great admiration; they are ready to excuse him all his misdeeds. But with Sybel's account their curiosity was by no means satisfied. They found themselves face to face with a prodigious being, a superman, without any of those touches which make a character

---

[1] In his "Kleine hist. Schrift.," iii. 184, he says of the conquest of Silesia: "What urged Frederick II to make this conquest was not the desire to increase his territory, but to uphold the peace of Europe. It is scarcely necessary to recall the very words of Frederick: 'My country needed a body, so I took Silesia.' Or again, 'A young and vigorous State,' etc." (see Memoirs and Correspondence).

real and living. True to his method, the historian, in the portrait he makes of him, leads everything back " to the incommensurable political genius of this man," who was a "politician of a great stock who sacrificed everything to the interest of the State." " Every other consideration," he added, " was secondary to him. Free trade or protection, feudal or democratic institutions, religious liberty or hierarchy, questions which for thousands of men are the determining principles of their lives, were nothing to him but good or bad means to an end, according to circumstances : he only had in view the aggrandisement of Prussia, and his enemies have sometimes been able to accuse him of being the most unprincipled opportunist there ever was. While Frederick the Great regarded the State as an instrument of civilization, Bismarck was always a pure utilitarian—always asking himself to what extent any art or science would contribute to the prosperity of the Prussian State."

But what we look for in vain in Sybel's work is the means employed by this " unscrupulous utilitarian " to bring about German unity. The historian makes a point of honour in having us believe that he never on any occasion tried to deceive his opponents : he makes him a sort of paragon of virtue, whose actions were only determined by noble motives, always inspired by a feeling of duty.

Nothing is more significant in this respect than the way he explains the origin of the three wars which presided over the foundation of the New Empire.

In the first place, there is the history of the Schleswig-Holstein question.

Never before had Sybel better exhibited the resources of his genius, fertile in expedients to attempt to wash the Prussian Government clean of any reproach of double-dealing. He examines with the greatest care the two questions invoked by the Germans to justify their intervention in the affairs of the duchies : the political or constitutional question and the question of law or succession.

The second of these questions, solved according to circumstances in two senses absolutely opposed to each other and always according to the Prussian interest of the moment, seems to him decidedly a bad one, and he abandons it, not without reproving with a certain asperity his fellow-countrymen who obstinately persist in using it still, and thus compromise a good cause.

The first one remains, the political question and the sound one, and on this he brings to bear all the weight of his argument. But he recognizes that this political question is very involved, for it is complicated with dynastic questions whose roots run back to the fifteenth century, and which require " the solution of the complicated rights of individuals, of princes and kings." He shows us the jurists of the Crown exerting themselves to decide whether it is the people's right and the State which has the highest authority, or whether it is the private right of princes : whether a right established for four centuries gives each agnate member of the family an intangible personal right, or whether the legal power of the State is invested in the right of controlling a new succession to the throne : in other words, whether the right of succession should be judged according to the principles of the Feudal System or according to those principles which, after the English Revolution, directed the affairs of the political world.[1]

---

[1] Among these accommodating jurists of the Crown there was one Helwing, of Berlin, who supported the rights of the Hohen-

In reality all this cleverly arranged, solemn preparation of rights was only intended to deceive the gallery. " The question of the duchies," said von Roon cynically, "is not a question of rights ; it is a question of force, and we it is who have the force." [1] The whole military party in Prussia said the same thing. " Just think," said General von Manteuffel to General Fleury, " I am the head of a division and have never yet been under fire."

Again, a curious thing was that these feudalists supported the people's right, which allowed Prussia to intervene in Schleswig-Holstein, while democratic Germany, by supporting Augustenburg, sided with feudal right.

What one would like to find in Sybel is that chapter of high human comedy in which Bismarck played the principal part : to see the consummate skill he displayed in encouraging resistance among the Danes by letting them be informed secretly that the English would support them in their demands [2] : the subterfuges he used to remove the scruples (Rechtsbedenken) of the King, who was a believer and was concerned as to the legality of the position : the manœuvres he used to bring Austria into the affair : the way he set about making Augustenburg, after he had recognized his imbecility, fall into the trap : how subsequently he was able, by means of the subsidized Press and the encouragement he gave to the Liberals of the duchies, " to set loose," as he said, " all the dogs,

zollern to the crown of the duchies. " This opinion was due to good nature," said Treitschke ironically, " but unfortunately it was untenable " (Treitschke, " Deutsche Geschichte," v. 579).

[1] Bernhardi, " Der Streit um die Elbherzogthumer," p. 163.

[2] See on this subject the " Memoirs " of Beust, i. 242.

who wished to bark, against the Danish power "[1] : the still more skilful way in which he induced legitimist Austria to propose to the Diet rigorous measures against Augustenburg : then the consummate skill he displayed in driving Austria from the duchies after having made her his accomplice : all this most dexterous policy, which was nothing but the putting into practice of a plan deliberately developed and which he had laid down as early as 1862 [2] :—

" *It is certain that the whole Danish business can have no solution for us, as we could wish it, except through a war : we shall have no difficulty in finding a pretext when the right time for entering upon it arrives* " : all this policy, I say, we do not find in Sybel's work. It seems, according to this historian, that in these events everything followed a logical and natural course and that Prussia was only obliged to intervene to put an end to a disorder which threatened to be prolonged.[3]

In the breaking off of diplomatic negotiations between Prussia and Austria which followed the Danish question, Sybel would have us believe, the same as ever, that the Prussian Government committed no

---

[1] Letter to Count Arnim.

[2] Letter, December 22, 1862.

[3] How much franker is the avowal of the historian Treitschke, who brands " the petty intrigues and clumsy and disgusting manœuvres of the diplomatists who would have us believe in the so-called rights of the Hohenzollern over the duchies," instead of frankly confessing the truth, which is that " we do not want another Court . . . that the particularism of the people of Holstein is already too marked : . . . that the matter at stake was the prosperity of a German territory, which must be made happy in spite of herself. . . . that the Germanization of the north of Schleswig was a pressing matter . . . finally, that Prussia should annex that country in order to be able to put into force a great German policy " (" Zehn Jahre deutscher Kämpfe," pp. 9–26).

wrong. If the Prussian fleet, in spite of the assurances she had given to do nothing without Austria, took possession of the port of Kiel, he cries : " How can you wish her to have done anything else: if Austria, by her geographical position, could not use that port, was that a reason why Prussia, otherwise situated, should not use it ? " [1]

When in the autumn of 1865 Bismarck left suddenly for Biarritz, where Napoleon III was at that time, Sybel assures us that it was less to sound the intentions of the French Emperor than "to ask of the powerful waves of the Bay of Biscay strength for his overworked nerves." [2]

After the war, if Prussia annexes Hanover and Electoral Hesse, you would never guess why she does it. It is to punish France for her stupid meddling in German affairs. The passage is worth quoting. This is it : " Prussia had undertaken this war only with the intention of reforming the Confederation and for the possession of Schleswig-Holstein, with no thoughts of any more extensive annexations. It was Napoleon, by his opposition to German unity, that forced Bismarck to give the King the necessary power to defend German interests by strengthening the individual power of Prussia." [3] When an advocate is reduced to such arguments, his cause must decidedly be a bad one.

The causes of the war of 1870 are a historical problem which Sybel wished to treat thoroughly. He knows too well that in the eyes of posterity the people who wished for it will carry a heavy burden of responsibility, and so he strives to make all the blame for it fall on France. To this question he devotes no less than half a big

---

[1] " Die Begründ.," iv. 105.
[2] Ibid. v. 212.   [3] Ibid. v. 253.

volume,[1] even at the risk of destroying the balance
between the various parts of his work. But in spite
of his trouble and pains we may well ask ourselves
whether he has carried the question any further.

At first it is very difficult to determine what might
be called the remote causes of this war. Was French
jealousy, as Sybel believes, of Sadowa, that " magnificent
victory which eclipsed Solferino and all Napoleon III's
victories," one of the causes ? It would then remain to
be determined what sort of Frenchmen desired such
a revenge.

It was not the educated class—the Liberals, who all
along had supported Prussia : it was not the mass
of people, who were under the Second Empire pro-
foundly indifferent as to what happened abroad : it
could only have been, then, the military and clerical
party. But what did they represent in the nation ?
I know, of course, that, once decided upon a campaign,
they had thousands of ways of exciting public opinion
and creating a factitious agitation. But until when
did they do this ?—at any rate only until the moment
when the relations became suddenly strained between
Prussia and France, following the question of the
Hohenzollern candidature, which consequently became
the real cause of the war.

But it is much rather on the German side, if we
wished to weigh the imponderables, that since 1867 we
could find the moral causes of the war. Their national
feeling at least showed itself to be more susceptible
and jealous than that of the French. The question
of Luxemburg, which to Napoleon was only one of
compensation which Bismarck had let him catch a
glimpse of at the price of his neutrality, raised in

[1] " Die Begründ.," vii. 234–416.

Germany a passion of national feeling which deeply surprised France. Sybel implicitly acknowledges that after Sadowa the German people, who now knew their own strength, did not consider the situation in the same way as they had before the war. Then why does he reproach France? He also avows that if the French Emperor had been a man of penetration he would have taken advantage of Prussia's preoccupation in Bohemia to take possession of Luxemburg. "No one in Germany," said he, "would have made that a *casus belli*." But to claim the duchy after the German victory seemed to him rather an ingenuous thing to do.

Although he admits all that, Sybel does not persist the less in saying that the national susceptibility of the French was greater than that of the Germans. He recognizes well enough, to tell the truth, that the Luxemburg question suddenly assumed in Germany "the proportions of a national event": that Bismarck, who had not counted on it, was rather surprised at first, but that, pulling himself together at once, he decided, in order to reassure public opinion, to allow himself to be questioned on this subject by a Liberal deputy, Benningsen.[1] Who cannot see that it was at that very moment that Bismarck saw, if he had not seen it before, how and by what means he could gather the Germans more closely around Prussia?

---

[1] Sybel himself gives us this detail, unknown until then and yet so suggestive. On this point all Bismarck's diplomacy resembles in a surprising fashion Frederick the Great's. When Bismarck wrote to Ambassador Goltz at Paris : "Go on beguiling the French," one might almost believe he could hear Frederick the Great speaking of those same French at the moment he was betraying them : "Be all smiles to those old duffers" (letter to Podewils, "Politische Correspondenz," i. 99).

A national war alone was able to do that.[1]

If war did not break out at that moment, we now know why : Bismarck reserved for himself the choice of the hour. All his skill henceforward was directed towards making France declare war.

There have been many discussions up to the present as to the origin of the Hohenzollern candidature, and there has been no enlightenment as to whether it originated in Madrid or Berlin. It would seem highly probable that Bismarck was the originator of it,[2] but until the Spanish archives make this certain for us by giving up the secrets they still hold, we can, at any rate, state that if he did not work it out entirely himself, he used it very aptly for the needs of his policy. After the revelations of the brother of the candidate himself, King Charles of Roumania, the certainty of this matter may be regarded as complete.[3] In Germany to-day there is no doubt about it. "France's suspicions," says Hans Delbrück on this subject, " are fully justified to-day.

---

[1] Sybel quotes the most interesting interview he had with Napoleon III, whom he saw at Paris in 1867, at the time when he was working there at his " History of the French Revolution." " Bismarck tried to make a dupe of me," said Napoleon, " and a French Emperor cannot allow himself to be made a dupe of." See, in order to correct Sybel on the whole of this question, Rothan's work, " La question du Luxembourg," completed by Lord Loftus's revelations, " Diplomatic Reminiscences," 2nd Series, i. 171 and 284.

[2] The recent revelations of Moritz Busch leave not a doubt in this respect. " Bismarck," he said, " confessed that this candidature was a trap he had set for Napoleon, and he added that neither King William nor the Crown Prince had the least suspicion of this manœuvre."

[3] " Aus dem Leben König Karl's von Rumanien," Stuttgart, 1894, ii.

It was the King of Rumania who, for reasons difficult to understand—they say he did not wish the responsibility for this war to rest upon his family—divulged the secret which the Minister for Foreign Affairs guarded with such jealous care."

After this declaration, we are forced to acknowledge that from the beginning Bismarck intrigued for the success of this candidature. He wrote a letter to Prim twelve months before the public knew anything about the affair.[1] What he evidently wished to do was "to feel the pulse" of public opinion in France, to see whether it would fly up at the idea of a Hohenzollern mounting the Spanish throne. Once he was informed on that point there was nothing left but to let things go, satisfying himself with intriguing covertly so that the Hohenzollern Prince should not absolutely refuse the candidature.

That is a thing which Sybel does not admit. One might almost say that he makes it a point of honour that in all the incidents of that candidature Bismarck always acted in a correct and loyal manner. We see this particularly in the account he gives of what might be called the three phases of the crisis : (1) the visit of Rancès to Berlin : (2) the double-faced negotiation of Bismarck with Prim and with Prince Anthony, the father of the candidate; (3) the Ems telegram.

As for Rancès' visit, we know what it was about. Two months after the publication of Salazar's pamphlet, which was the first openly to broach the

---

[1] Bismarck's letter to Prim at Madrid was carried by Lothar Bucher. See the "Memoires" of Moritz Busch. See also *Preussische Jahrbucher*, October 1895, p. 28 ; Lord Loftus's "Diplomatic Reminiscences," 2nd Series, i. 284.

Hohenzollern candidature, Rancès, a former Spanish Ambassador at Berlin, now at Vienna, came to Berlin for three days in a most mysterious fashion. He had more or less secret interviews everyday with Bismarck. Is it likely that during these interviews *there was no mention of the Hohenzollern candidature*, as Sybel declares? What proof does he give us of this assertion? None, unless it is his personal conviction. This, at any rate, was not the opinion of the diplomatic world in Berlin. This unexpected visit, coming just after the declaration of the Hohenzollern candidature, seemed a little dubious to the diplomatic corps. Lord Loftus, who voices their opinion, said: " Clearly it was not the mere desire to offer his compliments to Bismarck that brought Rancès to Berlin." He scents " a snake in the grass." The French Government, notified of it, is disturbed. Benedetti is required to ask an explanation of Bismarck. Explanations are made, but he is not satisfied. He seems to see in Bismarck's words that something is being kept back : he suspects " that he has not been told the truth." [1] Sybel, instead of examining impartially to see if anything in these suppositions might have some foundation, attacks " the suspicious mind of Benedetti, who concludes arbitrary results from nothing at all." [2]

If Sybel sees nothing abnormal in that, he would not see anything strange in the secret mole's methods practised by Bismarck at Madrid and Sigmaringen, advising Prim, on the one hand, to apply directly to the Prince, assuring him that the affair, which had

---

[1] " Ma Mission en Prusse," p. 308.

[2] " Die Begründ.," vii. 245. Lord Loftus's " Diplomatic Reminiscences," 2nd Series, i. 291.

not succeeded with the King, "might well succeed
behind his back," and exerting, on the other hand,
pressure on the Prince's father to make him accept
for his son the Spanish crown.[1]   Although he relates
these facts in detail, Sybel, through either his
psychological inaptitude or his bias, does not look for
its meaning.   Not for a moment does he ask himself
why Bismarck, who, in order to prevent the King
of Prussia from interfering, had just declared that
this affair had no political character, nevertheless
concerned himself about it—he who was nothing but
a politician.[2]

What reason does he give for this sudden change?
None, unless it is that a man may alter his opinion if
he likes.[3]   This reason is not good enough for us.

Yet it would have been easy for Sybel to justify the
conduct of the Prussian Government by showing that
if France made this Hohenzollern question a national
one, Bismarck was right in secretly pushing forward
that candidature in order to see how far French
pretensions would go.   But with his bias he did not
even think of that expedient.

With regard to the Ems telegram, Sybel's purpose

---

[1] See " Aus dem Leben König Karl's von Rumanien," ii.

[2] The thing which shows how much Prim was a mere
tool in this affair is his unasked-for declaration to the French
Ambassador at Madrid : " My consolation is that it was not I
who thought of such a candidature : *it was placed in my hands.*
As it was brought to me all prepared, I could not, in our present
situation, refuse it " (" Die Begründ.," vii. 262).

[3] He also said, without, I think, being deceived as to the value
of that reason, that the condition of affairs in Spain seemed
improved to Bismarck.   " The Government had just vigorously
put down two disturbances, and they could look forward to the
future with greater security."

is still more apparent. " An abridgment," he says ingenuously, " is not a forgery." It is sufficient, in order to be convinced, to compare the two copies. Everybody knows that the second had an offensive tone that was not to be found in the first. But who has any doubt about it nowadays ? Has it not been known for a long time that this telegram was the direct cause of the declaration of war ? " A telegram was brought to the Foreign Office," said Marshal Lebœuf before the Commission of Inquiry. " It was read in Council : I don't remember the words, my recollection of it is not accurate enough, but the dispatch was of such a character that an immediate change of face took place in the Council : mobilization was immediately decided upon." [1] But what was not known until Bismarck himself cynically confessed it, was that he himself, by skilful omissions, had given the communication its offensive tone. It was, indeed, an intentional mutilation, and as the German historian Philippson rightly said, " It made the King say exactly the contrary to what he had meant to say." [2]

It is difficult in the case of Sybel to measure with exactness the degree to which partiality and his lack of psychological sense contributed in preventing him from setting up for us real living historical characters, and in rendering with verisimilitude the drama or comedy

[1] Quoted by W. Ouchen, " Zeitalter des Kaisers Wilhelm I," i. 792. See also Lord Loftus, 2nd Series, i. 194 ; de Parieu, " Considér. sur l'hist. du second Empire," 1873, p. 22.

[2] *Journal de Genève*, February 13, 1895. Bismarck has found apologists for this " forgery " not among the least of men. " Blessed be the hand which traced those lines," said Hans Delbrück. " . . . If that had not succeeded, Bismarck would have found another. . . . A good diplomatist has always several arrows in his quiver " (*Preuss. Jahrb.*, xix. 739).

of history. It would seem that partiality carries it
in the explanation of events, and that the lack of
psychological sense makes itself felt particularly in
his synthetic portraits, when he gathers together
his observations and tries to make the features
stand out in an expression. Nothing illustrates
this better in his " History of the Foundation of
the German Empire" than the full-length portraits
he tried to make of the great actors in this drama.
Who, for example, would recognize Bismarck in this
description ?—

" Bismarck was then in his thirty-sixth year, at the
time when human life is at its highest development.
A tall stature, surpassing the majority of humble
mortals by a head and shoulders, a countenance bright
with good health, a glance full of intelligence : in his
mouth and chin, the expression of indomitable will.
. . . His conversation always full of telling outbursts
of wit, of coloured images and picturesque turns. ' He
took me for an egg,' he said of Frederick William IV,
' out of which he wished to breed a minister.' " [1]

How tame, colourless, and trivial is everything in
the expression of this description. What he says of
Bismarck might easily refer to any one. There is no
individual characteristic, no expressive and living word
which would thrust you at once to the bottom of that
extraordinary man's nature !

It is the same with his other portraits. In
William I he only sees the humble and submissive
Christian :—

" He always walked under the eyes of the Most
High. . . . His faith was the bread of his life, the
consolation of his sorrows . . . the only rule for his

---

[1] " Die Begründ.," ii. 143–5.

actions. Feeling himself powerless in the hands of God, he was strong in the face of the world." [1]

And the portrait thus proceeds for several pages in this honeyed and unctuous tone. With what diligence, we feel, Sybel applied himself to this ! He evidently said to himself that in order to celebrate suitably the merits of the founder of the German Empire, he must blow the trumpet of praises. He tries to do this, but how grossly and with what unctuousness !

In a similar way the genius in Moltke is not even indicated in Sybel's work. He is satisfied to point out what were the results of the "methodical calculations of a man who saw, foresaw, calculated, and understood everything, and who left nothing to chance," but you will look in vain for a more coloured picture of his activity. [2]

There are in the "History of the Foundation of the German Empire" a few anecdotes, but how frigidly they are told. Here is a fairly amusing one which he had from the lips of the Chancellor himself:—

"In March 1848 Bismarck was walking with King Frederick William IV on the Orangery terrace at Potsdam. The King was complaining that he could not get the revolution over. The Prince replied that the absence of courage compromised everything. 'Courage, again courage, and yet again courage,' he cried, 'and your Majesty will have the victory.' At

---

[1] "Die Begründ.," ii. 282–3.

[2] See, for example, what he says of Moltke's strategy, v. 104, et seq. : "Moltke recognized the impossibility of directing every detail from afar. He awakened the spirit of initiative in his subordinates, and the influence of this was felt throughout the scale of ranks in the Army Corps. . . . He was satisfied at the beginning of the war to give a general order : in detail what he foresaw was not always realized," etc.

this moment the Queen came out from behind a bush : 'Herr von Bismarck,' said she, 'how dare you speak to your King like that ?' 'Leave him alone,' answered the King, laughing, 'I shall soon put him down,' and he went on stating his prudent policy."[1]

Sybel evidently relates well, but he paints badly. Bismarck, who was the antipodes of this form of mind —Bismarck, to whom all history was contained in anecdotes—illustrated this one day in a rather striking fashion. As he was reading the volume of Sybel which contains the portrait of Radowitz, he exclaimed : " A Radowitz like the one described by the historian never existed." Then he set about making a portrait of the real Radowitz, the Radowitz he had known himself. " It is not with diplomatic documents that one can get to know men, but in their everyday life."[2]

Bismarck might have added, that to write psychological history a particularly subtle and alert intelligence is required, and in the absence of nimbleness of mind, good humour, or rather a sense of the irony of things, which is only perhaps, when all is taken into account, a certain modesty or self-effacement. This state of mind, the farthest possibly removed from any fanaticism and even bias, requires a basis of good-natured scepticism, which Sybel did not possess in any degree. He was, above all, a man of faith. He believed in the truth of certain political principles, and he also believed that these principles were always sufficient to give us the key to characters. In short, he had the bias of the doctrinaire.

---

[1] " Die Begründ.," i. 251.

[2] Quoted by Baron Alfred von Eberstein, " Kritische Bemerkungen uber H. von Sybels Begründung des deutschen Reiches," Wiesbaden, 1890.

But that, perhaps, was the root of his strength and contributed to his success. Such as it is, that lucid and deliberate exposition of the realistic policy which was enacted at the formation of the New Empire seems only the more striking on that account. If Sybel had not the fire which warms, he had at least the light which illuminates.

" I renounce," he said in his Preface, " any attempt to produce romantic effects . . . a sacrifice which is only imposed upon me by the desire to present historical truth in its integrity." [1]

Sybel, in short, believed that there is always something arbitrary in historical pictures, that the reconstruction of wholes is always problematical, and as he endeavoured to instruct and not amuse, he rather despised imagery. In his works he only wanted to bring out the spirit and deduce lessons. Hence the abstract character of his explanatory narrative, where the expressions " It seems certain that. . . . Before examining . . . let us see. . . . The first question that should be asked is. . . . If we sum up . . . we find," etc., are used at every end and turn.

But Sybel was not mistaken when he saw that thereby he would have a deeper influence on his contemporaries. At the time when he was writing, the most pressing task of the historian was to form the political judgment of the nation. Sybel was admirably adapted to do this. Clear-headed, lucid, and emphatic, with his rather meagre and dry, but incisive manner : with his irony rather cold, but certain in effect [2] : vigorous and rapid intelligence, ready

[1] Preface, p. vii.

[2] It is particularly in criticism that he has best succeeded. If he has no colouring he has touch. His portraits, sometimes

in retort, skilled in handling ideas and in present-
ing them in the most favourable light: with his
special talent of placing these ideas under the authority
of science, Sybel with his methodical work did more
than any one else in his country to spread those
National-Liberal political ideas which have become
those of the New Empire. Lord Acton has admirably
expressed it. He helped "to absorb and stiffen the
diffused, sentimental, and strangely impolitic talent of
the studious Germans: he inculcated in them a taste
for reality."

These are real services which the Germans could not
forget. Sybel was truly their political educator.

But after that critical work which prepared their
minds for the Imperial policy, there was yet another
piece of work to be done, that of glorifying the work
done by the Hohenzollern.

For this new work it was not a dialectician that was
wanted, but a poet or an orator endowed with that fire
of soul which was rather lacking in Sybel. Prussia's
victories had the power of bringing him to being: and
it is Heinrich von Treitschke, the corypheus of Imperialism, that we are now going to consider.

---

slightly caricatured, are not wanting in relief. Here is a pretty
successful one in three strokes :—

"Professor Bayrhoffer of Marburg was a little insignificant man
with a pointed nose and a thin, small voice ; until then he knew
nothing in the world except Hegel's logic : he only abandoned it
to plunge himself as exclusively as before in the principles of
Robespierre " (" Die Begründ.," i. 210).

CHAPTER IV

HEINRICH VON TREITSCHKE

FROM 1875 to 1895 a strange man was seen in a professorial chair at Berlin University: a sort of preacher, or rather a sort of apostle, whose orthodoxy consisted in preaching the excellence of Hohenzollern institutions. And he did this with a wealth of images, a richness of forms, which contrasted with the dryness of the subject. In its outbursts and passion his language reminded one of Thomas Carlyle's, but with such crudeness of expression that one of his audience assures us that half his words could never be allowed in print.

This man was called Heinrich von Treitschke: he was historiographer to His Majesty the King of Prussia and Professor of Modern and Contemporary History at the University.

When he appeared in his chair—a great, well-built man with a pleasant face, marked with a rather serious good-nature, his clear glance breathing loyalty—he made a great impression. But as soon as he opened his mouth you were disconcerted: a raucous, half-strangled, uneasy voice, like that of a deaf-mute, escaped from his throat: his movements were always uniform: " his head shook continually as if affected by some nervous disease " [1] : with all this a jerky

---

[1] P. Frédéricq, " L'enseignement supérieur de l'histoire en Allemagne," *Rev. de l'Inst. sup. en Belgique*, vol. xxv,

utterance, which did not seem to notice periods or commas, with strange stoppages in the middle of a phrase, as if the orator was obliged to stop suddenly to take his breath. You would ask yourself in astonishment what that meant. At last you would find the solution of the riddle. This orator was deaf and could not hear himself speak.

Yet the audience was full, and they applauded frantically. Even yourself, once you got over the strange first impression and became accustomed to his defective organ, would feel inseparably attached to his words. He was not, certainly, a true-born orator. There was nothing Attic or Ciceronian about him. He said himself of his eloquence: " I do not speak by any means in a fluent manner, and I do not make my audience's task an easy one. But at least with me they can be sure that they will never meet with any triviality. My words come from my heart, and it is in that I must finally place my hopes. I shall never be a refined orator, and the stupid newspaper panegyrics do not deceive me in the least." [1]

But if he was not a fluent orator, Treitschke led people by the vigour of his argument and the originality of his form. No one knew as he did the secret of drawing an audience. Students, officers, and officials thronged to his lectures. Women alone did not appear there, for this gallant Prussian professed, it would seem, with regard to the fair sex, Schopenhauer's opinions, which he expressed with a crudity that delighted his audience of young Teutons.

What made his success was the fact that throughout his lectures, always fiery and very "worked up" in tone, one could feel an ardent patriotic inspiration and

---

[1] Th. Schiemann, " H. v. Treitschke," p. 188.

an echo of the flourish of trumpets of 1870. This was the note which perpetually vibrated in his lectures. Treitschke actually lived under the effect of the great Prussian victories.

To this he added a most extraordinary gift of form. This deaf man had eyes that could see. In charming pictures he would call up all the places where historical incidents had taken place—towns, fields, and battle-fields.

He shows us Cologne and her marvellous cathedral, Bonn on the banks of the Rhine, melancholy and proud, with her seven hills surrounding her : Heidelberg with her castle, " covered with ivy and cut out as it were in the blossoms of the trees " : Dresden, " half-residential, half a foreign visitors' town, with the harmonious beauty of her whimsical style " : the Erzgebirge " with its Electoral Prince's castles hanging right over the precipice, its little mountain towns with pretty houses clinging to the sides of the hills, with their workshops buzzing with weavers and clockmakers " : Swabia " with its varied soil, its high wild plains, its alpine valleys covered with forests and laughing vines." [1]

Listening to this orator, so skilful in bringing to life the events of history, you would say to yourself that he must certainly be a writer. And you would not be mistaken. From the year 1879, with a wise deliberation, he wrote a great work—"A History of Germany in the Nineteenth Century," which he carried, in five volumes, as far as 1848.

With this work Treitschke gave his compatriots what they had lacked until then : a national history written in a popular and living style. The pictures therein are

---

[1] " Deutsche Geschichte im XIX^{ten} Jahr.," i. 309, ii. 302, iii. 503, 505, 585.

sometimes overcharged with colour.' The ultra-Prussian point of view prevails in it with a brutality which shocks you. From one end to the other you breathe a fighting atmosphere. But doubtless that contributed not a little to the success of the work in that Imperial Germany, barbed with iron and bristling with cannon. Henceforward she recognized her historian in Treitschke.

The University world was slower in acknowledging the merits of the work.

Accustomed to hold in small esteem works that were too literary or attractive in form, they could only see at first in this work partiality and excess.[1] Later they became more receptive. To-day one would even say that they wish to excuse their slowness by making Treitschke a sort of god. The historian had scarcely descended into the grave [2] than exaggerated praises were raised on all sides. A committee was formed, with Prince Bismarck as chairman, to erect a monument to him. To listen to these men, the Prussian historian eclipsed all the historians in the country. They forgot that in the scientific sphere of history there were greater men than he, to mention only Leopold von Ranke.

It is true that Treitschke is unequalled as an artist. No one in his country can rival him in the magic of his form. Added to this, he is the most brilliant representative of Prussian historiography.

Taine would have said of him that he is the most typical example of the group. The last of the line, all the qualities and defects of his predecessors were

---

[1] I think it was foreigners who were the first to acclaim the lasting qualities of Treitschke as a historian. See the article by A. Ward, *English Historical Review*, i. 809, 1886.

[2] Treitschke died in May 1896.

summed up in him. He carried their spirit, their
tendencies and method to the highest degree. As he
was the most powerful of them, his influence extended
over the widest sphere. To study him, then, is to make
oneself acquainted with one of the most powerful
factors, in its most vivid form, in German unity.

I

Treitschke, the great Prussian historian, was not
Prussian by birth or education. Born in an old Saxon
aristocratic family, with sentiments that were both very
particularistic and very conservative,[1] brought up by
a father and mother deeply attached to their King and
country, in his infancy he only imbibed, as he says himself, "the sweet milk of his Saxon fatherland." His
mother, however, who had grown up during the Wars
of Independence and who dreamed of nothing but the
heroes of that period—Bülow, Blucher, and Gneisenau
—developed in her children patriotic German feelings.
She made them read the famous verses of the warrior-
poets of that time :—

> Vaterland, ich muss versinken
> Hier im deiner Herrlichkeit.

How could this German patriotic passion, which was
the strongest feeling in Treitschke, identify itself with
Prussian politics ? The education he received in
school explains that.

It was not in the Universities alone that the apostles
of the Prussian idea taught. They were to be found

---

[1] H. von Treitschke was born at Dresden, 1834. His father
was General Eduard von Treitschke, who was in the service of
the King of Saxony, and who is frequently mentioned in the
"Memoirs" of the Duke of Saxe-Coburg-Gotha.

also in the secondary schools.   Treitschke, at Dresden, had for his master, in 1849, one of these men— Dr. Böttiger.   This doctor taught his pupils not to consider France the classical land of liberty, as the German Radicals taught at that time: but that, on the contrary, " nothing was more fatal to liberty than the spirit of the French people."   And to prove this he told them the history of the French Revolution in the manner of Sybel.

When this teaching was complete, he then showed them the only State that was able to give Germany what she lacked—liberty and unity: and to do this he told them the history of Prussia.

Treitschke profited wonderfully from these lessons. At fourteen years of age, when the crisis of 1848 was at its height, he had shown Republican inclinations. Without going as far as his comrades, who, he says, "wore next to their hearts the portrait of Robert Blum, that Christ offered up in sacrifice to tyranny," he tells us he offered up prayers for the election of General Cavaignac in France.   But a year later everything was changed.   The teacher entrusted to correct his opinions had converted him to other ideas.

At sixteen years of age Treitschke passionately denounced "the errors of the Frankfort Parliament," and severely condemned the "fatal policy of King Frederick William IV, who, by refusing to recognize the Imperial Constitution, gave the Radicals a pretext for crying treason." [1]

The University completed the political education of the young man.   Studying in various Universities, as is still done in his country, from 1850 to 1855, he gathered the celestial manna in turn at Bonn, Leipzig,

---

[1] Th. Schiemann, op. cit., p. 33.

Tübingen, Heidelberg, and Göttingen. It was at Bonn, where he made the longest stay, that he met his teacher, the historian Dahlmann, the man who, he says, had "the most decisive influence over his career."

Professor Dahlmann, who has left behind him in Germany a name rather than works, and the recollection of his teaching rather than a name, was one of those stolid temperaments, rather dogmatic and doctrinaire, who solve political questions by means of history. An ardent German patriot, Prussian, if not by birth at least by taste and aspirations,[1] he had been a professor first at Kiel, in that University which he called "an outpost of German culture in the North" to awaken in this people, too quick to forget, "the feeling of their German nationality."

But his first attempts had not been successful. The inhabitants of the duchies would not let themselves be convinced. They hissed the professor when he wished to prove to them that "Schleswig and Holstein were German countries," just as they hissed, a little later, one of his colleagues, Dr. Welcker, who wished, in the same University, to celebrate the twentieth anniversary of the Battle of Leipzig. The students, loyal subjects of His Majesty the King of Denmark, were not satisfied with this: instead of this anniversary they celebrated the recollection of some obscure fight—Schesteit—in which some Danish regiments had overthrown some Germans allied with some Swedes.

But Dahlmann was none the less on that account one of the most fervent apostles at Kiel of the Prussian idea, and the seed at length bore fruit.

---

[1] He was born in 1785 at Wismar, in Pomerania, then under Swedish rule.

Later he preached that idea in Hanover, at the University of Göttingen, where he was one of the famous "seven" whom the King, Ernst Augustus, dismissed for having protested against the suppression of the Constitution granted by his brother. After some years we find him again at Bonn, where a fruitful activity awaited him. There it was that Treitschke met him in 1852.

Dahlmann was what was called later a National Liberal, who strove against the influence of French ideas and recommended for Germany a Liberal Empire with Prussia at the head.[1]

For a moment, in 1848, he thought this hour had come. As a member of the Frankfort Parliament, it was he who drew up that famous Imperial Constitution to which Prince Bismarck was to render homage later by copying it for his Constitution of North Germany.[2] The failure of this enterprise caused the historian a feeling of grief that he never recovered from. In retirement at Bonn he wrote to his friend, Gervinus: "The best counsels in the world, when they come from any one who has no force at his disposal, are no longer of use to us. A master must assert himself, in the first place, wherever he comes from."

While waiting for the appearance of this master —and Dahlmann was certain he would appear—he prepared youth for his arrival. A powerful orator, he had a communicative warmth of soul. What struck

---

[1] Dahlmann undertook to prove that the constitutional ideas were embedded in the old German laws, and that in establishing them in Germany they were only giving the nation what was hers.

[2] The Prussian Crown Prince, afterwards William I, said of Dahlmann, in 1848 : "Dahlmann deserves the greatest credit for his idea of the new Constitution of German life."

one in all that he said was the force of his conviction. Thus it was that he influenced the young generation. He filled it with his faith by giving it the example of a blameless life and a most lofty character. " More than one young man," said Treitschke in the remarkable essay he devoted to his master, "has learned, by meeting this old man, the meaning of that wise saying: ' Knowledge ennobles the character.' "

And Treitschke was one of the first to let himself be influenced. " The day I met Dahlmann in my path," he said, " I saw clearly what I had to do and I undertook immediately to do it." [1]

What he acquired in the first place in his relationship with this man was the faculty of regarding life from the moral point of view.

From his early years Treitschke had set himself a high ideal of life. At fifteen years of age he wrote: " To be always upright, honest, and moral: to become a man, a man useful to humanity, a worthy man: that is what I mean to aim at."

To this ideal of life he was always faithful. From one end to the other his correspondence shows him to be a rough, frank, ardent, zealous man, unshakable in his principles, but full of kindness towards men.[2] Some of his actions do the greatest honour to his character.

With all this, Treitschke's was a rich nature, full of exuberance and vigour. He had a robust optimism, not that serene optimism of the self-satisfied, but the optimism of a man who has suffered and struggled

---

[1] Th. Schiemann, p. 47.

[2] It is worth noting, for example, that the oldest friend of Treitschke, who was one of the bitterest anti-Semites in the country, was a Jew, Alphonse Oppenheim.

and who has not allowed himself to be beaten by misfortune. When quite young he gave proofs of this. The deafness from which he suffered was accidental. It came upon him after a sickness of childhood—the measles. He endured this test with admirable courage.

"There opened before my enraptured gaze the joyous path of happiness, rich in hope," he wrote in an epistle in verse addressed to his father; "I ought to keep to it with all my strength and stand firm in the midst of the storms and commotions of the world." All his life Treitschke remained a man of struggle and of duty. Dahlmann had taught him that the fatherland required sacrifice on the part of all its children. He resolved to devote his whole existence to it. He needed courage for such an undertaking, for it was to demand the sacrifice of his dearest tastes.

Treitschke had a poet's nature. What he showed first in his youth was literary gifts. He began by publishing two collections of verses, "Vaterländische Gedichte" (1856) and "Studien" (1859). Later he wrote a play. Science had no attractions for him. With an imaginative turn of mind, he declared he had difficulty in submitting to the harsh discipline of political and social sciences, of law and history. He complained of allowing himself to be "too much controlled by his impressions." But his patriotism supported him. He had sworn to become a politician and a historian, and he kept his oath. He devoted himself energetically to the driest of studies and to those most contrary to his nature, and in the end he succeeded. At twenty-two years of age his scientific accomplishments were very considerable.

When he became a political historian, Treitschke adopted entirely the ideas of his master, Dahlmann.

Dahlmann was a Prussian Liberal who regarded
liberty as depending on the power and not on the
will of the nation, and who believed that the Hohenzollern's mission in Germany was to bestow on that
great country constitutional institutions.

Treitschke also became a Prussian Liberal.. He
wrote in 1860 : " It is only as a constitutional State
that Prussia can become a true centre for all the
Germans."

But even at that time we can see that he is more
Prussian' than Liberal. If he does not like what is
still feudal in the Hohenzollern State, and if he has
small liking for the squires—" those noblemen infected
with a narrow orthodoxy and full of prejudices "—he
does not the less on that account consider Prussia the
first among the German States. " It is Prussia," he
said, " who has done everything great that has been
done in Germany since the Peace of Westphalia."
He also said, " Her existence is the best political
work of the German people." And he draws this
consequence from it :—

" The institutions of Prussia, her law, army, navy,
posts, telegraphs, and banks, should be enlarged so as
to become those of all Germany."

Treitschke's first act as a historian was to work for
the purpose of spreading these ideas. For this
purpose he wrote a small work entitled " Sociology "
(" Gesellschaftswissenschaft," Leipzig, 1859).

What had sociology to do with Prussian politics?
This is exactly what he wished to show.

At the time when Treitschke published this work,
all the historical sciences had been renovated in
Germany by the application of the historical method :
this had happened first with law by Gneist and
Jehring, then with political economy by Roscher, and

finally with literature by Julian Schmidt.[1] And
all these historians arrived at the same result, namely,
that these sciences should be conceived from the
national point of view. Sociology alone had been
left outside this movement. This was the gap that
Treitschke resolved to fill. In his " Sociology " he
wished to shòw " that there would be no political
science distinct from society "; that is to say, that
"every effort of national life always tends towards
reforms at once political, social, and religious."[2]

At bottom this book was nothing else to him
than the opportunity of showing two things: firstly,
that the theory of nationalities conformed with the
biological data of peoples; and secondly, that Prussia,
the only German State "of purely German character,"
was the "centre" around which subdivided Germany
should be joined again. This is what he had to prove.

Treitschke had satisfied himself that in a country like
Germany, where science enjoyed so much credit, one
could get anything accepted if it had a scientific
gloss.   And thus it was that, after stating the principles
of sociology, he shows that the "stages of Prussian
politics" are predicted by this science. Sociology
also teaches him that in "little States monarchy has
never been anything but a caricature." Five years
before Prussia settled on the battlefield the question
of Schleswig-Holstein, Treitschke solved it by
sociology. "Political science," he said, "cannot speak
of a German Confederation without declaring why it

---

[1] We might even add, according to the Prussian national point
of view. This is especially true with respect to the history
of " German Literature from the Death of Lessing," by Julian
Schmidt, in which Treitschke admired " the inspiration at once
national and Protestant."

[2] " Die Gesellschaftswissenschaft," p. 55.

makes out quite a different case when dealing with Schleswig-Holstein annexed by Denmark, than when dealing with Hungary annexed by Austria. It is only when political science perceives the inseparable connection between political and national points of view that it has the right to discuss one of the cardinal questions of our time—the one which justifies the theory of nationalities." [1]

Was Treitschke deceived by his words? To see the contempt he professed elsewhere for "pure science," one would think he scarcely was. At the very moment when he was settling all these political questions by means of sociology he was attacking in his letters "the old German science which had done so little for the development of national life."

"Germany has thought only too much," he said; "it is time she acted." And in accordance with these ideas this great despiser of science wrote to his father: "I want to see men : to live their lives and visit their technical and agricultural institutions." [2]

Treitschke clearly did not like science save for the advantage one derived from it. He constantly constrained it for political and national purposes. He did not cultivate history in the silence of his study. He brought it into touch with reality. Whatever happened in the street or on the battlefields immediately had its counter-stroke in his lectures.

Treitschke was par excellence the man of the political present. Day by day in his ideas one can follow outside influences. With events his opinions were modified, and he is thus quite ready to become the leader of public opinion. It was of him in particular

---

[1] "Die Gesellsch.," p. 14.
[2] Th. Schiemann, pp. 71, 98.

that Lord Acton was able to say with truth : " They brought history into touch with the nation's life, and gave it an influence it had never possessed out of France : and won for themselves the making of opinions mightier than laws." [1]

II

The professorial career of Treitschke is divided into three parts of unequal duration and importance. The first, which might be called the period of initiation, goes from 1859 to 1866 : its theatre of action was in turn the Universities of Leipzig and Freiburg. The second period includes the years which Treitschke spent at Kiel and Heidelberg until 1875. The third, which extends until his death in 1896, covers his teaching at Berlin University.

Between 1859 and 1866 the great political events in Germany were the constitutional struggle in Prussia and the campaigns in Denmark and Austria. At that time Treitschke is still Liberal and hostile to the policy of Bismarck, in whom he sees " a sort of Polignac who seeks in war a counter-irritant to internal troubles." At the critical moment of the constitutional struggle in Prussia, Treitschke, who is frankly opposed to the Prussian Government, wrote an essay on liberty in which he says : " Whatever new and fruitful has been done in the nineteenth century is the work of Liberalism." But it is not difficult to see that even then Treitschke does not regard liberty as a Stuart Mill or a Laboulaye would—as being something good in itself.

He only wants it on certain conditions. In the first place it must be dependent on institutions. " Liberty," said he, rests on " national life wisely organized and on a good administration rather than on the power of parliaments." In short, the national question rather than political questions really occupies his attention. He expressed this in 1863 in a lecture given on the occasion of the fiftieth anniversary of the Battle of Leipzig: "One thing is still wanting—the State. . . . Our people is the only one which has no general legislation, which cannot send representatives to the great concert of the Powers. No salvo salutes the German flag in a foreign port. Our fatherland at sea has no flag—like the pirates."

The unity and greatness of Germany have a greater hold on his heart than political forms. He has but one desire—the German fatherland. These words, "the German fatherland," turn up again and again like a refrain in his speeches. And between 1863 and 1870 he made a great number of speeches.

He availed himself of every occasion—the anniversaries of poets or men of letters like Uhland, Lessing, and Fichte; meetings of singing and choral societies—to cry out in every key : "We have no German fatherland. The Hohenzollern alone can give us one." [1] His programme becomes clearer and clearer. He divests it, as of ballast, of all the Liberal claims, and he retains Prussia alone : "What I want," he said, "is a monarchical Germany under the Hohenzollern : the exclusion of the princely houses : Prussian annexations : now who can pretend that all that will be done pacifically ? " [2]

---

[1] In one of his letters dated 1859 we can see that he has found out William I. "All our hope is in him," he said. ". . . Yes, Germany is going to bleed once more for the liberty of the world, as she did two hundred years ago, but this time there will be a strong Prussia at her head, and the result will be better than that unfortunate Peace of Westphalia ! " (Th. Schiemann, p. 142).

[2] Ibid. p. 146.

Treitschke always expressed these feelings with great energy. No one was a greater enemy of *particularismus* than he. And what is most strange is that he was then expressing these opinions without hesitation in the midst of Saxon territory, at the University of Leipzig, on the eve of the war with Denmark. In accusation of the diplomatists of the Southern States, such as Malchus, Wangenheim, Beust, and Pfordten, he cried : " They are diplomatic mercenaries ready to enter the service of any State which will open a field for their ambition."

Beust was at that time the all-powerful Minister in Saxony. Treitschke was denounced to him in 1862 as a dangerous enemy : a year later the historian left the old Saxon University to go as Professor of Modern History to Freiburg University.

Treitschke was no less an opponent of Catholicism than of *particularismus*. In this University in the South of Germany, Catholic in spirit, he saw he had other struggles to wage, and he announced as the subject of his first lectures the history of the Reformation in Germany and the history of the Republic of the Low Countries, or, as he said, of the heroes of the Netherlands and the oldest seat of religious tolerance.[1] He immediately scandalized every one. The Bishop forbade his lectures to the Catholics. Treitschke retorted. He turned on the clergy, the gang of priests (die Pfaffen), as he said, who were plotting against him. He declaimed against the thickheaded Ultramontane stupidity and the hypocrisy of theologians unworthy of an honest man."

---

[1] Treitschke regarded this post as a " fighting one." He owed his nomination to the friendship of the Badenese Minister, Karl Mathy, a Liberal whom he had known at Leipzig, where he had been, a few years before, the manager of an important bank.

But he stood firm. Although he found the "soil extraordinarily hard to work" and the "seed slow in growing" he did not become discouraged. "This struggle," he said later, "has not been useless to me, for in it I have learned to know better the less known sides of German life. . . . I see more clearly every day that the opposition between Catholics and Protestants is infinitely more deeply founded than most people think. It is not a question of a difference between a few dogmas, but of the opposition between slavery and liberty."[1]

At the moment when Treitschke was strengthening his Prussianism, the Austro-Prussian conflict burst out. The whole of the South was against Prussia. At Freiburg, in particular, popular excitement was very great. All the Hohenzollern partisans were attacked. Treitschke in particular was singled out. The threatening mob crowded before his house. Offensive notices against "the Prussian" were pasted on his door. He just had time enough to pack his trunk and slip off to Berlin. Treitschke had no doubt but that a solemn hour in his life had just struck.

In fact, Sadowa was the crowning event of his life. On the next morning Treitschke found himself a new man. From the political point of view he definitely severed his connection with the Liberals and was entirely converted to the Prussian policy, which hitherto he had opposed more or less. His volte-face was as complete as it was rapid. Without further ado, moreover, he said: "A King who so quickly brought about so fine a stroke is right against everybody." "It must be recognized," he said, "that the glorious results of that day have been attained, not

---

[1] Th. Schiemann, p. 213.

as the reactionaries think by the Conservative party, but by the people in arms: but not yet by means of liberalism, but by the monarchical discipline of the army. This is what should not be forgotten."

No one could have bid his old companions farewell in a more cavalier fashion.

Treitschke needed, moreover, true courage to place himself at that time on the side of Prussia. His father, the old Saxon General, had not ceased for months to denounce the "misdeeds of the Hohen zollern." "So long as I can distinguish right from wrong, black from white," he wrote to his son, "I shall denounce the present tendencies of Prussia as hateful and harmful." When the rupture was complete, the brave old man cried: "We see all these things with sorrow, but we have not lost our trust in God. Force overrules right. That is possible. But right is always right. If God has decided other- wise for Prussia, we still have the satisfaction of having done our duty to the end, and of not having let ourselves be eaten by the wolf without a protest." [1]

But Treitschke would hear nothing of this. The poet had his vision. For in the Prussian arms he, too, could see the hand of Providence, which was punishing the Hapsburgs for their "anti-German sins." "In spite of my sorrow," he cried, "I am happy to have lived in such time. It is in spite of all a great State to which I belong, and all the anger of the conquered will not prevent me from crying out that this is a great day for Germany." [2]

---

[1] Th. Schiemann, p. 240.

[2] At the moment he sounded this note of triumph, one of his brothers, fighting in the Austrian ranks, fell seriously wounded at Sadowa.

At this moment Treitschke's activity as a professor was interrupted. In retirement at Berlin he wrote articles for the newspapers and began a career as a publicist which, running parallel with his career as professor, was to be of the most fruitful.

Treitschke was, perhaps, the first political writer of his time. He had all the qualities of a journalist : a simple, direct, familiar, and picturesque way of saying things : a living and concrete style.[1] He was, more-over, just the kind of writer to suit that generation of iron, which had been brought up to the rattle of sabres. Treitschke, a soldier's son, had something of the soldier in him. Had it not been for his infirmity he would have been put to a military career. No career seemed finer to him. I doubt whether among the writers on purely military subjects there is one who equals Treitschke in his contempt for the middle-class mind.

It is in vibrating and vigorous phrases that sound like clarion calls that he brands the " pacific aspirations of industrial peoples." " Among the English," he said, "the love of money has killed all feeling of honour and all distinction between right and wrong. They hide their cowardice and materialism behind fine phrases of unctuous theology. When we see the English Press turning their eyes to heaven in horror

---

[1] There were at that time two great organs which defended the Prussian policy : the *Grenzboten*, published at Leipzig, and the *Preussische Jahrbücher*, at Berlin. Treitschke had made his first attempts at journalism in writing for that periodical during his stay at Leipzig. At Berlin he became one of the most assiduous writers for the *Preussische Jahrbücher*, of which he became the editor, which post he held until 1889. To-day it is edited by Hans Delbrück, who, like Treitschke, is a professor at Berlin University.

at the boldness of the warrior peoples of the godless
Continent, one might think he was listening to some
droning priest. As if the mighty God in whose name
Cromwell's Ironsides fought, ordered us Germans
to let the enemy march undisturbed to Berlin. O
hypocrisy! O cant! cant! cant!" [1]

It is in this lyric tone, also, that he speaks of the
great human scenes of slaughter and their moral
significance, putting his audience on guard against the
"middle-class sentimentalism" which preaches universal
peace, in his eyes "the most dangerous of Utopias."
"Every intelligent theologian understands," he added,
"that the Biblical injunction 'Thou shalt not kill'
should no more be taken literally than the apostolic
order to give one's goods to the poor. It is only a few
Quaker dreamers who cannot see in what a lyrical tone
the Old Testament celebrates the splendour of holy
and just wars. . . . While there are men on the earth
they will fight : the doctrine of the apple of discord
and original sin are things which history unfolds on
every page." [2]

Elsewhere it is in a sombre tone which recalls the
implacability of the Hebrew poets that Treitschke
celebrates war. "It does not suit the Germans," he
says, "to repeat the commonplaces of the apostles of
peace or the priests of mammon, nor to shut their eyes
at the cruel necessities of the age. Yes, our age is an
age of war, our age is an age of iron. . . . If the strong
prevails over the weak . . . it is an indisputable law of
life. Those hunger wars which we still see among the
black tribes are as necessary for economic conditions
in the heart of Africa as the holy war which a people
undertake to save the most precious possessions of

---

[1] " Zehn Jahre," p. 281.   [2] Ibid. p. 408.

their moral culture. There, as here, it is a struggle for life : here for a moral good, there for a material one." [1]

Sadowa came at the right moment to give a striking confirmation to the historian's thesis. " For a long time we have put forward our utmost efforts to show that Prussia alone had the necessary moral force to organize Germany on a new plan : the proof has just been given on the battlefields of Bohemia. The dreamer may groan to see refined Greece fall under the rough hand from Rome, but the politician's clear head will perceive at this conjuncture the superior justice of history." [2]

Such a man evidently would be a valuable recruit to the Prussian Government. Bismarck saw at once the advantage he would have from him for his policy. He did everything to win Treitschke over to himself. But he did not succeed. The historian, it is true, had no malice. " At a time when the Ministry goes back to the best traditions of Frederick," he said, " every good Prussian should be on the Government's side." [3] But he was proud. He had just been in opposition to Bismarck's policy. He remembered that. And he did not wish his liberty to be taken from him. " I refused Bismarck's offers twice," he said in one of his letters, " because I did not wish to lose my reputation as an independent man, and I did not wish to serve a Government whose internal policy I had opposed." [4] Moreover, after Sadowa he thought the writer's occupation rather contemptible. " The man who holds the pen," he wrote, " feels bitterly the lack of value in his work. Every dragoon who strikes down a Croatian does more just now for the German cause than the

---

[1] " Zehn Jahre," pp. 275, 468.

[2] " Weltgeschichte ist Weltgerichte "—" Universal history is the tribunal of the world," he said.

[3] " Zehn Jahre," p. 153.   [4] Schiemann, p. 248.

most penetrating political brain with the finest cut
pen." [1]

With his fighting temperament, Treitschke needed
a more direct activity than that of a writer. Ten
months after his arrival at Berlin he took his seat once
more in a professorial chair. This was first at Kiel,
then at Heidelberg, until he came back to Berlin, where
he was to end in 1896 a glorious career.

At Kiel, where, since the Prussian annexation,
federal sentiments were still held, Treitschke struggled
in favour of Prussian centralization. "It is a mistake,"
he said, "to believe that Germany can become a
Federated State like Switzerland, America, or the
United Provinces—Germany should become a unified
and centralized monarchy."

Among the advocates of German unity, I do not
think that there is a more thorough one than Treitschke.
To listen to this Saxon, the King of Prussia should
have mediatized, after the war, all the rebel princes,
beginning with his own sovereign, the King of Saxony.
"Germany will not perish," he cried in merriment,
"even if this captain of Nassau takes the road to the
frontier with his cannon, his maid, and his seven
hens." [2]

Treitschke inaugurated there that Imperial policy
which made him the most detested Prussian in all the
little German Courts. "With Prussia victorious, the
sovereignty of the States is but a myth," he cried; "their
existence rests only on the goodwill and moderation of
Prussia. . . . It is only faithfulness to the Empire
that can assure the maintenance of the dynasties, just
as it is only treason against the Empire that can cast
them into the abyss. Let them look to themselves at

_____

[1] "Zehn Jahre," p. 91.   [2] Ibid. 113p. .

Munich and Dresden : if ever the old spirit of the Confederation of the Rhine should awaken, the Empire will take up the gauntlet, and in order to accomplish her historico-universal task, will not hesitate at the most radical means of bringing about political unity—those employed by the British Government when it united Scotland and England one day. Towards the disobedient or recalcitrant members, the monarchical Empire is not obliged to have the deference of a Federated State. . . . The issue of such a struggle, that is, of powerlessness against power, of selfishness against an ideal, cannot be in doubt." [1]

From that moment on Treitschke only regarded force in politics. Sadowa had performed the miracle of making a monarchical Liberal into a despotic Cæsarist.

The appearance of a man like Bismarck on the German scene was not unconnected with this strange metamorphosis. As with so many others of his fellow-countrymen, this extraordinary power imposed it on him. He had many heart-searchings. "What is thought," he cried, "in the face of action?" From that time on old Germany, thoughtful, learned, and artistic, seemed very trivial by the side of this hero of will power. He could see a civilization already springing from the Hohenzollern victories, and in a prophetic tone he cried, " It was Julius Cæsar's work that made the Augustan age possible: Louis XIV could only come after Richelieu." [2]

Treitschke always denied wishing to favour hero-worship or encouraging in his country the cult of great men. " The temptation to raise altars to genius," he said, " is, of all the dangers which threaten

[1] " Zehn Jahre," pp. 591–2.
[2] " Historische und Politische Aufsätze," ii. 250.

the historian, perhaps the greatest." [1]   From this danger he has certainly not escaped. His whole work is here to witness to it. No historian has attached more importance to the personality of great men. He even had a theory on the subject which he thus summed up : " The great man can only be born in a state of advanced civilization. He is the product of the race, of the moment, but it is he by his individual energy who solves the great crises from which nations arise regenerated. Peoples do not obtain a universal position save thanks to the great men who know how to utilize their forces. . . . We cannot, for example, imagine modern England without William III." [2]

It is true he did not deify all the heroes of history. He drew distinctions between them. He classified them into two categories, the good and the bad ones. The good ones in his opinion are those who " have faithfully placed their strength at the service of history," or, in other words, those who have devoted themselves entirely to the good of the State. The others are those men who, in their power, have only pursued selfish ends—the satisfaction of an insatiable ambition. A most subtle distinction which it was necessary to illustrate by examples. Treitschke chose for that purpose Napoleon I.

Treitschke might have given to the enormous study which he devoted to Napoleon I—a study which fills half a large volume in octavo—the sub-title : An Essay on the Folly of Greatness. To him the Emperor of the French is a monster. If he does not go so far as to refuse to admit any genius in him, at least he makes him an abnormal and evil-

---

[1] " Historische und Politische Aufsätze," i. 28.
[2] Ibid.

doing genius. He denies him the talents of a real statesman. " True monarchs," he said, " are recognized by their having been greater during peace than during war : but Napoleon never showed this." [1]

Even in war he doubts whether Napoleon revealed the qualities of a great leader: he calls him "a grandiose Attila, a monstrous Jenghizkhan," a representative of the most detestable kind of soldier, " he who likes war for itself alone." And setting out with this idea, Treitschke, before Taine, develops with great effect the famous comparison of the Italian condottiere which Stendhal had first laid down. " With his powerful brain," he said, " so different from the small Celtic ones, with his sudden and savage passions, Napoleon was from head to foot an Italian of the fifteenth century, who owed his strange fortune less to his genius than to circumstances which themselves have their explanation in certain peculiarities of the French character."

Thereupon Treitschke sets himself to lay down, by means of Bonaparte,[2] the psychology of the French people, a psychology of an extraordinary relief, in which the defects of the nation are shown up in a hard and brutal light, while the good qualities are carefully left in the shade.

Every one knows that psychology of the French people which the German historians have brought into fashion in the nineteenth century. The Frenchman is the turbulent, vain Gaul, a lover of equality and glory, chivalrous and gallant, ardent and generous, carrying his patriotism to heroism, yet without being able to devote himself to the accomplishment of his

[1] " Hist. und Pol. Auf.," iii. 74.
[2] The essay has the title, " The Political Life of France and Bonapartism " (iii. 43–427).

daily task,[1] lacking seriousness, having a contemptible
(künmerlich) notion of right which explains his frequent Revolutions and coups d'Etat at home and his
constaht aggressions against his neighbours abroad,[2] and
never understanding glory as other nations have done,
and having never, in the matter of government, "known
the middle path between subjecting others and being
subjected himself."

By means of this summary psychology Treitschke
explains the whole history of modern France since the
Revolution.   "The middle-class Frenchman, being
born subordinate," he said, "had never produced really
fruitful works in the political, moral, and artistic world.
Everything with him is uniform, law, the army, finance,
education, the Church, the University, even art and
science."[3]   "For all to obey the same idea," he said,
"to have the same faith, to this uniformity has France
sacrificed the inestimable advantages of independent
politics and the free movement of religious life:[4]
in politics the Frenchman is always a minor ; he alone,
in this century, has known complete absolutism :[5] with

---

[1] "The nation," said Treitschke, "has the habit of excusing
itself from any attempt at duty by a bon mot—a ' que voulez-vous,
c'est plus fort que moi' " (iii. 129).   Elsewhere : " It is clear that
there is none of that true democratic simplicity among the
French.   Even during the period of chivalry, it was they who
spread throughout the world the honour of chivalry and gallantry "
(iii. 56).   Finally : "Every Frenchman tries to shine. Envy is
his pet sin " (p. 57).

[2] "The wars of pillage (Raubkriege) of Louis XIV and the
conquests of Napoleon had no other origin.   The French have
a Roman conception of glory : national arrogance and military
pride " ("Hist. und Pol. Auf.," iii. 75).

[3] "The nation," he said, "does not let any one go beyond these
uniform ideas of the majority : it fears the destruction of the
all-powerfulness of the State " (iii. 60).

[4] Ibid. p. 58.   [5] Ibid. p. 62.

him the police have become the providence of the peaceful citizen and the terror of the disturber of order : [1] his spirit has always been refractory to the simple notion of liberty : he needs to be led, to receive a word of order, and that is why the political form which has always best corresponded to his genius is bureaucratic centralization." [2]

Napoleon—and in this alone he showed genius—understood what the people needed and gave it to them. His work was absolutely according to " the logic of French history," political and administrative centralization.[3]

It was also according to the logic of the history of the French people " to molest and dominate their neighbours." Napoleon admirably understood this instinct : all the wars of the Empire have their origin in it.[4] This is a warning to the Germans : they should

[1] " Hist. und. Pol. Auf.," iii. 60.

[2] " When the leaders of the German Liberals show us in the ' bold Frenchman the born Republican,' and in the German ' the docile monarchist,' they misunderstand the absolutely monarchical instinct of the French people. The French language alone knows the expression of sovereignty. . . . What is called the ideas of '89 is not in reality anything but a troubled chaos of despotic and liberal ideas which exclude each other. . . . The French bureaucratic centralization is the most odious one known. . . . It is Paris alone that awards the patents of genius to the French people. France is the only country in which the word provincial is synonymous with stupidity and narrowmindedness " (" Hist. und Pol. Auf.," iii. 50–70).

[3] " Napoleon found in centralized administration the form which suited him, and which unhappily will last as long as the needs and views of this people are not changed completely " (iii. 52).

[4] " The plan of Napoleon absolutely determined the policy of France in modern history . . . we can see that quite well to-day, when they are coming to the surface again " (Ibid. p. 83).

be on their guard, for their liberty and their national independence run the greatest dangers.[1]

It would be wrong to think that these opinions of Treitschke on French policy are inspired by hatred of France. On the contrary, Treitschke liked many things in the French temperament. " The nation," he said, " pleases me more than it does most of my fellow-countrymen." He admired the elasticity with which the nation recovered from evils that seemed irremediable. He willingly acknowledged the services which great Frenchmen had done to human thought : Pascal, Molière, and Mirabeau.

He attacked the Teutomaniacs, " those spiritual æsthetes," as he called them, who, in trying to prove by ethnology that the French race did not exist and other such nonsense, " bring ridicule upon the German name " : he admired the spirit of the French Reformation,[2] which gave the world the finest form of Protestantism—Calvinism. [3] When he heard his

---

[1] " The French will make the liberty of the world run the greatest dangers . . . if the German people do not mount guard " (Ibid. p. 83).

[2] " We Protestants," he said, " cannot see the sudden convulsions of the nation without regretting that criminal act which drove evangelical faith out of France. When among a bold and intellectual people there was no choice save between the Church and blank negation, terrible collisions have taken place and horrified society has sought safety in servitude."

[3] Treitschke has attributed whatever great things have been done in France rather too much to the Protestant spirit. If he acknowledges that " the parliamentary attempts of the French do not deserve complete contempt " (iii. 115), he gives the honour of them to the Protestant doctrinaires. He also says : " We Germans ought not to forget that France in these social struggles has suffered for the rest of the world " (iii. 228) ; and he recognizes that the French Radicals, whose ideas he certainly did not like, gave proof of a magnificent spirit of sacrifice and heroic valour (229).

fellow-countrymen thunder against "the vices of modern Babylon," he could not refrain from directing their attention to what was happening at home. " Are we," he said, "so superior to the French from the moral point of view that we can thus reproach them ? If the French are fond of women, we Germans are willing gluttons, and I don't know which of the two things is the better."

But while rendering justice to the qualities of the Frenchman regarded individually, Treitschke did not like his politics. He liked them all the less that, while between 1867 and 1869 he was writing this essay, he was a professor at the University of Heidelberg. There, in the country of the Necker and the Rhine, quite close to the French frontier, people were still under the influence of "the theories, as seductive as fallacious, of the Great Revolution." That was the "virus he must stamp out," and, under the cover of drawing a portrait of Napoleon, show that "such a historical monster" could not have been possible save with a nation like the French, which had never had "the sense of liberty."

To indicate, at the same time, what Germany had to do at home, Treitschke outlined for his fellow-countrymen the quite recent history of the formation of Italian unity with the central figure of Camille de Cavour, whom he clearly contrasted as a "good genius" with the evil genius of Napoleon.

I do not think that Treitschke ever felt a greater admiration for a man than for Cavour, unless it was, later, for Bismarck. The Italian, in his eyes, had all the gifts of the statesman : the sovereign clearness of mind, the simplicity of genius, common sense and moderation. Cavour had for a long time filled his attention. Even when he was at Kiel he made him the object of his meditations. "For a long time," he said in one of his letters, "nothing has so powerfully taken hold of me as the appearance of this man. His absolutely practical genius is immeasurable. It differs, it is true, from that of the great poets and thinkers who are so familiar to us Germans, but in the face of the world's riddles he is as great in his way as Goethe or Kant."

While Treitschke was writing these studies, in which reference to the politics of the day is manifest in each line, the political horizon of his country became obscured and war broke out between France and Germany.

If it had depended on him alone, this war would never have broken out, for he saw in it "the beginning of a struggle to the end between the two nations." But the way in which the situation was entered upon, showing him the Frenchman as the aggressor, awoke all his old illwill "against this people of lansquenets" who wished to rule the world. At the noise of the military preparations the warrior that was in him awoke, and he wrote the finest poem that appeared in Germany inspired by the war of 1870. He called it "The Ode of the Black Eagle." He says: "May thy wings rustle powerfully!—O Black Eagle whose clear gaze— looks upon the shining arms—of thy bands of Teuton heroes—O how it is long since thou didst fly away— from the Swabian castle of thy birth—that thou comest back victorious?—two centuries! Our people with joyful presentiments—followed the path which thou didst open—Shall we find our lost happiness—will the Empire of the Hohenstaufen return again?

"Hark! the shameless Frank—envies and longs for our happiness—and in his coarse rage—laughs at our old King—Arise, German warriors!

Valiant horseman, bestride thy charger! Hunter, leave thy retreat! All ahead for the last blood-red journey ! For the laurel of victory : Give us back Strassburg Cathedral—and give up the German river."

When victory followed victory, Treitschke's joy knew no bounds. At last he saw the realization of his dreams. This war assumed a symbolical meaning. He cried out one day : " In the great crises in the life of peoples war is always a less violent remedy than revolutions, for it guarantees faithful performance and its results seem like the judgment of God."

And now he sees infinite perspectives open out for Germany. For him the historico-universal rôle of his country begins. He sees her already "sweeping away the heavy vapours, the impurities and the disgusting debauches of the Second Empire." [1] This victory is not in his eyes the brutal triumph of force, but the triumph of an idea. A new era is opened for humanity, and Germany, "with her rich moral culture, will become the teacher of peoples." [2]

France in his eyes represented two things : revolutionary demagogism and clericalism. The victories of Prussia removed for a long while these two dangers from Europe. The new Empire that was being formed was to show the astonished world what was " a national and truly free State, based upon the recognition of the rights of the individual."

Treitschke had always been very Protestant in sentiments as well as the bitter opponent of Ultramontanism. He said, too, that Protestantism was "the mark of the German spirit."

German and Catholic were in his eyes two terms which clashed when brought together. " Never has the true German," he cried, " been able to submit to

[1] " Hist. und Pol. Auf.," ii. 559.
[2] " Zehn Jahre," p. 284.

any religious rule save that of his own conscience. The Jesuitic faith has always been foreign to the spirit of our people. . . . On this heretical soil it has never been able to take root."

And carrying his theory further still, he tries to prove that what has best upheld the cohesion of the German race in the world is Protestantism. " Everywhere," says he, " it has been the solid rampart of language and customs. In Alsace, as in the mountains of Transylvania and on the distant banks of the Baltic, as long as the peasant sings his old hymn:

A mighty Fortress is our God

German life will be in no danger of disappearing." [1]

After 1870 Treitschke, who had a little of the illuminati in him, thought that the Prussian victories would gather all the Germans to the unity of the Reformed Faith. He began to preach this new doctrine a little everywhere, in his lectures, in the pamphlets he published, in the Reichstag, to which he had just been appointed a deputy. Even as a politician he did not distinguish himself, save in the part he took in the Kulturkampf. He announced with the gravity of a Messiah that Germany, who, with Luther and Kant, had given to the world the Reformation, tolerance, gravity, morality and liberty, would be able at length to regenerate the universe. " The greatest future," he said, " is in store for Prussia, the greatest Protestant Power of modern history." And he added : " It is she who will help other countries to cast off the shackles of the Catholic Church and strengthen the national power of the State." [2]

---

[1] " Zehn Jahre," p. 313.
[2] " Luther und die deutsche Nation," pamphlet, 1884.

By destroying the credit of the revolutionary ideas of French origin, Prussia's victory seemed to Treitschke no less decisive. For a long time already the political writers of his tendency had attempted to cure the German people of what they called "the stupid French imitation." But all the Germans had not been convinced.

With these victories they began to open their eyes. Treitschke was jubilant. He saw that now there would be no further necessity to refute "the Utopias of natural right and middle-class liberalism," or to try to prove that "in the life of a State that only is true which is based upon the historical right of the nation." Sedan was entrusted with this task. The Liberals disappeared as if by enchantment, and in great joy the historian exclaims: "There are now no longer any but our Socialists, who are still fed with the scraps from the French kitchen." [1]

Treitschke had a strange notion of socialism. He still was at that stage of thinking that socialism is refuted by the experience of daily life. "The Socialist's great mistake is to think that the aim of life is to gain possession of material advantages. The true happiness of existence," he added, "should not be sought in what is attainable by all men and in what is common to them all. It does not consist in the possession of economic advantages or political power or art: it exists in the sphere of feeling, in the pure conscience, in the strength of that love which places the simple above the cunning; it is especially in the power of faith." [2]

We now arrive at a curious page in Treitschke's

---

[1] " Zehn Jahre," pp. 466 and 516.
[2] Ibid. p. 488.

life: his Prussian patriotism brings about in him a last metamorphosis : it makes him a religious man.

Until that time Treitschke had passed for an unbeliever. He even willingly posed as " an emancipated son of the Reformation," and one day he had deeply grieved his father, the old Saxon General, who was very religious, by confessing himself to be, in one of his letters, a freethinker. But Treitschke, in spite of the loss of his childhood's faith, had remained deeply attached to Christian morality. No one in his country, perhaps, had branded in more eloquent terms the corruption of his time. "Corruption has entered the moneyed world and the upper classes," he exclaims with reference to the Germans in Austria. "The Press of Vienna is the most shameless in Europe, without excepting that of France. The newspapers to-day are nothing but industrial enterprises, and the honest man who would presume to speak of morality to these literary speculators would be laughed at to his face. . . . And it is not merely the great political organs that are the prey of speculators. By the side of these newspapers swarms a cloud of dirty little sheets which positively live on extortion and piracy, for in that town of easy morals, venal consciences are numerous, and when a rascal's mouth must be shut, money is no object."[1]

Elsewhere, branding English hypocrisy, he cries: " In the Parliament that mercantile morality of the English was talked, which, a Bible in one hand and a pipe of opium in the other, spreads throughout the world the blessings of civilization."

Throughout his work you can notice that idealism which he wished to make the distinctive characteristic

---

[1] " Zehn Jahre," p. 370.

of the German race. He thought that if Germany had a mission to fulfil in the world it was to imbue the masses with more morality.

Now after 1870 he witnessed a strange sight: these victories on which he had counted so much to give examples of virtue to the world had resulted in quite the contrary effect. Triumphant Germany saw a new society arise, composed of most heterogeneous elements. A crowd of business men, more or less suspicious in character, Jewish financiers, stockbroking interlopers, rushed to the Prussian capital, which they made a field of speculations. All these people, of course, came to increase the ranks of the winning party, so that soon National Liberal meant in Germany what Opportunist meant later in France: men who made use of the Government to do business. The aged Ranke, from his solitude, saw with sorrow this transformation of manners, whose suddenness stupefied him. "Everything is falling to pieces," he said; "religion is overthrown: soon no one will be baptized nor will marriages be solemnized: the sacredness of an oath is no longer respected. There is nothing but industry and money. . . . The origin of all this evil is in our new institutions, and yet we cannot change them."[1]

Treitschke had also reached a similar state of thinking. He, who had called with all his prayers for the advent of this free and enlightened class, "found that the result did not come up to his expectation": the old ties were dissolved, and in this new society, eager for enjoyment, he could already see signs of decadence.

As opposed to this Liberal society, on the other hand, he saw that it was the old Prussian Conserva-

---

[1] L. von Ranke. " Zur eigen. Leben.," p. 597.

tives, those whose narrow and limited ideas, whose
sectarian spirit and formal rigidity he had formerly
combated, who now best realized his moral ideal.
Like that German Liberal who said one day to
Victor Cherbuliez: " Yes, these men are all of a
sort, limited in their ideas, rigid as bars of iron; but
most of them have a great quality, rare enough in
this century of jobbing—a perfect uprightness that
surprises me. Politics has turned most of us Democrats more or less crooked " [1]—like this Liberal,
Treitschke discovered that it was still these men
who best represented in his country the old ideas of
uprightness and morality. From that to identifying
himself with their policy was but a step, and
Treitschke was all the more prepared to take that
step as he had written as far back as 1867 : " The
Conservative tendency, whose rightfulness hatred
alone can deny in Prussia, will now find a fruitful
sphere of action." [2]   And this, no less significant :
" The true Prussian Conservatives are nearer to us
than the idle babblers who are satisfied only to talk
about unity in their patriotic speeches." [3]

The only question then was the devotion of the
squires to the Hohenzollern. Now it was their hatred
of liberalism and parliaments that he admired in them.
" What need is there of a parliament ? " he cried.
" Has such an assembly realized the hopes placed in
it ? Have we not our King ? And is our King a
docile instrument in the hands of a few financiers,
as was that shopkeeping merchant of Orleans who

[1] V. Cherbuliez, "L'Allemagne politique depuis la paix de
Prague" (1870), p. 133.
[2] " Zehn Jahre," p. 192.
[3] Ibid. pp. 28–9.

T

was wanting so much in royal prestige? Does our State depend upon a few fat bankers?" [1]

That was the last stage of the political evolution of Treitschke. The man who had begun his career as a pure " Gothaer "; the man who, later, under the influence of the victory of Sadowa and Bismarckian policy, had been transformed into an Imperial and Radical supporter of German unity, became, towards the end of his life, a reactionary Monarchist, anti-liberal and anti-parliamentarian. He dropped one after the other all his old Liberal friends, whom he reproached for lacking "that rather massive solidity which alone makes true statesmen ": he became the partizan of all reactions, religious, political, and literary. Carried away by the logic of his ideas, he came to detest all the manifestations of modern life, and ended by proposing for our imitation a Teutonic ideal of the Middle Ages —the king, a knight without fear and without reproach, redresser of wrongs and defender of the weak.

With this ideal, we can understand how Treitschke in his country gradually descended to the most retrograde notions. He became an anti-Semite. This might have been foreseen. The Jew, through his qualities and defects, is the antipodes of this conception of feudal life. Is he not the modern man par excellence, free from prejudices, revolted by abuses and violence? A Rationalist in politics and religion, he is indeed the son of that French Revolution in which he took no part, but which corresponded to the two great dogmas of his history : " divine unity and Messianism : that is, the unity of law in the world and the triumph on earth of justice in humanity." [2]

---

[1] " Zehn Jahre," p. 516.

[2] J. Darmesteter, " Coup d'œil sur l'histoire du peuple juif," 1881.

Treitschke had scented, in this modern emancipated man, who is an element of reform and progress in all countries, the great enemy of the Teuton and feudal Germany he wished to bring into being again. Thenceforward the Jew became his enemy. He opposed him with all the bitterness of a sectarian. He enlisted in the band of the pastor Stöcker. He wrote to justify this odious anti-Semitism a pamphlet in which one may read, among other things :—

"If we consider what the Jews have done, this powerful agitation which is manifested to-day is only the natural reaction of popular German feeling against a foreign element which has already taken too large a place in our life. . . . Do not let us deceive ourselves : the movement is deep and powerful. . . . It has penetrated right into the most educated circles, and among men who would reject with horror any notion of religious intolerance or national pride there is but one cry : 'The Jew is the cause of our misfortune!'" [1]

It was a strange sight to see history taught in the first University in Germany by a man who, in his attacks on the Jews, used arguments worthy of Drumont, calling the Israelite, for example, "an Oriental without a country, whose ideas are fatal to all higher national life, having no passion but that of interest, never of politics or patriotism, and corrupting the pure German virtues by his corrosive irony and by his venal and unscrupulous Press."

---

[1] "Ein Wort über unser Judenthum." "It would be an injustice to a Hohenzollern," he wrote on the death of Emperor Frederick III, "to believe that he was capable of becoming the Emperor of the Liberals, that is, of the Berlin anti-Royalists, of professors who have lost their way in politics, of a few vexed merchants and the great international Jewish power" ("Zwei Kaiser," Berlin, 1888).

From that moment, Treitschke loses all value as a scientific historian. The political writer, who a few years before had begun with profound studies in which one could feel the happy influence of Tocqueville, became a sort of bitter sectarian, a zealot of nationalism. Thereby, it is true, he acquired great force. He also, perhaps, powerfully developed his personality thereby. But his credit as a historian is considerably shaken by it.

There are men who, as they grow old, become wiser and more and more moderate. With Treitschke the opposite happens. As the years pass his excesses are more marked, and it is in this spirit that he wrote his great work, "The History of Germany in the Nineteenth Century," which in some respects is scarcely history, to such an extent does the author's partizanship burst out on every page, but as this work is one of the most extraordinary creations of the New German Empire, we shall now study it in some detail.

III

Treitschke said : " One can only be the author of one book. The point is to find that one." He had the luck to write that book : it is his " History of Germany in the Nineteenth Century," which became the work of his whole life. One might even say that he dreamed of it from the moment he began his career as a historian. " I want to write," he said in 1861, " a history of the German Confederation, brief, straightforward, and very plain, to show the sluggish masses that we lack the basis of all political existence, law, power, and liberty, and that there is no safety for us except by the annihilation of the small States. . . . I can think of no more necessary historical work than this

one: and as among those who are more learned than
I there is no one who has the courage to undertake it,
I shall attempt it, although I run the risk, while I am
writing it, of seeing the Confederation sink beneath
the malediction of the peoples, and when I take my
professorial chair again—and I will do so, for I know
now how fine it is to be a teacher of youth—this
work will have made me all the more able to influence
the new generation." [1]

In Treitschke's mind it was only a question at first
of making a large sketch "of what is already known
by collecting the scattered elements." [2]   But he was
not long in discovering that the work was more difficult
and longer than he had foreseen.   This discovery did
not rebuff him—quite the contrary.   When he saw
in it the occupation of his life, he rejoiced.

For twenty years, day after day, Treitschke collected
materials for this work.   From the year 1865 Prince
Bismarck had placed at his disposal the archives of the
Foreign Office, and said to him: " If you do not find
the linen of our politics of that time as clean as I could
wish, I hope, nevertheless, that you will never be obliged
to withdraw what you once said to me: ' Prussia, less
than any other State, has need to hide the past of her
federal policy.' "

When going deeper into his work, Treitschke enlarged
its plan considerably.   Instead of a history of the
German Confederation, it is the history of all Germany
during the nineteenth century that unfolds itself to his
eyes.   He read everything: newspapers, memoirs,
monographs.   And from all this he drew an immense
picture " of the life of the men," as he said himself,

---

[1] Th. Schiemann, p. 156.

[2] Ibid. p. 158.

" of the ideas and institutions which formed the new Germany." [1]

Treitschke conceived this history from a purely political point of view. He even ridicules somewhere in his work those historians of civilization who regard " Volta stooping upon his frogs' legs, or who count the lamps or the old pots down in graveyards." And yet he gives an important place to the manifestations of German life. As well as the great political subjects : the history of the Congress, the Prussian Kulturkampf, the organization of the Zollverein, which are pages of general history, each individual State is treated with marvellous care. Whether he is dealing with the great Powers, such as Prussia, Austria, Bavaria, Wurtemberg, or the central States, or even the very small principalities or free cities, we have a history in great detail, whose defect is almost that it is too detailed. Better still, in each State the provinces are studied in their proper character : with Treitschke you know what was in the nineteenth century Brandenburg, Posen, Pomerania, or the Rhine Province, and what sort of life the peasants, middle class, and nobles led there. And Treitschke does not describe this in general characteristics more or less vague : he tries to show up their life in its daily details. His process is that of the realist painters, who in a few typical facts give us a picture of the whole.

Treitschke is an incomparable chronicler. His history of the Congress of Vienna, for example, is a marvel. We see not only all the ministers and diplomatists pass before us—the great ones like Metternich, Nesselrode, Capodistrias, Consalvi and " the rich group of clericals": the smaller ones, such as the representatives of the

---

[1] " Deutsche Gesch. im XIX. Jahr.," i., Preface vi.

Hanseatic towns "with their group of intriguers, parasites, and beggars"; but also the people of the background, such as that enormous Lady Castlereagh, whom he shows us "with her curling-irons, her languorous airs, and loud toilets." And behind all this brilliant moving world, an amusing picture of Viennese life, "that town of Pheacians," as he calls them, with its eternal Sundays, and turnspits everlastingly turning.[1]

And if you consider that from one end of this vast history, which fills five volumes, to the other it is just the same: that there is in it a description of all the German towns according as their history is told: descriptions of the Universities, lectures, even of the smallest principalities, with amusing details about the Gothic customs of these remnants of another age: a description of all the great German fêtes, even of the historical pageants organized for such or such an anniversary, you will understand the charm that belongs to this work. German life is represented in it with a power of description which equals Macaulay, and with rather more research behind the details and something more brilliant in the form.

Such a work, which completely departed from the purely scientific conception of German historiography, could not be improvised. Treitschke wrote it slowly, giving a great deal of attention to form. His style is extraordinarily crowded, energetic, and picturesque.

Treitschke did not arrive at once at this concrete form. His passionate nature drove him at first into enthusiastic outbursts. In his first articles his phrases were those of an orator. Listen to him, for example, calling with his prayers for the political unity of Germany :—

[1] " Deutsche Gesch.," i. 602,

" All the books, all the works of art which reveal the nobility of German work : all the great German names which we regard with admiration : all that announces the glory of our spirit, proclaims the necessity for unity, conjures us to create in the political order that unity which already exists in the world of thought.   And our grief is tenfold when we think that each isolated work is so much admired, while our people as a whole are ridiculed abroad." [1]

Some of his invocations have remained famous in Germany,:—

" Germans, my dear fellow-countrymen," he cried at a school fête celebrating the fiftieth anniversary of the Battle of Leipzig, " you who dwell on the sea-shores where the lighthouses of Lubeck and the white cliffs of Arcona point out the fatherland to the sailor returning from a long voyage : you who come from the Helvetic Alps, mirrored in the great Swabian lake : you whose cradle is the grey Palatinate which dominates the Rhine; all you, of whatever race, what-ever canton you come from, join with me in crying, ' Long live Germany ! ' " [2]

But little by little Treitschke gets rid of his too oratorical phrases, he becomes more and more precise : for rather vague expansions of general ideas he sub-stitutes concrete words which bring up before one the image of things.   Already in his later essays the painter in him was revealed in the art of painting portraits and great historical pictures, and those who had read his sketch on Italian unity could not forget his most vigorous pages on the historical development of Piedmont, with the figure of Cavour, proudly set

---

[1] " Hist. und Polit. Auf.," ii. 86.
[2] " Zehn Jahre," p. 7.

up, radiant with truth, in his simple and pleasing realism.

But Treitschke only attained the perfection of historical narration with his history. His first volume was a revelation. At last Germany had a historian for whom the visible world existed, fit to grasp the drama and comedy of history, to describe in striking lines inanimate things, as this picture of the burial of Frederick William III will show:—

"The crowd lined the route in silence as, on the night of the 11th of June, the corpse passed down the long avenue of Unter den Linden on its way to the mausoleum at Charlottenburg, where the dead King had wished to lie by the side of his dear wife, Louisa. The lanterns were darkened: the moon alone, which came from behind the clouds, threw its pale light on the black carriages as they noiselessly glided over the soft sand." [1]

Elsewhere he shows us in a charming water-colour the King Frederick William III playing with his children " under the old trees of his park on the edge of the blue lake of Havel, condescending in the midst of them and even making the Countess von Voss, a strict guardian of etiquette, smile at his drollery." [2]

But it is especially as a portrait-painter that Treitschke distinguished himself. His historical portraits are certainly the most lifelike in all German historical writing. That, moreover, was an art in which his fellow-countrymen have never excelled. Bismarck said one day that what particularly distinguished an Englishman from a German is that the first attaches importance to the physical appearance

---

[1] " Deutsche Gesch.," v. 20.
[2] Ibid. i. 148.

of people and the other does not. " When Shakespeare painted Hamlet," he said, "he showed us a fat man, slow in movement, and when we saw the man we understood the character." [1]

But such a reproach cannot be offered to Treitschke : under his pen historical persons positively come to life. It is not so much the rapid vision of Michelet or Carlyle as the realistic portrait of Flaubert or Tolstoi. You see Baron Stein with his " little, thickset body, the large nape of his neck, his broad shoulders, his deep brown and sparkling eyes, his owl's nose over his thin lips "; Talleyrand with " his high cravat, his horrible mouth with black teeth, his little deepset, grey, expressionless eyes, his dreadfully common, cold and impassive features, incapable of blushing or of betraying the workings of his mind ";[2] King Leopold of Belgium, " small, tired, but distinguished features, with a sly and melancholy look, speaking in a slow, deep voice, always taciturn as much in his affairs as in his amours ";[3] King Maximilian of Bavaria, " the most middle-class of all the Kings, with his head that brought to mind at once a retired French colonel and a Bavarian brewer, stopping people in the street and talking familiarly with them."[4]

And Treitschke is not a painter of details only, but of whole pictures : his great historical scenes are admirable. I do not know anything more attractive than the painting he makes in his third volume of the patriarchal life of the Gothic Courts of North Germany, petrified in their superannuated customs.[5]

---

[1] Bewer, " Bei Bismarck," Dresden, 1891.

[2] " Deutsche Gesch.," i. 616.

[3] Ibid. iv. 83.   [4] Ibid. i. 611.

[5] " Altständisches Stilleben in Norddeutschland " (" Deutsche Gesch.," iii. 456–556).

His description of the Court of the old King of Saxony, Frederick Augustus, is a real genre picture. "The King had retained at Court the customs and etiquette of 1780, to the great joy of the people of Berlin. He had a fine talent for music, but he would only exercise it on Silbermann's old grand piano. On Sunday, when he went to Mass, the children of the better class families collected along the paths in his park to admire the magnificent cortège of the King: the grooms, the chamberlains and the adjutants walked in front: the King, in a magnificent old dress, his hair dressed as a Brutus wig and powdered, his hands concealed in a large muff, was at the head. Behind him walked the Princes Anthony and Maximilian, nearly as old as he, also carrying muffs, with their soft hats under their arms. A strange sight, at which only the simple Dresden people could have assisted without laughing. . . . The King was never met on foot in the street. Even when there came a menagery which he wished to see, he made the elephants, lions and serpents come into his park."[1]

What gives a great charm to Treitschke's narrative is his language, full, ample, musical, sometimes clothed in too sumptuous a style, but always of powerful effect.

Treitschke's vocabulary is of the richest. A rare thing for a German, he gives one at times the impression of being a most skilful juggler of words. One might say that language has no secrets for him. He said, moreover, that form should not be despised. "There is as much affectation in despising it as in running after it too much." And he added with Goethe: "The thought which ripens alone brings the accurate expression as the flower brings the fruit."

---

[1] " Deutsche Gesch.," iv. 506, 507.

In the matter of form, which at bottom is the matter of thought, Treitschke gives proof of a wonderful virtuosity. He foreshortens admirably in words—as, for example, when he says of the Czar Nicholas: " He was a subaltern of the best style, incomparable when required to drill a regiment, but in reality neither a general nor an administrator." The eccentric King Ludwig of Bavaria is described in a most attractive fashion in three strokes : " This intellectual artist was not in character when he had to speak his native tongue, which he treated cruelly. When he desired a work of art he willingly renounced all pleasure, but when he saw a pretty woman pass, nothing could hold him back. He would then declare his love to her with quite an Hellenic ardour, which was bound to cause a bit of scandal in our modern middle-class, sedate society."

To these qualities Treitschke added others : he was a witty German. Indeed, if one tried to discover what was his principal quality as a narrator, one would find it to be humour. His humour is of a very German kind : it resembles that of the Badenese poet, J. V. Scheffel, or that of Bismarck in his table-talk. When he was leaving the University, Treitschke showed his companions a rough sketch he had made, in which he ridiculed with much humour two German scholars who had come to blows as to whether the fish which swallowed Polycrates's ring was a herring or a pike.

Treitschke remained for the rest of his life the man of that rough sketch. Everything removed from his Teutonic ideal of purity of manners and military strength, of Prussian common sense, realistic spirit, he poked fun at with the same good-humour. He had in store a great number of jokes about the ridiculous side of life in the small States. On that subject his humour was astonishing. Hear him, for example, relate the military exercises of the Hamburg militia :—

" The greatest pleasure of the Hamburg people was to be present at the exercises of the citizen militia, which was composed of seven battalions of line troops, light infantry, cavalry, and artillery. These troops from the height of their greatness looked down upon the poor Hanseatics, who formed the regular army. What a great day it was when you saw these troops march through the streets of the town. The drum beat, ' Come, comrade.' The burgomaster with his three-cornered hat, his comic-opera sword at his side, reviewed the troops outside the gates of the town. After the parade there was a great drinking-bout : warriors, a little fuddled, re-entered the town with the vivandières, marching at walking pace, while the little street boys who went before them sang, to the air of ' Carry the pig to market,' the old national song :—

> The Hamburgers have won the victory,
> Ho ! Ho ! Ho ! "

Treitschke always excels in genre pictures. The anecdote is his forte. No one can tell as he tells the " stormy scenes in the Wurtemberg Landtag, the picturesque and amusing side of the college student, the story of the undercurrents at the Congress, the rivalries between the great men of little countries." He was thoroughly acquainted with all the scandals, the life at the Berlin theatres, the Philistine customs of the Radicals of Young Germany. In another part he gives us wonderful information about Rhenish Catholicism, on the return of the Jesuits to Austria, and on the religious ideas of Prince von Metternich. And he does all this with spirit and good-humour.

What could be prettier, for example, than this picture of the family life of King Frederick William IV and his Queen Elizabeth ?—

" Queen Elizabeth was certainly the person who had the greatest hold upon the King's heart. He devoted to her an unlimited tenderness, which surpassed, indeed, the degree of tenderness permitted to a king. When, bathed in tears and broken down with emotion, he rose from the bed where his father was laid dead, he said : ' Elizabeth, support me: it is now that I need strength.' When overburdened with affairs he returned to her, she always received him with the same evenness of temper, the same joy and love : it was only when a sudden access of temper put him beside himself she said, looking about the room : ' I am looking for the King.' She tried to make her happy family life as intimate as Court etiquette permitted. At the feast of Christmas-night the royal couple went down to walk in the castle grounds, and on the New Year's Eve the night-watchman had to come to the palace to announce with his trumpet the new year." [1]

Here is a picture of the same kind of the life of Queen Victoria and the Prince Consort about 1840 :—

" What pleased the English in this Court was the good behaviour of the house, the family life of the Queen, the punctuality with which she bore a child every year as quickly as the laws of nature permitted. The Court became once more a sort of social force, although it did not become, as in the time of the Stuarts, the centre pivot of life in the capital: however, the high society in London, frivolous at bottom, had at least to control their outward appearance according to the decent manners of the Court. For the first

---

[1] " Deutsche Gesch.," v. 17.

time since the accession of the House of Guelph the Court entered somewhat into the life of the nation, though less deeply than was imagined." [1]

In a humorous vein, there are in Treitschke's work several portraits that are not lacking in flavour, as, for example, this sketch of Lord Palmerston: "Lord Palmerston laughed at the sanctimonious airs of his fellow-countrymen, and confessed with all the sincerity of a 'bon vivant' how much he liked women and the pleasures of the world. Even in his old age he liked to be called Lord Cupid. When in the evening he came out from a long sitting of the Second Chamber with his elastic step, a flower in his button-hole, his umbrella across his shoulder and his tall hat slightly tilted to the back of his head, all his fellow-countrymen were delighted with this apparition of the old freshness of British life. His whole person exhaled an air of joyous satisfaction: with his strong, square Anglo-Saxon head, his bright eyes, which, wide apart from his nose, recalled at once the power of the bull-dog and the cunning of the fox. He was a good master to his servants and tenants, and he knew, according to the old custom of English nobility, how to find good places for his cousins and friends. And yet he had never been reproached for wittingly putting a fool into office." [2]

If the talent of drawing lifelike and amusing portraits, of telling good stories with spirit, sufficed to make a great historian, Treitschke would certainly be the first in his country. But something else is needed beside that. Beside a clear understanding of political problems, great impartiality is required. Had Treitschke that impartiality ?

---

[1] " Deutsche Gesch.," iv. 126, 127.   [2] Ibid. iv. 27.

When we open his history, the first thing that strikes us is the violence of his tone.   On every page we find phrases like these :—

"Metternich was the greatest liar and rascal on the Continent." [1]

"The Jews are the carrion birds of the misery of German peasants." [2]

"Whatever Government that France may take, she will always be the country of police, of soldiers lowered to the service of policemen, of partial tribunals, of phrases in Parliament, of the besottedness of the people and of Catholic fanaticism." [3]

"These Teutomaniacs were in reality hypocritical scoundrels." [4]

The Grand Duke Constantine's marriage is related in the following fashion: "On a sign from the Czarina the mother sent her three daughters, and the coarse Constantine threw the handkerchief to the youngest of them." [5]   The Court at Brussels becomes "the great matrimonial agency for the Courts of Europe." [6]

You have no need to go very far with this reading to see that you are not dealing with a real historian. The real historian respects his opponents, even though his ideas be diametrically opposed to theirs.   And this is all the more to be regretted as Treitschke has so much talent.

The historian says somewhere that in "their scientific discussions his fellow-countrymen often lose sight of the rules of good taste and politeness."   According to this, he himself is a national writer in the fullest sense of the term.

---

[1] "Deutsche Gesch.," iv. 265.   [2] Ibid. iv. 529.
[3] Ibid. iv. 423.   [4] Ibid. ii. 390.
[5] Ibid. iii. 85.   [6] Ibid. 86.

But was he always so, and did he always wish to be so?

Treitschke had a violent and passionate nature. His dearest friends acknowledged that he could not suffer contradiction. "He spoke freely," said one of them, "but he did not listen if any one answered him, and he was astonished if any one disapproved of what he said. He persisted in his point of view, and ended by breaking with his best friends." [1]

It must be acknowledged that these are bad conditions for writing history. What man can boast that he alone has the truth? Treitschke recognized this, and at first made praiseworthy efforts to acquire this impartiality. "I lack the calm style of a historian," he wrote to Sybel in 1864; "I become heated too quickly, but with time I hope to become a historian." Later he wrote again: "My blood is too hot for a historian: I read Thucydides to acquire the real historical style." Then suddenly Treitschke changes his opinion and begins to say that history should be written "regardless (Rücksichtlos), with anger and passion." [2]

He writes in one of his letters: "To be called an impartial historian is a reputation for which I have no aspirations: to ask that of me is impossible. . . . That anæmic objectivity, moreover, is surely contrary to true historical sense. . . . All the great historians have frankly acknowledged their partiality: Thucydides was an Athenian: Tacitus an aristocrat. . . . Let the facts be accurate: that is everything for the historian: for the rest, his judgment is his own." [3]

---

[1] *Die Nation*, No. 31, 1896, May 2nd.
[2] "Deutsche Gesch.," v. Preface.
[3] Th. Schiemann, p. 226.

Whence this change of opinion? It was a consequence of the Prussian victories. At the outset of his career Treitschke had a passion, the passion of patriotism, which still had, at least, something noble and generous in it. It often made him distort the history of foreign countries. He admitted it at first with a frankness that does him honour. "I cannot forget," he wrote of Louis XIV, "that it was by mounting on the shoulders of our country that France became the first Power on the Continent."[1]

"Competent judges like Mohl," he wrote elsewhere, "have asked me if I ever did sufficient justice to Napoleon's power of organization. I can understand such a reproach. The wounds which the Emperor inflicted on our country are still too open to be forgotten. It is not easy for a German to do justice to the arch-enemy of Germany."[2]

But towards 1880 it is no longer this patriotic passion that rouses him: he is taken up with questions of Prussian policy. He sees nothing beyond that. He brings everything down to that. He becomes a sectary of "Prussianism," and it is in this spirit that he writes his history.

The whole secret of Treitschke's great partiality is to be found in that.

IV

Treitschke never concealed the fact that he conceived his history from a strictly Prussian point of view. On the contrary, he gloried in it. The reason he gives for it is this: "In politics one can only judge by what has succeeded." This philosophy conformed with the ideas

---

[1] "Historische und Pol. Aufsätze," iii. 79.
[2] "Zehn Jahre," p. 207.

of his country. That was the theory called by Renan the "zoological" theory of history, so dear to the Prussian historians. Treitschke is their most brilliant representative. It is by means of physical causes, so to speak, he explains the origin of Prussian success in Germany. "Radical theories," he said, "would have the State arise from the free will of the sovereign people. History teaches us, on the contrary, that most often States arise against the will of the majority of the people, by conquest and by submission, and just as war, even in times of high civilization, always keeps its plastic power of making States, so the home policy of peoples is not determined by the changes in public opinion alone, but by the acts of governments." [1]

Thenceforward the whole history of Germany is explained, in his opinion, by the history of Prussia. It was Prussia alone which made German unity, " less by the deliberate action of the Government than by the inherent power of her institutions: or what comes to the same thing, by the spirit that directed her political evolution."

We have already heard this explanation of the history of Germany by means of the psychology of the Prussian people, but no one had yet developed it with the eloquence and wealth of images of Treitschke. He passionately tries to show that the Prussian people realized the purest German virtues, and thus became the representative par excellence of the German race.

What did these virtues consist of? Treitschke enumerates them with complacency: in the first place, independence of character, pride, immovable faith in their right, and the cult of conscience. These virtues, said Treitschke, " the German people possessed in the

---

[1] " Deutsche Gesch.," iv. 350.

highest degree. It is true they had no art, but that
was doubtless a cause of superiority. In the sands
of Marches," said he, "no saint ever grew up: in
the rough courts of the Ascanian Margraves no
Minnesingers were heard to sing. The industrious
monks tried harder to win the reputations of skilful
farmers than the laurels of the artist or the scholar:
the merchants of the towns led the roughest existence with their hard work: it was only by military
force and powerful national pride that the State of
Brandenburg rose above its neighbours."[1]

Setting out with this idea, Treitschke shows that
this work was accomplished by the kings and nobility,
the authors of the two great institutions which had
made Prussia's strength—the administration and the
army.

The kings of Prussia, in Treitschke's eyes, are
models: a hard and resisting race, tempered by hard
work on a poor soil and by the continual struggles they
had to sustain against their neighbours, they were prepared already for their great mission by these rare
virtues. They became so entirely when they embraced
Protestantism.

Treitschke tries to prove again with a great abundance of arguments that Protestantism and German-
ism are synonymous terms: "The Jesuitical faith," he
said, "always remained foreign to the spirit of our
people. The rich spiritual forces of the New Roman
Church developed proudly in their Roman fatherlands:
but on this hostile German soil, among this people of
inveterate heretics, they could never take root. Here
no Tasso or Calderon sung: here no Rubens or
Murillo painted. Scarcely one of the lazy gluttons of

---

[1] "Deutsche Gesch.," i. 25.

German monks rivalled the scientific zeal of the worthy fathers of Saint-Maur. The Society of Jesus brought up among the Germans many pious priests and able statesmen . . . yet all the Jesuitical civilization remained the work of Roman brains, just as did the sensual, intoxicating forms of its cult."[1]

What is strange in the theory of Treitschke is not that he asserts that Prussia, the best incarnation of the German spirit, should conquer Germany according to that inevitable law that the strong puts down the weak. Others had said this before him : no, what is strange are the consequences which he draws from it.

Two things having made up the strength of Prussia, the care for material interests and a regard for the army, says he, these two things then *must have created* the New Germany, which comes to the same thing as saying that Prussia was a machine so well constructed that she acted, so to speak, in an automatic fashion without requiring the will of any particular man. And going from one deduction to another, Treitschke thus arrives at the conclusion that the Zollverein and the reform of the Prussian army were the two great makers of German unity : that this unity was brought about alone, then, in the chanceries and on the battlefields : that it is consequently nothing but the work of functionaries and officials—that is to say, finally, of the Prussian aristocracy.

To arrive at such a paradox as this—"that the squires brought about German unity"—Treitschke wrote in five large volumes a "History of Germany in the Nineteenth Century." He writes it in almost every line of the work: "In German affairs," he

---

[1] " Deutsche Gesch.," i. 20.

says, "our high nobility has shown itself to be more clear-sighted and readier for sacrifice than the middle class."[1] And elsewhere: "It was the same Governments who condemned the exhibition of the national flag and opposed the establishment of a German Reichstag, which they considered as revolutionary heresy, who are in reality the creators of the New Germany."[2]

With all this, then, what became of the part played by the Liberals, in whom Treitschke saw in 1861 "the authors of everything great that had been done in national life during the nineteenth century"? In his history he reduces their part to nothing, or practically nothing. He recognizes unhesitatingly, it must be confessed, the services rendered to the German cause by those men of letters and thought who were not of the nobility—Fichte, Niebuhr, and Schleiermacher. He even speaks with a certain effusion of the Liberals who had faith in Prussia, like Pfizer, a Swabian, who, "not having even seen Berlin," wrote in 1830 an argument in favour of the Hohenzollern policy. Dahlmann, too, the father of the National Liberals and their successors, the Sybels, Dunckers, and Freytags, who twenty years later were to become Imperialists, found grace in his sight. But all the other Liberals, especially those of a deeper dye, he denies they had any part whatever in the work of unity. On the contrary, he laughs at their efforts, at their exhibitions of the national flag, as if it sufficed, he said sarcastically, "to hoist a flag or utter a patriotic speech to bring about unity." He forgets that he, too, made speeches, and that these speeches, with so many others, helped to

---

[1] "Deutsche Gesch.," ii. Preface.
[2] Ibid. iii. 350.

form that public opinion without which the unity could never have been brought about.

There is a fact in the history of modern Germany which illustrates this in a striking fashion. It was at the famous session of the Chamber of the North German Confederation when Bismarck caused himself to be questioned by Benningsen upon the Luxemburg question. That was in 1867, less than a year after Sadowa. At that time the real significance of the Prussian victory was understood. In spite of her successes, Prussia was no longer free to act, or rather, to realize these successes, she was obliged to follow in the wake of German public opinion. This opinion it was still that controlled.[1]

Treitschke could not relate this incident of modern German history, as his history stops at 1848, but he has nowhere shown in his work the great services which the voice of the people rendered to national unity.

It was the nation itself which created the unity. If Prussia was the instrument she was the soul. The idea of a German fatherland was by no means a Prussian idea. Born after Jena, it was especially alive among the enlightened circles of the nation, in the Universities, among the students. It was the professors who propagated it and made it penetrate into the deeper strata of the people. But Treitschke will hear nothing of this. A reactionary and rigid Prussian,

---

[1] This opinion was gagged later by new victories, but it could not be destroyed for all that, and in spite of its temporary eclipse the future belonged to it. After Sadowa, Victor Cherbuliez already said : " There is in the world a mysterious power, full of artifices and ruses, which plays with the greatest politicians and draws from their most skilful undertakings consequences which they neither desired nor foresaw."

he admits but two factors in this unity : the nobility and the Kings of Prussia.

Treitschke's partiality does not stop at that : he goes further and insists that these kings and nobles were irreproachable from all points of view. Of these squires, "so much decried as narrow-minded Conservatives," he makes "men more Liberal than the self-styled Liberals."[1] "They have not," he says, "their doctrinarianism nor their middle-class selfishness,"[2] ",they are practical and have an understanding of diplomatic and political affairs."[3] Evidently in 1881 Treitschke saw all the Prussian nobles through Bismarck and Moltke.

With regard to the Kings of Prussia Treitschke's task was more delicate. In spite of all his goodwill, the historian will never succeed in making us regard Frederick William II as a model of domestic virtues, Frederick William III as a wise and penetrating politician, and Frederick William IV as a sovereign who had any notion of the greatness of the historical rôle of his house.

Treitschke does not attempt this, but he manages in a most skilful fashion not to make any false steps. He ignores the defects in the characters of these kings. If they were lazy, dissolute, and weak-willed like Frederick William II, he lays the blame upon the difficulties of the time : if they were obstinate cowards without any insight into their policy, like Frederick William III, the historian prudently leaves all these defects of the king in the shade, and makes up for it by praising the virtues of the private man, " of the good father of a family " : if he can in no way dissimulate

[1] " Deutsche Gesch.," iii. 8.
[2] Ibid. iv. 499.   [3] Ibid. iii. 86.

the enormous mistakes in policy of the king, he does it
with so light a touch that you ask yourself where the
blame begins and the praise ends. What gentleness,
for example, in this portrait of the most pitiful of the
Kings of Prussia, Frederick William IV :—

" It was a world of magnificent plans that
Frederick William with his artist's imagination had
conceived, and now he was master the natural goodness of his heart, which would not let him have
sorrowful faces around him, urged him to realize
them. . . . All the harshness of the old regime he
hoped to soften : pardon for the demagogues, for the
Poles, whom he defended as poor oppressed people :
liberty for the Press, and above all religious liberty.
The wrath of the Catholics, with reference to the
episcopal quarrel of Cologne, he hoped to calm by
magnanimous concessions. . . .

" For a long while he had suffered, too, from the
parsimonious habits of the Court of Berlin : to keep up
a sumptuous Court worthy of the Hohenzollern he
hoped to gather around him all that Germany possessed great in the arts and sciences. . . . Alas, if among
so many plans there could only have been found
one a little more developed, one which could have been
realized ! But the practical realization of a plan was
what mattered least to this dreamer. But, entirely
given up to the ideal play of his schemes, he was
discouraged by the first obstacle he met in his way,
and he finished nothing.

" Of all the Hohenzollern he was the least warlike,
the most anxious to preserve peace, more peaceful even
than his father, and he was the only one who, during
his reign, waged no war. On the front of one of his
Museums he had these words of the Cæsars engraved :
' Melius bene imperare quam imperia ampliare,' a

saying that might well suit the master of a universal empire, but which was scarcely in place in the mouth of the King of a small, incomplete State with absurd frontiers.

" He was least of all a swordsman, and this short-sighted King always unwillingly rode on horseback. . . . All his officers could see that he performed his military duties from the promptings of conscience, but without any liking for them. . . . He had no enjoyment but when he could return to his ego, or when, delighting his audience and himself, he would let flow the stream of his thoughts and sentiments in ardent discussions. ' I had no rest until I had spoken,' he wrote one day to a friend. . . . Only those who did not know him accused him of play-acting, for at bottom there was no vanity in him. . . . But to pour out his heart, to play with the brilliant images of his imagination, and to manipulate with an unequalled mastery his mother tongue, was a necessity to him. . . . From this point of view he little resembled his grandfather, Frederick the Great, who also was a born orator, but who always spoke to say something, and who never forgot that royal words only live in posterity if they are actions." [1]

When not dealing with the Kings of Prussia Treitschke is pitiless towards royalty. There are in his work not fewer than twenty-four portraits of sovereigns, Germans and foreigners. I do not think that there is one of them presented in a favourable light. This royalist by conviction, who had the same ideas of kings as were held in the Middle Ages, the master who redresses wrongs and protects the feeble, expresses himself about all foreign kings with the

---

[1] " Deutsche Gesch.," v. 7–9.

sectarian passion of a demagogue of 1848.   Never
has been seen in a work such a hecatomb of crowned
heads.   They are nothing but rascals, perverse and
vicious beings, debauchees, maniacs, or dangerous
fools, who seem to have sprung from the smaller
houses.

We see pass before us the sly kings who, in that
position which should raise them above the ordinary
level of men, see only an opportunity of exercising on
a large scale their natural wickedness.   Duke Charles
of Brunswick: the King of Wurtemberg who declared
one day that his " masters were Tarquin and Nero " :
the Austrian Emperor Francis II, whom he gives as
an example of the " crowned rascal."

" He was a Florentine with vulgar inclinations, who
had stuck on his face the mask of a jovial and good-
natured Austrian to deceive those who approached
him.   And so, in spite of his evil appearance and his
cold and hard eyes, in spite of the extraordinary
resemblance he had to certain members of his family,
Philip II among others, everybody believed in the
childish innocence of this false and heartless despot.

" His political system was of the simplest.   After
the years of trouble through which they had passed he
wished to enjoy his rest : he wished again, like a zealous
counsellor at Court, to add insignificant notes in the
margins of the bundles of acts that were presented
to him : to play the violin in his spare time : to cut
up paper and varnish cages." [1]

Another king, the King of England, George IV, is
treated still worse.   After acknowledging in him no
good quality except taste in the selection of his cravats,
the historian concludes :—

[1] " Deutsche Gesch.," i. 604.

" This god of fashion was now nothing but a vulgar libertine, a young man grown old, a drunkard, one of the vilest natures that ever dishonoured a throne. . . . He did not even have the only virtue that has never been disputed to his race—courage : this effeminate person had never shown any." [1]

After the rascals and the debauchees come the narrow-minded ones, a good example of whom he sees in Czar Nicholas I, " incapable of feeling the aspirations of his people, and never having exhibited on the throne the qualities of a mediocre official or a corporal."

A most numerous class is that of the puppets and inoffensive coxcombs who in the sovereign's calling saw only an opportunity to shine. In this most amusing gallery Treitschke shows us " the old stick-in-the-mud royalty," like King Frederick Augustus of Saxony, " a rigorous observer of a superannuated etiquette, and full of Gothic prejudices." Another group, less numerous this one, is that of the " good fellows," like King Maximilian of Bavaria, suited " for any calling you like except that of king." There is, at length, a last category, that of the " middle-class kings." This last class Treitschke particularly detests. For this class he keeps his most biting satire : two princely houses in particular have stirred up his passion : Orleans and Coburg.

In the Orleans family, Louis Philippe particularly seemed to him a good example of the middle-class king.

" The pride of the French princes," he said, " was as foreign to him as the sense of his dynastic duty. In that arid soul the spell of the past and the thousand-

---

[1] " Deutsche Gesch.," iv. 543.

year-old right of the Capetiens awakened no response. He was a careful father of a family, concerned principally to recover the great fortune of the Orleans, which owed its origin to a great extent to the letting of the gambling parlours of the Palais-Royal. He wished, at all events, to assure his family a fortune in any eventuality (ein ruhiges Hauswesen). When he received the royal dignity he gave up his fortune to his children, keeping only the interest, which, by the way, he knew well how to make fructify with the co-operation of his friendly banks. ' I tell you,' he would constantly repeat, ' my children will not have a morsel of bread to eat.' " [1]

Among the Coburgs the representatives of that spirit are more numerous : Leopold I, the King of Belgium, is the first that Treitschke maltreats even worse than the Kings of France :—

" He was a tall, slender man, with tired and delicate features, with dark and melancholy eyes ; he wore a very smooth black wig, and spoke in a deep deliberate voice, always silent as much in his political affairs as in his amours. In England he was called ' Mr. Little by Little,' ' Marquis Very Gently.' In the German Courts, where he was not well liked, he was called ' Leopold the Sly.' He preached the philosophy of well-regulated interest. At the first communion of one of his nephews he gave him the following rule of conduct : ' You must learn to give shape to your egoism so as to be able later to exploit it like a productive mine.' He was thoroughly acquainted with the merchant's art. To gain partisans to his policy he could suppress his avarice and scatter money with both hands, but his intimacy with the Bourse soon

---

[1] " Deutsche Gesch.," iv. 19.

made up his losses. . . . He was the second middle-class King of the revolution. . . . With the houses of Orleans and Coburg a new generation of men insinuated themselves into the high European nobility : they had dealings with affairs and always had a Bourse list in their pockets. . . . As indifferent to feelings of honour and historic piety as the Italian tyrants of the fifteenth century, they were at bottom haughtier than the princes of the old aristocracy." [1]

All the Coburgs, after the King of Belgium, have their turn, and the Prince Consort is not spared the least.

" Prince Albert was, like all the Coburgs, a prosaic nature, unenthusiastic and devoid of religious feeling, and who had no difficulty in habituating himself to the English custom of finding everything ' very interesting.' At Brussels he was initiated into the mechanical conception of the world of the statistician Quételet, who explained all the phenomena of social life, even moral phenomena, as the work of blind natural forces. He valued the mechanical arts more than the fine arts, technique more than science, the ingenious more than the ideal. . . . In the English Court, more-ever, the little German Prince was in the position of a princess married to a foreigner ; he belonged no more to his own nationality and could not avail himself of it. Indeed, he became altogether English. Although he still spoke his mother-tongue in the family circle, and although his affectionate spouse allowed him to make use of his knife to eat his fish, to the great scandal of British hearts, he had completely forgotten the habits of his own country. And when some years after his marriage he visited Germany again, he affected

---

[1] " Deutsche Gesch.," iv. 83.

so much British habits that he reviewed the garrison
at Mayence in a grey overcoat, to the great indignation
of the Prussian generals, who asked each other whether
this young man had really forgotten that German
Princes were accustomed to honour the flag in uniform.
With the cold and joyless English life he lost the jovial
character that distinguishes the real German ; be became
stiff, formal, harsh and unthinking in his opinions, so
much so that in spite of all the efforts he put forward
to bring up his children well he only succeeded with
one or two of his daughters, and absolutely failed in
the case of the heir to the throne."

We can see quite well that this Coburg's greatest
crime was to have become an Englishman. A stout
Prussian, our historian was one of the leaders of that
very numerous group in Germany who saw in the
Englishman the national enemy. He detested the
English. If he still acknowledged certain qualities in
the Frenchman, "the strong idealism of his race, his
chivalrous and generous character," if he admired, as
he said, "the people of Molière and Mirabeau," he
could see nothing in the Englishman. To him he was
a "Baconian, a shallow utilitarian, a narrow and selfish
islander, a hypocrite who, with the Bible in one hand
and a pipe of opium in the other, spreads throughout
the universe the benefits of civilization."

Treitschke exhibits this hatred of the English people,
of which he was to give so curious a proof at the death
of Emperor Frederick III,[1] most frequently through-

[1] In the obituary notice which he devoted to the Emperor
Frederick III, Treitschke positively accuses the English doctor,
Dr. Morell Mackenzie, of having " killed the august patient."
" The patient," he said, " was placed in the hands of an English
doctor, who soon by the unheard-of lies in his bulletins soiled the
good reputation of our old and honourable Prussia. With increas-

out his history. The moment an Englishman appears
he ridicules or abuses him. The only exception he
makes is in the case of Carlyle, " the only Englishman,"
he says, " who absolutely understood the Germans,
and the first foreigner to rise to the height of German
thought." [1]

Witticisms that are always successful with a very
Teuton public are those about the English. Treitschke
excelled in calling up in his lectures grotesque British
figures, accompanying them with " Hip, hip, hurrah ! "
which set his audience laughing.[2]

When dealing with English policy the Prussian
historian can see nothing but commercialism and im-
morality, British pride, pitiless to the weak. " It was
Great Britain which waged the most hideous war
that a Christian country has ever waged : the Opium
War." [3] Elsewhere, speaking of the Eastern question,
he declared that Europe should have seized this occasion
to put a stop to British ambition by ending the crushing domination of the English fleets at Gibraltar,
Malta, Corfu, and giving the Mediterranean up to
the Mediterranean people." [4]

When he speaks of the commercial Englishman who
" sacrifices everything to the consideration of profit and
despises everything that has not a direct connection
with advancement in life," we feel that Treitschke
is contrasting with him in his own mind the idealism
of the German race. He shows this even in rather

---

ing anxiety the Germans began to feel that this dear life was
in the worst of hands. The result passed their worst forebodings.
When Emperor William gave up his last breath, it was a dying
Emperor who succeeded him " (" Zwei Kaiser " (pamphlet,
20 pages), Berlin, 1888).

[1] " Deutsche Gesch.," iii. 685, iv. 409.
[2] Ibid. i. 606.   [3] Ibid. v. 53.   [4] Ibid. v. 64.

an amusing fashion with regard to Queen Caroline, whom he selects as an example of " German innocence and purity." " . . . Queen Caroline," he said, "was a true German nature, natural and frank, lacking moderation perhaps, a little fantastic too, but sincere, brave, capable of loving, and too fond of the truth for the hypocrisy of that English Court. . . . In that inhospitable isle she was slandered and covered with mud." [1]

This is because in Treitschke's mind a German nature cannot be vile. His work, from one end to the other, is a hymn in honour of German virtues. The German race alone have truly known idealism, frankness, pride, absolute self-forgetfulness,[2] and an invincible attachment to right. [3] And his history is there to prove that the truly great men of his country have corresponded to that ideal.

When he approaches literature, it is in a lyrical tone that Treitschke analyses the great works of the classical period and the fine scientific efflorescence of the beginning of the century. "The Germans knew," he said, "that for a long time they had enriched the treasure of traditional European culture with new forms of the ideal, and that they occupied in the great commonalty of civilized people a place which no one in the world could fill in their stead. Enthusiastic youth spoke of German profundity, German idealism, and German universality. The national pride of that idealistic race was satisfied with the notion that no other people could completely follow German thought in its daring flight or attain the freedom of our universal sentiment." [4]

In all spheres—painting, music, architecture, poetry,

---

[1] " Deutsche Gesch.," v. 147.   [2] Ibid. v. 279.
[3] Ibid. ii. 154.   [4] Ibid. i. 195.

politics, and military art—Treitschke tries to show forth the original qualities of the German (die deutsche Eigenart). He finds at least one of these realized in every great man. With Baron Stein, for example, it is the pitiless frankness of the Teutonic jouster: with Scharnhorst "it is depth of feeling and inflexibility of character which are hidden under simplicity of habits and modest good-nature " [1] : with Grimm and Niebuhr it is "sincere, profound German science with its unconscious intuitions of genius."

On the other hand, woe to the Germans who have profaned this ideal! Treitschke is pitiless to them. Even Prince Hardenburg finds no favour in his sight. He finds nothing-German in "that refined dilettante and diplomatic nature who wrote in an elegant and clear hand, in very modern German, perfectly intelligible things, but in which that rather massive force, that taste for detail and the profundity of which the strong German natures alone are capable, were lacking." [2]

We recognize in Treitschke's ideal the type of German dear to Tacitus, the man of the forests, of indomitable courage, rough and hard, chaste, without elegance and refinement, but substantial and with only one vice—drunkenness. He tries incessantly to resuscitate him in his history. Does he always do it well? There are doubts about that. He tells us somewhere in his work that when the Allies penetrated into France in 1814, there was seen walking in the streets of Paris a little man who aroused the laughter of the street urchins by the strangeness of his dress. He wore a large collar doubled back over a greasy coat. His long and badly-combed hair fell on his shoulders. He had in his hand a great knotty stick. " He was Vater Jahn,

---

[1] " Deutsche Gesch.," i. 290.   [2] Ibid. iii. 253.

the father of the German high schools, who wished to
revive the habits of the Germans at the time of the
aurochs, and who, by his strange appearance, meant to
show the civilized and corrupted French what was the
true German nature (die reine deutsche Eigenart)."

I am afraid that Treitschke acts rather the same as
Vater Jahn; by detailing throughout his work its
coarseness and roughness, by railing against everything
that might "adulterate its German purity," by de-
nouncing for that purpose all the misdeeds "of
the cosmopolitans," he had revived in his country
all the old race hatreds against the Muscovites,[1] the
Sarmatians, the Danes, the French, the English, and
the Jews.

And this work is as vain as it is criminal. The
Germany which, at the beginning of the century,
prided itself on the greatest spirit of tolerance, the
most human and comprehensive cosmopolitanism,
seems to have lost those fine virtues. These new
Prussian prophets it is who have driven them away.
In 1870 Ernest Renan denounced this evil: "The
excess of patriotism," he said, "injures those universal
works whose basis is the saying of St. Paul: Non est
Judæus neque Græcus. It is exactly because your
great men eighty years ago were not over-patriotic
that they opened that wide path in which we are their
disciples. I am afraid that your ultra-patriotic
generation, by rejecting what is not pure German,
will prepare for itself a narrower audience. Jesus and
the founders of Christianity were not Germans. . . .
Your own Goethe acknowledged that he owed something to that 'corrupted France' of Voltaire and
Diderot. Let us abandon those fanatical opinions to

---

[1] " Das Moskowitenthum " (" Deutsche Gesch.," iv. 87).

the nether regions of opinion. Let me tell you, 'You have fallen.'" [1]

Treitschke is in the first rank of these prophets of evil. He it is particularly who has uttered the loudest cry of the nationalist barbarian: "We have allowed ourselves to be led astray too much by the great names of tolerance and enlightenment (Aufklärung)." He was the foster-father of that generation which said with Herwegh : "Enough of such love; let us now try hate." And that is why his work has been sinful.

The only excuse he can make is that he thought he was performing a holy work. This is the excuse of all sincere fanatics. Now he has shown himself to be sincere. It is through love of his country that he became so narrow in his ideas and so exclusive in his principles. And thus it is that this Liberal, who one day took Tocqueville as his model, became the apostle of intolerance.

His fault was that he wanted to write history. Treitschke was a sort of Veuillot backwards, a debater of great power, a stern and eloquent moralist. But to write history on a large scale he had—except beauty of form—none but negative qualities. Now· see what happened. He who by principle claimed that history should be "scientific in method and practical in object," he who would have it purely political, treated it for the most part as would a historian of customs, a chronicler. Doubtless he examines with great diligence all the political questions which present themselves, and on many of these he has thrown, thanks to his work and his knowledge of unpublished manuscripts, new light, but, at bottom, men occupy his attention rather than

---

[1] Renan, "Nouvelle Lettre à Strauss" ("La Réforme intellectuelle et morale," Paris, 1871).

institutions. While he fully relates in twenty-six pages the scandal of Lola Montèz and the King of Bavaria, he only gives fifty—that is, not twice as many —to relate the most important act in the political history of Germany between 1840 and 1848, the assembly of the Prussian Landtag.

Treitschke is interesting in himself to the highest degree by reason of his vigorous personality, but it must be acknowledged he is not a real historian. A man of sentiment and imagination, he must be enamoured, enthusiastic—he must fulminate or curse. He is not capable of studying a question scientifically in itself: he must hate or love it. At bottom Treitschke reminds us of Carlyle—a Carlyle of greater common sense perhaps, less vapourish, more direct and good-natured, of a more frank and pleasant spirit (there are some exquisite pictures of an affecting nature which Carlyle, always in a passion, never knew), less irritating too, because he does not pose; but after all a Carlyle—that is to say, a moralist rather than a historian.

CONCLUSION

DECEMBER 3RD, 1870.—To-day the Emperor and Empire are irrevocably established: thus ends the interregnum of sixty-five years: to-day the terrible gap of an Empire without an Emperor is filled up."

Such is the brief note to be found in the note-book of the Crown Prince Frederick William, who was to be for two months the unhappy Emperor Frederick III. The Prince might have added: "This Empire is partly my work."

He was, in fact, the only one of the Hohenzollern who desired it before the victories. Indeed, it had been the dream of his life. He belonged to that generation of Liberals of 1848 who from their youth had lived with the idea of the resurrection of a democratic Empire under the Hohenzollern. His most intimate friends, his dearest confidants—artists, poets, men of letters—were the Germans who had been most enthusiastic for it. What the historians announced in the name of science they sang in fiery verses. Such a one was the poet Emmanuel Geibel, one of the friends of the Prince, who in 1834, when the others were speaking of political rights and demanding a constitution, only wanted one thing: "a successor to Barbarossa." At night he dreamed of it on the banks of the Rhine, "in the midst of hills covered with vines, which shone in the light of the moon," and he seemed to see the great shade of Charlemagne "walking with the sword in his hand and the purple mantle on his shoulders."

At every great crisis of national life Geibel had called upon this saviour. In 1840, at the time when Nicholas Becher was singing "They shall not have our free and German Rhine," the poet cried " No, what we desire is not that servile well-being, the bloody uncertainty of the time of the Gallic equality. What we want is the German Empire. Persist, my people! . . . Necessity will speak aloud in the thunder of battle. The green springtime is coming: it is the Empire, full of power and glory."

Similarly, in 1848, it was not liberty that this poet demanded, but " a man."

" O Fates," he cried, "give me a man—one man alone. We need a man, a grand son of the Nibelungs. . . . Rather than rot away with an internal cancer I would meet the enemy on the field of battle. Thrice blessed will be the hour when the cannon-balls will rain on the banks of the Moselle! . . . War! War! Give us a war to take the place of the quarrels that are drying up the marrow in our bones."

And the poet (vates) foretold the ransom of this holy crusade: " The old Minster of Strasburg makes its bells speak thus: ' German art taught me in better times to erect towers reaching to the stars, and yet I still languish in the slavery of the Gaul!'"

After Sadowa the warrior-poet is satisfied: his songs are now only a hymn of joy in honour of King William.

"Anointed of the Lord, thou hast at last restored to us the right of self-respect." But that was only the prelude to the great victory. After Sedan, it is the cry of the victor: " Sodom, the city of insolent joy, will now tremble beneath the flaming sword of Germany ! ” and at the end : “ Now we are delivered from the Gaul : we have rooted out from our hearts the evil seed of lies and everything else that is Gallic in our thoughts, words, and actions (das Welchthum auszumerzen in Glauben, Wort und That !).”

Prince Frederick was not so bellicose as his friend the poet, but he, too, in his way, was a poet, and in those holy wars which he had not wished for he saw his ' House’s glorious mission to build up again the old German Empire : in 1870 he reached the realization of his dreams, and, like the poet Geibel, intoxicated by victory, he could cry :—

“ I salute you, holy rain of fire, tempest of rage that dost burst out after so many hours of sorrow ! We become healed in thy flames and my heart answers thee with beatings of joy. Eagles of the powerful flight, forward ! Germany already breathes again and tunes her harps to celebrate her victories ! ”

It seemed that this day of victory should have been his day. Was he not the representative of that Young Germany of men of letters, historians, poets who had given an actual shape to the longtime vague idea of a German Empire ? And for several months, in the midst of the roar of cannons, while the old Prussians fought the battles, he could experience all the joy of the great page of history that was being opened before his country. At his headquarters he was surrounded by German Princes, who already paid him homage as future Princes of Germany. It was like a picture of the Germany of to-morrow. There, no rigid Prussian discipline was felt : everything there was done in splendour. All the Princes seemed very modern, worldly, and emancipated. The Duke of Weimar took charge of the Comedy. French pieces were played there, "Trou Madame."[1] They dined, kept late hours, drank champagne to celebrate the victories. There was a perpetual come and go in this camp. They met all sorts of people there, newspaper correspondents—Englishmen sometimes, whom it was found that the Crown Prince "received very cordially."[2] The Prince himself, in the midst of all these people, represented quite well the New Germany, the Germany of the future. Although simple and modest in his tastes, he had, nevertheless, a taste for his part. Handsome, tall, imposing, and very decorative, he had a particular way of wrapping himself in his camp-cloak, as in an Imperial mantle, with a studied simplicity which emphasized the only decoration he wore : the iron cross of the first class, which he had won on the battlefield of Weissenburg.

No one more than he had the notion of the glorious future of his race. He spoke of it, in the evening, to his friends, particularly to Gustav Freytag. He told him that a splendid Empire was needed which would link up the chain of the ages. Gustav Freytag, the most Prussian of his Liberal friends, was not of that opinion.[3] He thought that " the finest Imperial mantle was not worth the simple blue uniform of the

---

[1] Wilmowski, " Feldbriefe," Breslau, 1894.

[2] G. Freytag, " Der Kronprinz und die Deutsche Kaiserkrone," Leipzig, 1889.

[3] Gustav Freytag says that Prince Frederick, although simple and familiar, had an unfailing notion of his rank and estate. " He thought," said he, " a great deal of title, of the hierarchy and honours. All the ceremonial details of the organization of receptions was an important thing to him : a new crown, the aims of the Prince and Princess Royal, were serious things to him."

Hohenzollern." [1]   But he took care not to contradict his royal companion; he kept that for the posthumous revelations which were to show that he had never shared "the chimeras of that noble mind."

By the side of the Crown Prince's brilliant head-quarters, that of his father made a sorry figure.   There you would meet scarcely any one but old Prussians—plain generals, wrapped up entirely in their military duty and avoiding display.   The old, undemonstrative King was silent.   Even to the Princes who formed his suite, like Luitpold, Crown Prince of Bavaria, he was very reserved. [2]   With him, display was reduced to its minimum.   The table never had more than thirty-five covers.   "The menu was the simplest—the menu of Ems," said his Prime Minister, "a soup, three dishes, cheese and beer, red and white wine."   At times champagne was drunk to celebrate a victory, but lights were put out early.

From time to time, across the background of princes and generals loaded with crosses, you would see pass the great silent shadow of Moltke.   And he was more taciturn than the others.   "With him," said Prince Luitpold spitefully, "it is impossible to know anything."

All these men were the representatives of the old Prussian policy—the policy "narrowly Hohenzollern." And when one considered the brilliant victories, it

---

[1] "The old German Empire has left a very bad impression to the North Germans with its centuries of humiliation and its mountains of national suffering to renew it again" (G. Freytag, "Lebenserinnerungen," p. 30).

[2] "He treated him with great attention," said his Prime Minister, Wilmowski, "but never took him into his confidence about the plans of battle until the time when they were to be delivered—that is, when every one knew them."

seemed that this policy was going to disappear for ever. Was it not Young Germany which was rising to the sound of the trumpets of victory, a democratic Germany which all these squires had never liked and still mistrusted? When for the first time the Crown Prince brought them the wishes of the Princes, "the re-establishment of the German Empire," they gave the proposal a most frigid reception. The King said that no title in his opinion was as good as that of King of Prussia, and Bismarck, then, was of that opinion. Yet as the victories increased the situation changed, and the necessity of the Empire became a political fact. Then a strange thing was done: in the hands of these men of iron, that Liberal German Empire dreamed of by the Crown Prince and his friends became a great Prussia.

The strength of Prussia was made of military force, economy, and exact administration. The only point, then, was to extend these institutions to the whole of Germany. The great maker of States, Bismarck, foresaw the wry faces, but he said: "Look now, Prussia is like a flannel vest; it is not pleasant at first —it irritates—but it is warm and holds onto the skin."

From that moment began a long duel between the Prince who had wished for the Empire and those who, holding the power, wished to make it according to their fancy. The Prince was Liberal. He had been brought up during that period of censure and opposition to the narrow and annoying bureaucracy, in those years when it was not the power of the army but popular movements which marked the progress of the State, and remained deeply attached to these ideas. His marriage with the daughter of Queen Victoria had no doubt contributed in strengthening him in this point of view. At this time he was regarded by all the Liberals as their true leader. They did not at that time rail against English institutions and against the Coburgs. On the contrary, believing that unity would only come with liberty, they expected these benefits with the accession of the Crown Prince.

In 1861, at the time when the Prussian constitutional conflict was most acute, the Liberal opposition knew that the Crown Prince was with them and gloried in it. Later, he protested against the annexations, which, he said, injured the good fame of Prussia, which she required to make moral conquests in Germany. This time, all the Liberals were not with him. After the organization of the Empire, their defection was complete. All his old friends left him for the camp of Bismarck.

The Imperial Prince was a general without an army. Like the great majority of Germans, these Liberals had the cult of force and the sentiment of discipline. They could not resist success. Not long before they had done homage to the Crown Prince, vying with each other in celebrating his liberalism, the nobility of his sentiments, the height of his character, and the culture of his mind. On the morrow they were no longer of that opinion : with Bismarck, their new idol, it was exactly the opposite that they celebrated.

The future Emperor was reproached for his liberalism. They bore him malice for disapproving of the political methods of the Chancellor, to whose brutality he could never become accustomed.

He was reproached, moreover, for not being Prussian enough, that is, for not sharing sufficiently the prejudices of the sect, of not detesting the English, the French, and the Jews. The English particularly ! Had he not married an Englishwoman ? And Gustav Freytag, his old friend, took upon himself to denounce the misdeeds "of the Englishwoman." In the first place, her husband liked her too much! Had he not been seen writing to her every day during the war, at the risk of delaying the post? He had on his table the portrait of that woman, "whom he looked at with tears in his eyes at times."[1] Was it to be endured that a future King of Prussia and Emperor should thus let himself be ruled by sentiment and allow a woman to take such an Empire from him?

From that it was but a step to asking whether he was really the man capable to leading Germany to her new destinies, and his friends cut him. One after the other they abandoned him. Some of them still paid him attention, as, for example, Freytag, who, while severely criticizing his policy, still respected the man. But, in reality, could they tolerate on the Hohenzollern throne an idealistic nature, devoid of practical sense?[2] If at least in 1870, to prepare himself for his career as King, he had settled in the country, as a landed proprietor, to make use himself of his land, to inspect his cattle and measure his hay, and thus initiated himself in the administration of circles, in the wants and desires of the countrymen, in the interests of rural economy,[3] he would have prepared himself for his calling as King: but he had done nothing: and as, on the other hand, he was devoid of any spirit of initiative, and had no creative genius and no gift of commandment, he was only fit to be scrapped as old iron.

Another companion of the Crown Prince, David Strauss, the author of the "Life of Jesus," who had always been Liberal in politics and very progressive in spirit, had allowed himself to be won over to Bis-

---

[1] G. Freytag, "Lebenserunnerungen," p. 136.
[2] Ibid. p. 47.   [3] Ibid. p. 68.

marck's policy, and he cried: "We cannot forget, moreover, that it was the Prussian nobility that gave us a Bismarck and a Moltke." If this old Liberal, who had written a most biting pamphlet about Frederick William IV, entitled "A Romanticist on the Throne," [1] now began to deify the squires, who was left to be trusted?

Prince Frederick was deeply moved by these defections. Kept apart from all affairs, having nothing to do but to review once a year the army corps of the South of Germany and to open museums and art galleries, he contracted a sort of melancholy. " Lassitude and melancholy, his usual company, attacked him." [2] His wife's efforts were not always successful in driving away these dark thoughts. "His courage was no longer that of a man who shortly was to wear the Imperial crown." [3] Even before he fell ill he thought of abdicating in favour of his son, and his friends were not the last in advising him to take such a step.

But illness came and did its work. It settled upon him implacably, coming as if at the desire of his old companions. His death was received as a sort of deliverance by those people who thought they saw in his son, Prince William, a true Hohenzollern. This was the time when Bismarck said to Moritz Busch: "The Prince wants to take the government into his own hands: he is energetic and determined, and he has no desire to put up with parliamentary

---

[1] In this pamphlet, published in 1847, he branded "in a descendant of Frederick the Great an encourager of a double pietist and Conservative reaction." Strauss preferred the warlike and realistic pietism of the Moltkes and Bismarcks.

[2] G. Freytag, " Lebens.," p. 68.   [3] Ibid. p. 73.

regents—a proper soldier of the Guard! He has no pleasure in seeing his father visited by professors, by Mommsens, Virchows, and Forchenbechs! Perhaps some day he will be the *rock of bronze* which we need!"

This was because Prince William seemed just the man of the Prussian realistic historians. He had been brought up according to their lessons. Taking his first place in public life in 1870, he formed part of that ardent and bellicose generation whose patriotism had been swelled by the great victories.

A strange transformation was taking place in the Germany of that time. The race, formerly slow and deliberate, now became somewhat agile and excitable. The old peaceful customs disappeared. No more men were to be met smoking large porcelain pipes. The cigar and cigarette appeared everywhere. A feverish activity took hold of all minds. Industry, commerce, and banking assumed prodigious proportions. And a strange thing in this growth of public life was that the character of the old military and dynastic Prussia seemed to penetrate still more into all the corners of society.

Heinrich Heine, at the beginning of the century, had difficulty in recognizing his old Rhenish Provinces after the Prussian annexation. The happy countries of La Crosse had lost all their charm with the advent of the spiked helmet and Prussian drill. Even the Customs officers, stiff and serious in their uniform, seemed to him to be made of wood.

To-day it is the whole of Germany that is transformed. Prussia is spread over her like an immense camp that has only a regular and mechanical life about it. Old dreaming, romantic Germany is completely stifled by the realism of the barracks. For twenty years letters and the arts have been dead. The only literature that has flourished has been military literature. With the works of the General Staff, the correspondence of Moltke, the speeches and letters of Bismarck, the works on tactics by Du Verdy Du Vernois, and the "History of Germany in the Nineteenth Century" by Treitschke, the great work of the period is an essay on the philosophy of war, "The Nation in Arms," by Major Colmar von der Goltz.

Nothing could be stronger than this work, and nothing could give one a better notion of the transformation of Germany into a vast Prussian military camp. It is quite a brutal defence of militarism, in which we hear the celebration in a lyrical tone of the moralizing virtue of the great human scenes of slaughter, of the benefits of the warrior State, the inferiority of the industrial State, and the mission of the army as an educator of the people and a centre of national culture.

"There will be wars as long as the people on this earth wish to acquire terrestrial advantages, as long as they are filled with the desire of procuring for future generations the space they require to live in, at ease and in peace and comfort, as long as these peoples under the leadership of great minds attempt, without keeping themselves within the narrow limits of their daily needs, to realize some political ideal of civilization. We must accept what the gods send us . . . wars are the lot of man . . . they form the inevitable destiny of nations. In this world men will never enjoy everlasting peace."

And these words, like a leitmotiv, appear in all the works of the New Empire. Written in an energetic style, which contrasts in its precision and brevity with the diffuse character of the old German prose, these words had immediately a great success. It is not of these Prussian military writers that Schopenhauer would have been able to say what he wrote in 1840: "German writers will do well to allow themselves to become impregnated with this truth, that they must think as much as possible in elevated thought, but that they must express that thought in the language of everybody."

It was in these ideas that the young Prince William was educated.[1] He was one of the most characteristic productions of the New Germany. No one was more impregnated with the spirit of the age than he, nor underwent more emphatically the double Prussian education of the school and the barracks.

At school the future Emperor showed himself to be a diligent, well-disciplined scholar of an indifferent understanding for intellectual things, little inclined to philosophizing, but practical, active, alert, fond of all games, violent exercises, endowed with an iron will, and, in spite of this, generous, grandiose, and haughty. He always wanted to be the first, and he tried to be so by his serious and thorough work.

In his father's house he had as teacher a most remarkable man, Dr. Hinzpeter, one of those practical minds, little inclined to be dogmatic, who give him a most elevated notion of his calling as king. He only had to tell him the history of his House to show him his duty. Dr. Hinzpeter was one of those historians who believed that Prussia is the navel of Germany, and Germany that of the world, and who, by definite reasons, like Dr. Pancrace, show us the historical mission of Germany in the world. The future Emperor opened wide his ears. After 1870 the great enemy of his country was no longer France but England.

---

[1] William II was educated at Kassel Gymnasium.

Y

"When the spiked helmet and the red trousers march side by side, let Carthage beware," he said to his French master.[1] This indeed was the cry of New Germany triumphant, and in his ambitious patriotism the young Prince of fourteen years of age already revealed himself.

At the University[2] he got something else : Bismarck-worship. It was the moment when in Germany (1877) the recognition of the work of the Iron Chancellor was passing into adoration for the man. Curiously enough, until then Prince William had not been a partaker in this infatuation. Trained in infancy by the Countess Reventlow—a native of Schleswig-Holstein who had preserved, with the painful memory of 1864, a decided dislike for the Chancellor—the future Emperor, who underwent the influence of that lady, had little love for Bismarck. But, at the University, a professor saw to the correction of his sentiment ; it was Professor Maurenbrecher, a Bismarck fanatic.[3] "When the Prince left the University," says he, "he had become, thanks to me, a fervent admirer of Prince Bismarck. I am proud to have achieved that result ; and, though I had never written my books, I could still testify to myself that I had employed my life gloriously."

---

[1] F. Ayme, "Guillaume II," 1897.

[2] William II studied at the University of Bonn.

[3] W. Maurenbrecher was a historian who claimed that Bismarck had succeeded in proving the truth of the national thesis. "We historians," said he, "cannot prove the justice of our political judgments by means of experiments repeated at will. . . . It is the statesman who furnishes the proof. . . . Thus Prince Bismarck has become the *convincing experiment* as to the truth of the historians' view of the German mission of the Prussian State. . . . The *hypothesis* was earlier Prussian history ; the action of Bismarck was the *proof.*"

He was obliged later on to pitch it lower, the good professor! for he lived long enough to see the black ingratitude of his young pupil. But at that moment he was under the charm of the youthful adoration which he was conscious of having inspired in the Prince-Imperial. Never, indeed, was there more frantic admiration of the Chancellor! The young Prince had his spring-rash. All on the outside and very exuberant it was; he put into his Teutonism an ardour which seemed excessive in a royal prince. He boldly paraded his hatred of the English, opposing his family. Narrow nationalist, and vibrant in his narrowness, he publicly congratulated Pastor Stöcker on his crusade against the Jews. He was to be found in company that was at once military and pietistic, at the mystic receptions of Count Waldersee, where he spoke of "bringing the masses to a sense of respect for authority and to a love of the monarchy."

How was it possible not to be full of confidence in a Prince who was young, vibrant, daring? *There* was there not at least a true Hohenzollern? Had he not given every proof of it, by his words and by his acts?

The historians were particu'arly jubilant: was there not a little of their work there? Thus, when his father, the Emperor Frederick, two months after accession, descended into the tomb, one of these— H. von Treitschke—could not hide his joy: "Life belongs to the living. It is with a thoroughly hopeful confidence that the nation turns its eyes upon the young Emperor. All that he has hitherto said to his people breathes strength and courage, piety and justice. We know now that the good disposition of the time of King William is not lost to history, and already in these first days of mourning we have lived through a great hour in the history of Germany." [1]

But the illusion was not to endure long. From the first, disquieting signs were plainly visible : instead of that "Hohenzollern" simplicity which they awaited, they found themselves confronted, not only by a superb Emperor loving glitter and splendour and losing no opportunity of adding to the dignity of the throne, but also by a Prince who got himself up like the hero of a Wagnerian opera, displaying in every circumstance a taste for theatrical production contrary to all their habits : in place of a statesman wary but efficient, they saw a man of feverish activity, discoursing about everything and willing to be in every business—at once soldier, diplomat, orator, musician, architect ; playing the preacher on the vessels of the State, and next day striking up a bellicose fanfare—in place of the Bismarckian despotism which they tolerated because they found it reason-able, they encountered a despotism odd and whimsical, whose caprices were given out as special divine revelations. The disciples of Strauss and of Haeckel had fully forgiven old William in regard to his in-voking God for the battles of Rosbach and Sadowa : *that* God they tolerated when it was a question of rekindling the faith of the faithful in the cult of Hohenzollern ; but when they saw the new Emperor invoking God to act in opposition to their ideas, they rebelled. It seemed to them that this Emperor's head was slightly turned ; and, disrespectful critics having dared to call their sovereign "an end-of-the-

[1] "Zwei Kaiser," Berlin, 1888.

century Emperor," *they* did not dare to protest very much. [1]

On top of that, out burst the Bismarck affair. A thing believed to be impossible had come to pass: the Emperor had dared to lay a sacrilegious hand on the idol; at once, the charm was broken. The whole enlightened part of the nation declared against him. The Emperor had committed a double crime: a crime of black ingratitude against the founder of the German Empire, and a crime of *lèse-nation* in wounding the deepest of popular feelings.

The people who appeared most affected were the National Liberals. Twice the Emperor had ruled against them: the first time in determining to take the initiative in social reforms which they opposed. They hoped to see him return to them. As a matter of fact, when the Emperor on digging into the social question came to the tufa — that is to say, the redoubtable problems of capitalism and the social organization—and when he stopped short in dismay: these men, who only asked to believe, had hopes of seeing William II return to the politics of the old stager

---

[1] Article by Maximilian Harden in the *Frankfort Gazette*, criticizing in a charming apologue the adage "Speech is silvern, but silence is golden." It contains this, *inter alia*: "Towards the end of the tenth century, a young mystic, Otho III, reigned over the Holy German Empire. Subject to attacks of epilepsy, he abandoned himself, like all epileptics, to colossal illusions. . . . He wished to renovate everything, to rejuvenate everything, to reform everything. . . . Having an absurd idea of his own omnipotence and of the origin of his mission, he plunged into mystic fantasticalities, and his ideas became more and more confounding. The characteristic of this *fin-de-siècle* reformer was, reforming backwards." See also the "Caligula" of Quidde, Leipzig, 1894.

whom he had dismissed; perhaps recall him. He
did nothing of the sort. Saddened, they assisted at an
awakening of the old reactionary spirit of the time of
Frederick William IV, feudal and pietistic in character.

The chasm between the Emperor and his old masters
was bound to be dug deeper still. At bottom, he
and they had nothing whatever in common. Consider, indeed, the physiognomy of that idealist soldier
with the clear and quick mind; of that man wholly
modern and contemptuous of classical studies, revolutionary by temperament, who has not the slightest fear
of breaking with a past which cramps him, who scorns
patient study of facts and trusts only to the inner light
of his genius—is there not *there* a kind of mind that
must clash with the settled habits of those men of
science and method who claim to represent the best
German traditions? So their grief was profound. It
seemed to them that all possible calamities were about
to descend upon Germany. " I asked myself," says one
of their most illustrious representatives, Felix Dahn,
man of letters, " if since the death of William I and
the fall of Prince Bismarck we had fallen from our high
position. I had sorrowfully to answer myself in the
affirmative; and I continued: It is necessary that that
should be said, for our enemies without and within
have known it this long while ; we reveal nothing that
they are not already making merry over. The agonizing
feeling of uncertainty as to direction is spreading widely
among the German people, and just among those men
who have been and who remain most zealous partisans
of the Empire, of Prussia, of the Hohenzollerns: is it
patriotic to disenchant them? "

It was only the beginning of the disenchantment.
William II was going to make them taste to the dregs
the bitterness of the cup.

Shortly after the retirement of the Chancellor, the Emperor was seen presiding over an academic commission which he had convoked at Berlin to reform secondary education. There, his fist on the hilt of his sword, as disallowing all reply, he proceeded to unroll a programme of academical reforms so utilitarian in character that it might have been drawn up by Dickens's *Thomas Gradgrind*, who, for every order of education, would have nothing but facts ("Stick to the facts, sir").

The stupefaction which this discourse produced in those literati and scholars—who, despite the realism of their politics, remained deeply attached to classical culture—may be imagined.

A little earlier, the most illustrious of their representatives, Treitschke—a man who nevertheless could not pass as an adorer of science exclusively, raised the cry of alarm : " It might be said," he exclaimed, " that the noise of arms has called forth a new race of Bœotians, and that it is about to stifle the knowledge of arts and science. Why laugh at the Russians, who put generals into the managership of their botanic gardens, when we are doing the same to-day ? " [1]

William II produced on these people the impression of a sheer barbarian, more sensitive to the rich than to the beautiful, to the appearance than to the matter, regarding the arts solely as the sumptuous decoration of his greatness.

Moreover, full of confidence in his judgment, he laid down the law about everything. Has he not been seen to impose by force on the jury of the *Salon* a very mediocre portrait by a lady painter, Mme. Parlaghy, which had been twice refused ? Then,

---

[1] " Zehn Jahre," p. 384.

contrary to the decisions of a committee charged with judging the rough models for a statue of the Great Elector, to refuse the selected design? And, every time, he has found himself in opposition to the majority of cultured and lettered people of his country.

It is true that in history the Emperor expressed the same ideas as the historians.

"Why," said he, "do so many Germans criticize their Government? It is because youth does not know how our nation has developed. Now that the Empire is created, what is necessary is to make youth understand that this new form of State ought to be conserved. . . . If the school had done what is rightfully to be expected of it, it would, before everything else, have itself forced the duel with Social Democracy. Now, I should have the instruments with which I could work and which would aid me by making me more quickly master of the movement."

Yes, he repeated what he had been taught; but he added to it certain ideas, and a method which was in complete disagreement with that of the historians. Did he not say, indeed, that history ought to be taught backwards?

If there is one thing of which the Prussian historians are proud, it is their historic method, which claims to elicit the political institutions from the study of the past. It is in virtue of this method that they have expounded their theory of the German Mission of Prussia.

But the Emperor William has retained out of their lessons the practical results only, and he mocks the method.

That was strikingly seen when he entered into conflict with two of the most illustrious representatives of the Prussian historical school, Sybel and Treitschke.

There exists in Germany a national history prize called the Verdun Prize. It was founded in 1844, at a period shrill with Gallophobia, shortly after the ostentatious celebration of the thousandth anniversary of the Treaty of Verdun, in consequence of which Germany came to have an existence separate from France. In 1894, the Academy of Berlin, charged to adjudge the prize, had unanimously indicated the historian H. Sybel —on account of his great work, " Establishment of the New German Empire "—as worthiest to obtain it. It was the Emperor's business to ratify this decision. Nobody had any doubts on the subject. Nevertheless, without a word said, he was pleased to obliterate with a stroke of the pen the name of H. von Sybel; and he awarded the prize to an estimable erudite Herr Erdmansdorffer, a professor at the University of Heidelberg, and author of a sufficiently indigestible work on the Great Elector.

The thing caused an enormous sensation in the University world. Was not Herr von Sybel a Prussian historian entirely devoted to the Hohenzollerns ? Yes, but he did not write history according to the good methods indicated by the Emperor. The latter had announced that, in a history of Germany, the Prussian sovereigns ought to be clothed with a " heroic greatness." Now, Herr von Sybel, far from having done that, had in his " History " given the first place to Bismarck. Nothing more was needed to irritate the spiteful sovereign. His last word had been *Suprema lex regis voluntas.*[1]

Shortly afterwards it was the turn of Treitschke;

---

[1] [" The king's will the supreme law."]

who, to be avenged on the politics of the " new course,"
riddled the young Emperor with epigrams. Then, in
his new volume (1895), under colour of pourtraying
his [1] granduncle, the romantic Frederick William IV,
he wrote of William II :—

" It was a world of magnificent plans, which, with
the fancy of an artist, Frederick William had imagined,
and which, now that he was master, he wished to
realize. For a long time, consequently, he suffered
from the parsimonious habits of the Court of Berlin ;
to keep up a Court, sumptuous, and worthy of the
Hohenzollerns, he hoped to unite all that was great
in the arts. He was never content but when he was
allowing the flood of his thoughts and feelings to run
. . . 'I was not easy until I had spoken,' etc.—thus
he once wrote to a friend."

The allusions are transparent, and the Imperial rancour would no doubt have struck at the old professor
—he was threatened with having the Archives closed
to him—if death had not put an end to the quarrel.

From that moment, there was nothing more in common between these men and the sovereign whom they
had long regarded as " their finest work."

Their old age was sad. Under the stroke of unhappiness, their eyes were opened. They understood
that they had taken the wrong road. Suffering from
despotism, they became again, like the old hermit of
Fredericksruhe, the friends of liberty. It is true that
they at least could argue that they had once loved it.

And that made them clear-sighted and just. At
the end of their lives, they recognized that the Empire
in being was not the one of which they had dreamed.

It cannot be denied that these men, however limited

---

[1] [The Emperor's.]

their political conceptions, had a high ideal. Perfectly upright in their private lives as they were, very honest as they were in their intentions, the Germany on which they called in their prayers was a great, strong, powerful Germany, but also an enlightened and moral Germany. Behold! after twenty years, they saw that the new Germany did not in the least answer to their ideal. Intoxicated by the heady flavour of victory, she had putrefied in the sunshine of happiness. Not virtues had shot up, but vices. What was everywhere displayed was pride, boasting. Those who had sung out, in every key, that " war, like tempest, was going to purify the atmosphere," recognized that what was going on in Germany " scarcely allowed of faith in the purifying action of the last war." [1]

Perhaps the isolation of old age had been necessary to that perception; perhaps also the contempt of a young sovereign, barbarous and ungrateful, who had never had anything but contempt for scholars and professors. Be that as it may, the most courageous of these men, Treitschke, uttered it with his usual frankness. For this purpose he even profited by the occasion offered by the twenty-fifth anniversary of the battle of Sedan. On the 19th of July, 1895, less than a year before his death, he delivered in the Aula of the University of Berlin a patriotic speech which had great vogue in Germany.

After having recalled the glorious memories of the " great year "; after having shown that the Empire had not disarmed its enemies within, nor those without, he added : " All our habits have become coarser: politics and life. . . . If politics have become coarser, the proximate cause lies in the disquieting transformation

---

[1] Colmar von der Goltz, " La Nation armée," p. 453.

of our public life. A great proportion of the things which we formerly held to be an appanage of the Roman Empire in its decadence is really a product of that intensive urban culture which is invading us in its turn. A democratic society never seeks its leaders among the men of talent, as imagined by the dreamers —for talent remains always an aristocratic thing—but among the moneyed men or the demagogues, or both. Respect, which Goethe named as the final goal of all moral education, vanishes from the new generation with dizzying rapidity : respect for God, respect for the bounds which Nature and society have put between the two sexes : respect for country, which grows fainter from day to day in presence of the phantom of a pleasure-taking humankind. The farther culture extended, the flatter it became ; the profundity of the antique world was despised, and nothing was reckoned important except what served immediate ends. Nowadays, when everybody talks about everything, in the manner of his newspaper or his encyclopædia, it is a rare thing to encounter a mind possessing that creative power, and that courage to avow its ignorance, by which the truly original are distinguished. Science, which at one time even went too deep in its descent into the unfathomable, now loses itself on the surface. . . . In the boredom of an empty existence, pastimes such as betting on the racecourse assume a real importance; and, in view of the fact that we now have heroes of the circus and juggler heroes, we disgustedly recall the monstrous and costly mosaic of the twenty-eight wrestlers at the Baths of Caracalla. All of which is a serious sign of the times." [1]

[1] Treitschke, " Zum Gedächtniss des grossen Krieges," Leipzig, 1895.

All these remarks are extremely fine and extremely proper; but, on getting to the bottom of things, the least we can do is to ask ourselves whether those who complain to-day are not the prime authors of this state of affairs.

Who, then, if not they, developed in the youth of Germany that boastfulness, that national pride, and that jingoism which they deplore?

If there is one virtue the acclimatization of which in their country has not been attended to, it is humility. By force of preaching that the German ought not to be a naïf and credulous person, they have awakened in him an exaggerated self-confidence which has quickly degenerated into presumption.

Again, when they complain of "the invading barbarism, of the lowering of general culture and of mind," whom do they tax, if not themselves? Was it not they who first of all proclaimed that Germany was suffering from scientific plethora; that she had thought only too much and that it was time for her to act; that what gave strength to a country was not Intelligence, but Will? Was it not Treitschke himself who, in an access of barbarism, contemplating the ruins of the Coliseum, exclaimed, "That! why, it's only ruins!" Was it not Treitschke, too, who repeated, for the purpose of appropriating, the remark of Massimo d'Azeglio: "A good business-man is more necessary to the State than a poet"?

After that, is there room for astonishment when the men whom they have formed, pushing their ideas to their logical consequences, have come to say, with William II, that science is useless if it does not aim at practical and positive ends?

Finally, when they groan over the loss of their liberties, they have only to remember that it was they, first of all, who made those liberties cheap, when Bismarck—to gratify their social, political, and religious spite—made those "laws of exception" against the Catholics and the Democrats.

They suffer now from what they call "the perversion of the public mind" and "the lowering of character"; but have they not contributed hereto also —by legitimatizing, in the name of history, the worst political crimes; and by building pedestals for the Human Providences?

Their Human Providence, they have had him: Bismarck, and what a Bismarck! Doubtless, in him they admire one of the greatest political geniuses that have been; and, if they have loved him so much, it is because he gave them a country. But their admiration and their love have become boundless. They have made a fetish of that man. They have excused everything in him. They have been seen deifying imposture: " Blessed be the hand that falsified the Ems telegram!" exclaimed one of them.[1] The Bismarck whom they have glorified is the "greatness of flesh" which Pascal speaks of; the worst of the century, after Napoleon: he is the grand carnivore, specially organized for the struggle for life; the man without scruples, to whom all means of attaining success were good, who bent the corners of the cards when luck did not serve him; the man who despised the human race, and whose table-talk was the disgrace of humanity: he is the man, totally void of sensibility, who averred that the greatest pleasure of his life was when he killed his first hare, in the chase; that vindictive and jealous man who passed his nights in calling to mind the injuries which had been done him and which he had been unable to

---

[1] Hans Delbrück, in the " Preussische Jahrbücher."

avenge. The man whom they have exalted is the man of all the lies—from the day when, on the eve of war with Denmark, he said to Bernstorff: "The pretext which you invoke is worth nothing. If you want war, I engage to furnish you with a *casus belli* of the first water, inside twenty-four hours"; until the day when, pencil in hand, he mutilated the Ems telegram in order to give it the aggressive air which must precipitate war. Did he at that time see the enormous responsibility of his act: the thousands of brave soldiers about to cut each others' throats; the ruins, the disasters, the griefs; two nations armed to the teeth, ruining themselves with armaments—one to keep what it had taken, the other to try to get it back? He saw nothing of all this; and, according to his own statement, he "never ate with so good an appetite."

Such is the man whom the Prussian historians have offered for the admiration of future generations. The cult of Bismarck in Germany has reached proportions which the cult of Napoleon never attained in France. Bismarckian literature is to-day the richest in Germany. Even Goethe is outdistanced.

And what is there at the bottom of this admiration? Crude justification of the policy of force. It is to this end that Germany has had the most idealistic and most widely human writers in the world. The chastisement has not been slow in coming. Ernest Renan was predicting it already, in the fine letter he wrote to his friend, David Strauss—also grown to be an admirer of force: "Excess is bad; pride is the only vice which is punished in this world. To triumph is always a mistake, and in any case there is something unphilosophic about it. *Debemur morti nos nostraque.* Don't imagine yourselves to be better sheltered from error than others.

For the past year your newspapers have shown themselves no doubt less ignorant than ours; but quite
as impassioned, quite as immoral, quite as blind. . . .
Your German race has always the air of believing in
Walhalla; but Walhalla will never be the Kingdom
of God. . . . Ah! dear master, but Jesus did well
to found the Kingdom of God; a world superior to
hate, to jealousy, to pride; where the most highly
esteemed is not, as in this sad time through which
we are passing, he who does the most evil—he who
strikes, kills, insults; he who is the most lying, the
most disloyal, the most badly brought up, the most
perfidious, the most hardened against pity and pardon
—but he who is mildest, most modest, farthest from
all boastfulness. . . . War is a tissue of sins, a state
contrary to nature. . . . Have you remarked that
neither in the Sermon on the Mount, nor in the
Gospel, nor in primitive Christian literature, is there
one word which puts the military virtues among those
which win the Kingdom of Heaven?"[1]

Renan was right: the great scandals that have
recently occurred in Germany, those defenders of the
throne and altar who have been seen recently rolling
in the mire, the secret corruption that has been revealed
in the elections—that corruption which made the
historian Sybel say, when speaking of the French
elections under the Second Empire, "other countries
which are not acquainted with these customs to-day
have nothing to envy of France"[2]—all this, is it
not, after all, the heritage of that policy for which no
name is bad enough: the policy of Bismarck, of secret
undercurrents, of the reptile Press, of spies and frontier
provocations?

---

[1] Renan, "La Réforme intellectuelle et morale," pp. 184, 192.
[2] "Die Begründung," vi. 100.

And if we consider that this policy had its warmest defenders in the recent Prussian historians, we are right in saying that they are the authors in the first place of this degeneracy of manners. By so acclaiming strokes of force and cunning, in spite of the moral varnish with which they have covered their theories, they have helped to pervert the public mind. As the philosopher Renouvier said admirably, "They have awoken and stimulated the dangerous taste of the past, ending in the fatal universal evolution, in the supremacy of history over reason, of deeds over rights, of force over justice." Through their historical theories they have been the propagators of the worst political maxims, for the refutation of which humanity already has shed seas of blood.

They must be surprised after that with the results; they have worked for social democracy.

In truth, nothing lasting is based upon deceit and lies : sooner or later that work comes back to you.

INDEX